VIDEO
GUIDE

BARRY NORMAN'S VIDEO GUIDE

Barry Norman and
Emma Norman

A Mandarin Paperback
BARRY NORMAN'S VIDEO GUIDE

First published in Great Britain 1995
by Mandarin Paperbacks
an imprint of Reed Consumer Books Ltd
Michelin House, 81 Fulham Road, London SW3 6RB
and Auckland, Melbourne, Singapore and Toronto

Design copyright © 1995 Reed International Books Limited
Text copyright © 1995 Barry Norman, Emma Norman

The authors have asserted their moral rights

A CIP catalogue record for this title
is available from the British Library

ISBN 0 7493 1994 1

Printed and bound in Great Britain
by Cox & Wyman Ltd, Reading, Berks

This book is sold subject to the condition
that it shall not, by way of trade or otherwise,
be lent, resold, hired out, or otherwise circulated
without the publisher's prior consent in any form
of binding or cover other than that in which
it is published and without a similar condition
including this condition being imposed
on the subsequent purchaser.

CONTENTS

Introduction vi

Top Tens viii

User Guide x

Action/Adventure 1

Comedy 24

Drama 58

Family 105

Foreign 116

Horror 126

Musicals 131

Mystery/Thriller 139

Science Fiction/Fantasy 159

Westerns 167

Index 173

INTRODUCTION

As I was saying in the last edition of this book: you will not find all these videos in your local store. You will probably not find all of them in a big, specialist store. Some indeed you will not, for a while, find anywhere at all because the films are so recent that they have not been released on video yet. But they will be, sooner rather than later. It's just a question of being patient.

Seeking out videos can be an irritating business. We know and you know that the titles should be available. All the films listed here – except the very latest ones – have already been issued on video. But where are they? Every week in my office at 'Film 95' I receive a score or more of letters from desperate people asking where they can find a video of such-and-such a film, as if somehow I was privy to a secret source unknown to anyone else. But, alas, I am not. All I can suggest to these unhappy people is that they contact the British Video Association, 21 Poland Street, London, W1, and throw themselves on its mercy. If the BVA doesn't know where or how a video is to be located, the chances are nobody does.

Since we compiled the first edition of this book things have changed. Censorship has become much harsher. Originally we included Quentin Tarantino's 'Reservoir Dogs' in the naive belief that a film as good as that was bound to get a video release soon. For similar reasons, and also because far more gruesome horror flicks have been made since 1973, we also included 'The Exorcist'. We were wrong. Both of them are still banned. Since the new Criminal Justice Act means that the censor's decision to grant a certificate can be challenged in court, it seems almost certain that Tarantino's 'Pulp Fiction' and Oliver Stone's 'Natural Born Killers' (based on a Tarantino story) will also be denied a video release.

Those who support these new regulations (especially politicians) self-righteously insist that they prevent violent films from falling into the hands of children. But, unless we are all very careful, they can also mean that nothing deemed unfit for a child will fall into the hands of adults either. And adults have rights, too. The claim that violent films, videos and TV cause violent crime is quite unproven; it's merely a useful cop-out for politicians to deflect attention away from the fact that bad social conditions, not images on a screen, are responsible for society's ills. Films have become too violent, certainly. But restrictions in this country have also become too worryingly stringent.

As for the rest, we have again restricted entries to around 1,600 in the belief that when you're out shopping for a video you will want a book you can slip into your pocket or handbag rather than some great tome that's even heavier than your shopping.

The basic format, too, is much the same. For ease of reference the films are divided into ten loose categories – loose because very few films are simply dramas, or simply comedies, or even simply Westerns. And, as an added bonus, we have plucked ten choice war movies from the various sections and included them in our Top Ten lists.

You will not, of course, agree with all our ratings; sometimes Emma and I didn't agree with each other. Nor will you agree with the choice or placing of the films in our Top Ten lists but then part of the fun of any such book as this is the passionate discussions it can provoke, among readers as well as compilers. As to those Top Ten lists, I should point out that they don't actually represent our personal favourites among ALL films but merely our favourites among those available on video.

One more thing: may we suggest that you keep this book beside you at all times? After all, it's just as useful for checking out the movies on TV as it is for helping you to find a video.

Barry Norman

WRITING a third edition of the 'Video Guide' meant that my father and I were able to make further changes to some of our decisions – not that we were wrong before, just a little hasty perhaps. Some videos have now gone, others have been added, and not just new releases. Old favourites like 'The Philadelphia Story' have become more widely available since our last book, and so it was high time it was included here.

There have only been a few changes to our Top Ten lists, because unfortunately such classics don't come round that often. Had it been available on video it's possible that 'Reservoir Dogs' would have made it into the mystery/thriller Top Ten but, at the time of going to print, it remains uncertificated.

Again, I'd like to take this opportunity to tell my father what a joy it is working with him and to wish you all very, very happy viewing.

Emma Norman

TOP TENS

These are our recommendations for ten special videos in each genre which should be readily available, or at least easily obtainable, by your local store. There are of course many other great films we would have liked to include, but for one reason or another they are sadly less easy to find on video.

The more astute of you will notice that we have slipped in an extra genre. War films are in fact included largely within the Action/Adventure section of the guide itself.

■ ACTION/ADVENTURE
The Adventures of Robin Hood
Lawrence of Arabia
The Godfather
Jaws
Thelma and Louise
Romancing the Stone
Indiana Jones Trilogy
True Lies
The Untouchables
The Fugitive

■ COMEDY
Bringing Up Baby
Gregory's Girl
To Be or Not To Be (1942)
Life Is Sweet
The Man with Two Brains
Tootsie
Ninotchka
A Fish Called Wanda
Monty Python's Life of Brian
Sleepless in Seattle

■ DRAMA
Citizen Kane
Gone With the Wind
Casablanca
The Third Man
Raging Bull
Schindler's List
All About Eve
In the Name of the Father
One Flew Over the Cuckoo's Nest
The Remains of the Day

■ FAMILY
The Wizard of Oz
It's a Wonderful Life
The Railway Children
Great Expectations
Snow White and the Seven Dwarfs
Local Hero
Moonstruck
Field of Dreams
The Jungle Book
Aladdin

■ FOREIGN
La Regle du Jeu
Ran
The Seven Samurai
Cyrano de Bergerac
Women on the Verge of a Nervous Breakdown
Man Bites Dog
Jean de Florette/Manon des Sources
Farewell, My Concubine
Un Coeur en Hiver
Cinema Paradiso

■ HORROR
The Silence of the Lambs
An American Werewolf in London
Psycho
Misery
A Nightmare on Elm Street
The Omen
Cape Fear (1991)
The Hitcher
Halloween
Wolf

■ MUSICALS
Singin' in the Rain
High Society
Kiss Me Kate
Cabaret
The King and I
The Commitments
Seven Brides for Seven Brothers
Oklahoma!
The Sound of Music
Oliver!

■ MYSTERY/THRILLER
Witness
Jagged Edge
Suspect
Someone to Watch Over Me
Chinatown
The 39 Steps
In the Heat of the Night
The Maltese Falcon
Klute
Sea of Love

■ SCI-FI/FANTASY
ET The Extra-Terrestrial
Close Encounters of the Third Kind
2001: A Space Odyssey
Star Wars Trilogy
Terminator 2
Back to the Future Trilogy
Alien/Aliens
Total Recall
Star Trek VI
Ghostbusters

■ WAR
Apocalypse Now
The Cruel Sea
M*A*S*H
The Bridge on the River Kwai
The Great Escape
Platoon
Zulu
The Dam Busters
A Bridge Too Far
Henry V (1989)

■ WESTERNS
The Searchers
Stagecoach
Unforgiven
Butch Cassidy and the Sundance Kid
High Noon
Shane
The Magnificent Seven
Dances with Wolves
Red River
The Outlaw Josey Wales

USER GUIDE

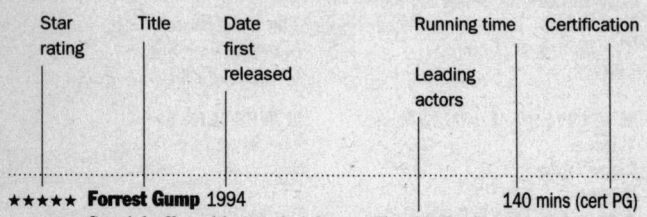

Star rating | Title | Date first released | Running time | Certification

Leading actors

★★★★★ **Forrest Gump** 1994   140 mins (cert PG)
Special effects hit new heights as *Tom Hanks* plays the simple hero who, one way or another, is present at every important event of the past three decades. Don't miss it, it's a gem.

Star ratings

★★★★★	Not to be missed
★★★★	Excellent
★★★	Very good
★★	Worth watching
★	OK

Certification

U	Universal
PG	Parental guidance
12	12 and over
15	15 and over
18	18 and over

ACTION/ADVENTURE

★★★ **Above Us the Waves** 1956 99 mins (cert U)
Gripping wartime drama of British submarine crew attempting to destroy enemy ship. *John Mills* tops impressive cast.

★★★★★ **The Adventures of Robin Hood** 1938 102 mins (cert U)
Glorious swashbuckler with *Errol Flynn* as the dashing outlaw, *Olivia de Havilland* a feisty Maid Marian and *Claude Raines* the evil Prince John.

★★★★★ **The African Queen** 1951 103 mins (cert U)
Magnificent romantic adventure. Prissy missionary *Katharine Hepburn* and drunken riverboat captain *Humphrey Bogart* brave a treacherous journey down the Congo to destroy a German battleship during WWI.

★ **Air America** 1990 112 mins (cert 15)
Mel Gibson and *Robert Downey Jr* as CIA pilots in Vietnam. Goodish action, weak on comedy and storyline.

★★★ **Alive** 1993 121 mins (cert 15)
True story of plane crash survivors resorting to cannibalism to stay alive during their long ordeal. Sensitive subject neatly handled.

★★★★ **All Quiet on the Western Front** 1930 140 mins (cert PG)
Outstanding WWI drama examining the disillusionment of young soldiers in the trenches.

★ **Another 48 Hours** 1990 95 mins (cert 18)
Eddie Murphy and *Nick Nolte*'s continuing love/hate relationship as they take on the Iceman. Not a patch on the original.

★★★★ **Apocalypse Now** 1979 153 mins (cert 18)
Francis Coppola's hypnotic version of Joseph Conrad's 'Heart of Darkness' set in Vietnam. Poignantly played by *Martin Sheen*, *Robert Duvall* and *Marlon Brando*.

★★ **The Assassin** 1992 104 mins (cert 18)
Bridget Fonda as killer saved from execution by government agent *Gabriel Byrne* in order to act as official hit woman. Able support by *Harvey Keitel* and *Anne Bancroft*. Original French version, 'Nikita', is better.

★★ **Attack of the 50 Foot Woman** 1993　　　　　89 mins (cert 12)
B-movie remake with *Daryl Hannah* as the mild-mannered wife
of a cheating husband who, after an encounter with an alien
spaceship, becomes enormous. A B-movie is a B-movie is a
B-movie.

★ **Backdraft** 1991　　　　　136 mins (cert 15)
Feuding firemen brothers, *Kurt Russell* and *William Baldwin*,
fight arsonist and each other. Mediocre story enlivened by
Robert De Niro as fire investigator; spectacular fire sequences.

★★ **Back in the USSR** 1994　　　　　99 mins (cert 12)
Frank Whaley, a bored American tourist in Russia, meets a
mysterious woman and her friends and becomes embroiled
in counterfeiting and the Red Mafia, represented by *Roman
Polanski*. Never quite works as a thriller or a comedy.

★★★ **Ben Hur** 1959　　　　　217 mins (cert PG)
William Wyler's 11 Oscar epic pits *Charlton Heston*'s revenge-
seeking galley slave against the Romans. Somewhat earnest
story but marvellous chariot race.

★★★★ **Beverly Hills Cop** 1984　　　　　105 mins (cert 15)
Fast-talking, wise-cracking cop *Eddie Murphy* takes LA vacation
to find friend's killer. Highly enjoyable, undemanding and
humorous entertainment.

★★ **Beverly Hills Cop 2** 1987　　　　　99 mins (cert 15)
Dumb sequel that contains, if possible, even more movement
and violence but far less plot.

★★★ **Beverly Hills Cop 3** 1994　　　　　104 mins (cert 15)
Eddie Murphy returns to form though the plot's as predictable as
ever. This time the maverick detective is back in LA on the trail
of drug-running cop-killers.

★★★★ **The Bounty** 1984　　　　　128 mins (cert 15)
Most convincing version of the story of the Bounty mutiny,
starring *Anthony Hopkins* and *Mel Gibson*.

★★★★ **The Bridge on the River Kwai** 1957　　　　　161 mins (cert U)
David Lean's powerful drama of POWs constructing bridge for
Japanese captors. *Alec Guinness* superb as the obsessed Colonel.

★★★★ **A Bridge Too Far** 1977   175 mins (cert 15)
Richard Attenborough's honest, absorbing, star-studded portrayal of WWII Allied operation that led to defeat at Arnhem in 1944.

★★★ **Captain Blood** 1935   119 mins (cert U)
Errol Flynn as doctor turned dashing pirate. Plenty of romance, sea battles and bags of swashing and buckling.

★ **Christopher Columbus: The Discovery** 1991   120 mins (cert PG)
George Corraface's Columbus heads out to sea as *Tom Selleck*'s King of Spain gazes wistfully after him. *Marlon Brando* deserves better than this. We all do.

★★★ **Cliffhanger** 1993   112 mins (cert 15)
Breathtaking stunts as ace mountaineer *Sylvester Stallone* chases robber *John Lithgow* across treacherous mountain terrain. The film that revived Stallone's career.

★★★ **The Colditz Story** 1954   97 mins (cert U)
British POWs plan to prove that 'escape proof' German castle is anything but, in ever-popular wartime escape saga.

★★★★ **The Cruel Sea** 1953   126 mins (cert PG)
Gripping action/adventure involving the crew of a warship during WWII. Among the best of British war films.

★★★ **The Dam Busters** 1954   125 mins (cert U)
Host of English actors grace exciting, intelligent WWII tale of Barnes Wallace and his bouncing bomb. Brilliant music too.

★★ **Days of Thunder** 1990   107 mins (cert 12)
Tom Cruise and *Nicole Kidman* in a 'Top Gun' on the racing circuit. Very flashy, but little substance. *Robert Duvall* lends some much needed weight.

★★★ **D-Day the Sixth of June** 1956   106 mins (cert PG)
Lengthy romance set around the WWII Normandy invasion. *Robert Taylor* leads the troops; *Dana Wynter* is the crumpet.

★★ **The Dead Pool** 1988   91 mins (cert 18)
Dirty Harry, *Clint Eastwood*, in his fifth, rather lacklustre outing; here investigating a bizarre death list.

ACTION/ADVENTURE

★★ **Demolition Man** 1993   114 mins (cert 15)
20th-century cop *Sylvester Stallone* and villain *Wesley Snipes* are defrosted to pursue each other in 21st-century, crimeless society. Some nice ideas never fully explored, though action's satisfying.

★★★ **The Desert Fox** 1951   88 mins (cert PG)
James Mason is superb as Field Marshal Rommel facing defeat, disillusionment and death in desert warfare.

★★★ **The Desert Rats** 1953   88 mins (cert U)
Good star-studded tale about a British captain, *Richard Burton*, warding off German troops in North Africa. *James Mason* plays Rommel again.

★★ **Diamonds Are Forever** 1971   120 mins (cert PG)
Sean Connery's penultimate outing as 007 James Bond, this time in Las Vegas. With *Jill St John* and *Charles Gray*. Otherwise the mixture as before.

★★★★ **Die Hard** 1988   131 mins (cert 15)
New York cop *Bruce Willis* flies to LA for a family Christmas and finds he alone can rescue his wife and others held hostage by evil *Alan Rickman*. Great stuff, with Rickman outstanding.

★★ **Die Hard 2** 1990   120 mins (cert 15)
Bruce Willis returns to take on terrorists, this time at Dulles airport. Same as before, though not as much fun. Willis does seem to be in the wrong place at the wrong time more often than is good for him.

★★★ **The Dirty Dozen** 1967   150 mins (cert 15)
Macho, stellar cast play hard-case jailbirds sent to infiltrate enemy lines to redeem themselves in wartime action/adventure.

★★★★ **Dirty Harry** 1971   103 mins (cert 18)
First and best outing for *Clint Eastwood* as the magnum-packing, sharp-shooting detective assigned to bring in crazed killer.

★★ **Double Impact** 1991   100 mins (cert 18)
Twins – *Jean-Claude Van Damme* twice – separated at birth reunite to avenge their parents' murder by the Triads. Corny plot and dialogue. Good action, though.

★★★ **Dragon: The Bruce Lee Story** 1993   121 mins (cert 15)
Excellent depiction of kung fu karate king by *Jason Scott Lee* (no relation) in gripping story combining action and romance.

★★★ **Dr No** 1962   111 mins (cert PG)
First of the Bond movies sees *Sean Connery* creating 007. Still one of the series' best.

★★ **The Eagle Has Landed** 1977   135 mins (cert 15)
Nazi plot to assassinate Churchill provides reasonable star vehicle for the likes of *Michael Caine*, *Robert Duvall* and *Donald Sutherland*.

★★ **El Cid** 1961   184 mins (cert U)
Spectacular action movie sees the Spanish hero, *Charlton Heston*, romancing *Sophia Loren* as he attempts to drive the Moors from his country.

★★ **The Enforcer** 1976   96 mins (cert 18)
Dirty Harry Callahan, *Clint Eastwood*, and female partner *Tyne Daly* on the trail of terrorists. Third in the Dirty Harry series and looking tired.

★★★ **Escape from Alcatraz** 1979   112 mins (cert 15)
Reasonable action yarn with *Clint Eastwood* escaping from the reputedly ultra-secure prison in story based on fact.

★★ **Escape from Sobibor** 1987   142 mins (cert 15)
Alan Arkin leads biggest escape ever attempted from a Nazi concentration camp in solid, made-for-TV movie.

★★★ **Excalibur** 1981   140 mins (cert 15)
John Boorman's lavish, quirky rendition of King Arthur fable. The cast is both impressive and surprising.

★ **The Exterminator** 1980   101 mins (cert 18)
Violent vigilante *Robert Ginty* wreaks revenge on the gang that paralysed his friend. Run-of-the-mill mayhem.

★★ **Firefox** 1982   127 mins (cert 12)
Unconvincing *Clint Eastwood* Cold War vehicle in which Clint plays US pilot sent to Moscow to steal state-of-the-art Russian jet fighter.

★★★ **The First of the Few** 1942   117 mins (cert U)
Impressive biopic starring *Leslie Howard* depicting the life of R J Mitchell, inventor of the Spitfire.

★★ **The Fortress** 1993   100 mins (cert 15)
Title refers to futuristic prison from which there's no escape – ha, ha, heard that one before. *Christopher Lambert* is the prisoner who refuses to be caged.

★★★★ **48 Hours** 1982   97 mins (cert 18)
Sharp, fast thriller in which cop *Nick Nolte* 'borrows' jailed conman *Eddie Murphy* for two days to help catch a cop killer.

★★ **For Your Eyes Only** 1981   127 mins (cert PG)
Roger Moore as 007. Stunts and traditional action replace earlier technical wizardry.

★★★★ **From Here to Eternity** 1953   118 mins (cert PG)
Pre-WWII American military drama. Excellent performances by *Burt Lancaster*, *Deborah Kerr* and *Frank Sinatra*. Best remembered for sizzling sex scene on beach.

★★★ **From Russia With Love** 1963   118 mins (cert PG)
Sean Connery as James Bond nicely supported by *Robert Shaw* as psycho assassin.

★★★★ **The Fugitive** 1993   140 mins (cert 12)
Brilliant action/adventure based on TV series. *Harrison Ford* as the innocent doctor on the run for murdering his wife and ardently pursued by sheriff *Tommy Lee Jones*. Fantastic, fun and exciting.

★★★ **Full Metal Jacket** 1987   116 mins (cert 18)
Stanley Kubrick's contribution to Vietnam war movies shows *Matthew Modine* undergoing the horrors of training and actual warfare.

★★★ **FX: Murder by Illusion** 1986   107 mins (cert 15)
Fast-paced caper about movie special effects man hired to protect a supergrass. *Bryan Brown* and *Brian Dennehy* star.

★★ **FX 2: The Deadly Art of Illusion** 1991   109 mins (cert 15)
Mixture much as before – *Bryan Brown* again using his skills to give the cops (especially *Brian Dennehy*) a hand. Just as well he never seems to have a movie to make.

★★★ **Gallipoli** 1981   110 mins (cert PG)
Gripping study of the people and events involved in futile, suicidal WWI Australian campaign against Turks. *Mel Gibson* at his best under Peter Weir's direction.

★★★★ **Geronimo** 1994   215 mins (cert 12)
Gripping account of how the Apache chief was forced to surrender by the double-crossing US government and cavalry, splendidly told by director Walter Hill. Stars include *Gene Hackman* and *Wes Studi*.

★★★ **The Getaway** 1994   115 mins (cert 18)
Enjoyable, sexy remake of the 1972 film directed by Walter Hill. *Alec Baldwin* and *Kim Basinger* play bank robber and wife caught up in violence and double-dealing. Brisk action, humorous script, nice performances.

★★★ **Gettysburg** 1994   261 mins (cert PG)
Impressive account of the longest, hardest and bloodiest battle of the American Civil War. Stars include *Martin Sheen*, *Tom Berenger* and *Richard Jordan*.

★★★ **Glory** 1989   122 mins (cert 15)
Harrowing account of first black regiment in American Civil War. *Matthew Broderick* and *Denzel Washington* excellent, as are battle scenes.

★★★★★ **The Godfather** 1972   175 mins (cert 18)
Best gangster movie ever made. Definitive Mafia story awash with talent. Francis Coppola directs. *Marlon Brando*, *Al Pacino* and *James Caan* head Corleone family.

★★★★★ **The Godfather Part II** 1974   200 mins (cert 18)
Only sequel to match its forerunner continues Corleone saga minus James Caan. Compelling story of corruption of power.

★★★ **The Godfather Part III** 1990   160 mins (cert 15)
Most lavish but weakest of the family series. Still worth watching if only for *Andy Garcia*'s performance and Francis Coppola's direction.

★★ **Goldfinger** 1964   112 mins (cert PG)
Sean Connery, licensed to kill, takes on evil *Gert Frobe*. *Honor Blackman* is the unusually feisty Bond girl.

ACTION/ADVENTURE ■

★★★★ **Goodfellas** 1990   146 mins (cert 18)
Martin Scorsese's violent, riveting depiction of Mafia soldiers in New York. Explosive performance from *Joe Pesci*; *Robert De Niro* and *Ray Liotta* give excellent support.

★★★★★ **The Great Escape** 1963   173 mins (cert PG)
Plethora of stars play Allied POWs masterminding mass breakout from WWII German concentration camp.

★★ **Greystoke: The Legend of Tarzan** 1984   129 mins (cert PG)
Rich and faithful version of the Tarzan story. *Christopher Lambert*'s the man raised by apes, *Ralph Richardson* his baronial uncle bringing him home.

★★★ **Gunga Din** 1939   117 mins (cert U)
Ripping yarn with *Cary Grant*, *Douglas Fairbanks Jr* and *Victor McLaglen* as three soldier comrades involved in 19th-century uprising in India. Owes little to Rudyard Kipling.

★★★ **The Guns of Navarone** 1961   157 mins (cert U)
Multi-national commandos are dispatched to destroy WWII German gun. Cracking action/adventure with *Gregory Peck*, *David Niven* and *Richard Harris*.

★ **Hard Target** 1993   95 mins (cert 18)
Ridiculous shoot-'em-up in which *Jean-Claude Van Damme* uncovers a fatal man-hunt racket. Despite facing an army of baddies and an arsenal that would put the US army's to shame, our hero emerges without so much as a graze – we're talking macho!

★★ **Heartbreak Ridge** 1986   130 mins (cert 15)
Muscular army action stuff from *Clint Eastwood* as grizzled sergeant knocking rookies into shape before they invade Grenada, for God's sake. I mean, that was hardly the world's most important war.

★★★ **High Sierra** 1941   96 mins (cert PG)
Somewhat overplotted action/film noir with strong lead performances from *Humphrey Bogart* and *Ida Lupino*.

★★★ **The Hunt for Red October** 1990   135 mins (cert PG)
Exciting suspense thriller about a Soviet naval captain, *Sean Connery*, stealing a state-of-the-art nuclear submarine to help him defect to the West.

★★★ **Ice Cold in Alex** 1960   129 mins (cert PG)
John Mills stranded in desert in charge of ambulance, a nurse and a Nazi soldier. Splendid WWII action/adventure.

★★★★ **Indiana Jones and the Last Crusade** 1989   127 mins (cert PG)
Best of the series sees *Harrison Ford* taking on the Nazis while searching for his father, *Sean Connery*, and the Holy Grail.

★★ **Indiana Jones and the Temple of Doom** 1984   117 mins (cert PG)
Weakish sequel to 'Raiders of the Lost Ark'. *Harrison Ford* as Jones, *Kate Capshaw* as Jones's girl.

★★ **An Innocent Man** 1989   114 mins (cert 18)
Brutal, overlong action movie. *Tom Selleck* wrongly imprisoned and out for justice and revenge.

★★★ **In the Line of Fire** 1993   118 mins (cert 15)
Clint Eastwood as the veteran FBI agent charged with protecting the US president against murderous sociopath *John Malkovich*. Good stunts, good performances.

★★★ **Into the West** 1992   102 mins (cert PG)
Two young Irish boys save a horse and flee to the coast followed by father *Gabriel Byrne*, gypsy *Ellen Barkin* and police. Magical, mystical and pleasing.

★★★ **In Which We Serve** 1942   114 mins (cert U)
Noel Coward's WWII drama centring on the survivors of a torpedoed destroyer. Dated but still splendid. *Richard Attenborough* makes his debut.

★★★ **The Italian Job** 1969   100 mins (cert U)
Michael Caine and *Noel Coward* in crime caper. Complicated plot involves creating world's biggest traffic jam in Turin. Good fun.

★★ **I Was Monty's Double** 1958   100 mins (cert U)
True WWII story of actor, *Clifton James*, who was recruited to impersonate Field Marshal Montgomery in a bid to fool the Nazis.

★★★★★ **Jaws** 1975   125 mins (cert PG)
Spielberg's terrific thriller of seaside resort terrorised by shark. *Roy Scheider*, *Robert Shaw* and *Richard Dreyfuss* as both hunters and hunted. If you haven't seen it, you haven't lived – and you certainly shouldn't go swimming.

★★ **Jaws 2** 1978   117 mins (cert PG)
Scheider's back again, so's the shark, in just about adequate reprise of the original. (Two further sequels – 'Jaws 3D' with *Dennis Quaid* and 3D effects and 'Jaws 4' with *Michael Caine* – are unworthy of attention.)

★★★ **The Jewel of the Nile** 1985   104 mins (cert PG)
Fast-paced but slight sequel to 'Romancing the Stone'. *Kathleen Turner*, *Michael Douglas* and *Danny DeVito* reprise roles.

★★★ **The Karate Kid** 1984   126 mins (cert PG)
Bullied teenager *Ralph Macchio* turns on tormentors when Japanese handyman *Pat Morita* teaches him the martial arts. (Two sequels provide more of the same, less entertainingly.)

★★ **Kickboxer** 1989   100 mins (cert 18)
Violent karate champ *Jean-Claude Van Damme* swears revenge on the kickboxer who maimed his brother. Fairly vicious stuff notable, if at all, as Van Damme's first starring vehicle.

★★★ **Kindergarten Cop** 1990   111 mins (cert 12)
Mean policeman, *Arnold Schwarzenegger*, goes undercover as primary school teacher in a tale too violent to be funny.

★★ **King Kong** 1976   135 mins (cert PG)
Good special effects and sympathetic attitude towards gorilla in competent remake. *Jessica Lange*, on her debut, reprises Fay Wray's role.

★★ **King of New York** 1990   103 mins (cert 18)
An excessively violent film but a powerful performance by *Christopher Walken* as a newly-released prisoner taking on New York's druglords.

★★ **K9** 1989   102 mins (cert 15)
Alsatian and cop *James Belushi* pal up to catch drug pushers in feeble action movie.

★★★ **The Krays** 1990   119 mins (cert 18)
Hard-hitting portrait of the psychotic Cockney brothers who ruled London's East End underworld. The Spandau Ballet brothers, *Gary Kemp* and *Martin Kemp*, are surprisingly good as Reggie and Ron.

★★ **Kuffs** 1991   102 mins (cert 15)
Christian Slater takes over his dead brother's San Francisco private police force in a decidedly soppy teenage action flick. Slater fans will probably like it, though.

★★ **Last Action Hero** 1993   136 mins (cert 15)
A magic cinema ticket enables young lad to enter cinema screen but also lets movie hero *Arnold Schwarzenegger* and evil *Charles Dance* come out. Despite numerous star cameos, film spoofs and money oozing from every stunt pore, it's downright dull stuff.

★★★ **The Last Boy Scout** 1991   105 mins (cert 18)
Ultra-violent action/thriller pickled with comic one-liners and hectic car chases. *Bruce Willis* stars as down-at-heel PI; *Daman Wayans* is his ex-footballer sidekick.

★★★★ **The Last of the Mohicans** 1992   122 mins (cert 12)
Superb adventure. *Daniel Day-Lewis* helping English colonel's daughters, *Madeleine Stowe* and *Jodhi May*, through war-torn and Indian-infested American frontier in 1757. *Wes Studi* gives us one of modern cinema's nastiest villains.

★★★★ **Lawrence of Arabia** 1962   222 mins (cert PG)
David Lean's magnificent epic which brought instant stardom to *Peter O'Toole* as the enigmatic adventurer.

★★★ **Lethal Weapon** 1987   110 mins (cert 18)
Fast-action cops and robbers pairing *Mel Gibson* and *Danny Glover* as the good guys. Violent, trashy and fun.

★★ **Lethal Weapon 2** 1989   111 mins (cert 15)
Inevitable sequel to the above. Perhaps even more violent. Again *Gibson* and *Glover* risk all to catch baddies.

★★★★ **Lethal Weapon 3** 1992   118 mins (cert 15)
Best of the series. More humour accompanies the action as a story of police corruption unravels. *Joe Pesci* returns as *Gibson* and *Glover*'s hapless side-kick.

★ **Licence to Kill** 1989   133 mins (cert 15)
Timothy Dalton as 007 again; *Robert Davi* particularly good as the heavy; *Carey Lowell* the more than usually liberated crumpet. Otherwise the mixture as before.

ACTION/ADVENTURE

★★★ **Little Caesar** 1930   80 mins (cert PG)
Edward G Robinson shot to stardom in this dated but classic 1930s gangster movie based loosely on the exploits of Al Capone. His 'Is this the end of Rico?' is one of the great lines of the movies.

★★ **Live and Let Die** 1973   121 mins (cert PG)
First licence to kill for *Roger Moore* as James Bond. Lots of wild chase sequences. Paul McCartney title song.

★★★ **The Long and the Short and the Tall** 1961   101 mins (cert PG)
Vivid war drama of British patrol in Malayan jungle. *Laurence Harvey* is rather miscast but *Richard Todd* and *Richard Harris* are first-rate.

★★★ **The Longest Day** 1962   169 mins (cert PG)
Mammoth re-creation of Allied invasion of Normandy. Stirring battle scenes and all-star cast: *John Wayne*, *Henry Fonda*, *Robert Mitchum*, *Sean Connery*, *Richard Burton*, etc.

★★★★ **The Long Good Friday** 1980   105 mins (cert 18)
Tough, exciting British gangster thriller. Great performance by *Bob Hoskins*; fine support from *Helen Mirren*.

★★ **Mad Max** 1979   105 mins (cert 18)
Futuristic, innovative action movie. *Mel Gibson* is the policeman out to avenge the murder of wife and child.

★★ **Mad Max 2: The Road Warrior** 1981   90 mins (cert 18)
Visually impressive, action-filled sequel sees *Gibson* protecting small community against marauding group.

★★★ **Mad Max 3: Beyond Thunderdome** 1985   107 mins (cert 15)
Mel Gibson's futuristic warrior exiled to desert. Stunts, chases and *Tina Turner* flesh it out a bit.

★★★ **Magnum Force** 1973   124 mins (cert 18)
Clint Eastwood's second outing as Dirty Harry Callahan. Not quite up to the original but still gripping as Clint hunts down murderous cops.

★★★ **Married to the Mob** 1988   104 mins (cert 15)
Enjoyable comic adventure of gangster's moll *Michelle Pfeiffer* trying to cut ties from the Mob. *Matthew Modine* is her police protector.

★★★★ **Mean Streets** 1973   110 mins (cert 18)
Martin Scorsese's riveting study of young hoods in Little Italy. With *Robert De Niro* and *Harvey Keitel*.

★★★ **Memphis Belle** 1990   107 mins (cert 12)
Spectacular dramatisation of the 25th and final mission of B52 bomber crew during WWII. Young male talent form crew.

★★★ **Moonraker** 1979   126 mins (cert PG)
Roger Moore as 007 in James Bond adventure that increasingly resembles an animated comic strip with gadgets. *Michael Lonsdale* makes a good, weighty heavy.

★★★★ **Mutiny on the Bounty** 1935   135 mins (cert U)
Charles Laughton at his most splendidly hateful as Captain Bligh; *Clark Gable* charismatic as mutiny leader Fletcher Christian.

★★ **Mutiny on the Bounty** 1962   177 mins (cert 15)
Disappointing remake, this time with *Trevor Howard* as Bligh and *Marlon Brando* as Fletcher Christian.

★★★ **The Name of the Rose** 1986   131 mins (cert 18)
Atmospheric mystery story of a monk turned detective. *Sean Connery* investigates murders in a 14th-century monastery. Early appearance by a young *Christian Slater*.

★★ **Navy Seals** 1990   113 mins (cert 15)
Dreary action/thriller with *Charlie Sheen* and *Michael Biehn* as members of the US Marines' crack commando unit.

★★★ **Never Say Never Again** 1983   134 mins (cert PG)
Sean Connery returns as Bond, certainly for the last time, in a stylish but overlong remake of 'Thunderball'.

★ **New Jack City** 1991   100 mins (cert 18)
Poor thriller with *Wesley Snipes* as New York drug baron. Predictability and stereotypes wherever you look.

★★ **Next of Kin** 1989   108 mins (cert 15)
Patrick Swayze as a country cop tracking down mean mobster *Adam Baldwin* through the rougher parts of Chicago. *Liam Neeson* as Swayze's brother.

★★ **Nico: Above the Law** 1988   99 mins (cert 18)
Steven Seagal flexes the occasional muscle in undemanding role as Chicago cop out to protect a senator. Not much demanded of the viewer's brain either.

★★★ **No Escape** 1994   115 mins (cert 15)
A futuristic prison camp on an impenetrable island is where *Ray Liotta* lands up. Some nice ideas never fully explored but Liotta is good playing the hero for once.

★★★★ **North by Northwest** 1959   136 mins (cert PG)
Sparkling Hitchcock adventure with *Cary Grant* as innocuous advertising executive mistaken for spy.

★★★★ **Northwest Frontier** 1959   129 mins (cert U)
Kenneth More as dashing British soldier guiding train bearing native prince through war-torn India. *Lauren Bacall*, *Herbert Lom* and *Wilfrid Hyde White* are among the other passengers. Great Empire stuff. Lips never stiffer.

★ **Nowhere to Run** 1992   95 mins (cert 15)
Nowhere to hide. Outlaw *Jean-Claude Van Damme* helps *Rosanna Arquette* defend her homestead against evil property developer *Joss Ackland*.

★★★ **Octopussy** 1983   130 mins (cert PG)
Thirteenth James Bond movie sees *Roger Moore* smoothly outwitting the evil *Maud Adams* and dastardly plot to nuke US forces.

★★ **On Deadly Ground** 1994   97 mins (cert 15)
Steven Seagal saves Alaska and preaches ecology to the oil barons in an action-packed, preposterous piece of posturing. *Michael Caine* is the bad guy.

★★ **The Package** 1989   108 mins (cert 15)
Gene Hackman becomes the fall guy in an East-West Cold War conspiracy while conducting prisoner *Tommy Lee Jones* to Washington.

★★ **Passenger 57** 1993   84 mins (cert 15)
Wesley Snipes as an airline cop on board a plane hijacked by psychotic *Bruce Payne* on way to trial. Rather appealing, though corny and predictable.

★★ **Patriot Games** 1992   117 mins (cert 15)
Harrison Ford foils IRA plot to blow up a British royal, *James Fox*, so he and wife *Anne Archer* become targets of terrorist *Sean Bean*. Daft but quite exciting.

★★★ **A Perfect World** 1993   135 mins (cert 12)
Kevin Costner as an escaped convict forming a relationship with the young boy he takes hostage. *Clint Eastwood* doubles as the Texas Ranger on his trail and director.

★★★ **Platoon** 1986   120 mins (cert 15)
Oliver Stone's harrowing depiction of US soldiers' lives – and their atrocities – during Vietnam war. *Tom Berenger* and *Willem Dafoe* are outstanding.

★ **Point Break** 1991   120 mins (cert 15)
Ludicrous action picture about surfing bank robbers. With *Patrick Swayze* and *Keanu Reeves* riding those waves. Unbelievable nonsense.

★★★ **The Poseidon Adventure** 1972   117 mins (cert PG)
Disaster movie on the high seas as starry cast panic aboard sinking liner. Oscar-winning special effects.

★★ **Predator** 1987   107 mins (cert 18)
Arnold Schwarzenegger heads SWAT team on rescue mission in jungle, but someone or something keeps killing them.

★★ **Predator 2** 1990   108 mins (cert 18)
Frenetic sequel, this time with *Danny Glover* and *Gary Busey* up against the predator on the streets of LA.

★★ **Quigley Down Under** 1990   120 mins (cert 12)
Tom Selleck arrives in turn-of-century Australia as trouble shooter for evil ranch owner *Alan Rickman* – easily the best thing in it. A Western down under.

★★ **A Rage in Harlem** 1991   110 mins (cert 18)
Racy, sometimes effective combination of sex and violence in quest for stolen gold in 1950s Harlem.

★★★★ **Raiders of the Lost Ark** 1981   115 mins (cert PG)
First rousing adventure of intrepid archaeologist Indiana Jones, *Harrison Ford*. Expertly directed by Steven Spielberg.

★★ **Rapid Fire** 1992   95 mins (cert 18)
The late *Brandon Lee* – son of Bruce – brings class to typical kung fu action/thriller.

★★★ **Reach for the Sky** 1956   135 mins (cert U)
Solid account of exploits of WWII flying ace Douglas Bader – *Kenneth Moore* – who heroically overcame the handicap of a double leg amputation.

★★★ **The Red Badge of Courage** 1951   69 mins (cert U)
John Huston's American Civil War story – truncated and nearly massacred by MGM – with *Audie Murphy* as the young soldier guilt-stricken over his cowardice.

★★ **Red Heat** 1991   104 mins (cert 18)
Arnold Schwarzenegger as Russian cop sent to Chicago to partner *James Belushi* on hunt for Red drug pusher. Not as much violence as you'd expect from director Walter Hill but authentic – first film shot in Red Square.

★ **Revenge** 1990   124 mins (cert 18)
Set in wilds of Mexico where *Kevin Costner* goes to stay with wealthy rancher *Anthony Quinn* but falls for his abused wife, *Madeleine Stowe*. Soon turns from romantic thriller to brutal, boring chase.

★★★ **The Right Stuff** 1983   193 mins (cert 15)
Story of first American astronauts in a sort of space Western adapted from Tom Wolfe's bestseller. Better than its box-office performance would suggest.

★★★ **The River Wild** 1994   113 mins (cert 15)
Exhilarating thriller with *Meryl Streep* negotiating rapids and whirlpools on a family canoeing trip that takes a horrifying turn when *Kevin Bacon* turns up.

★★ **Road House** 1989   114 mins (cert 18)
Patrick Swayze as a nightclub bouncer with a remarkable (and unlikely) past charged with cleaning up a Missouri road house. Lots of violent action.

★★★ **The Roaring Twenties** 1939   106 mins (cert PG)
Dated but still classic gangster story. *James Cagney* and *Humphrey Bogart* involved with the rackets after WWI.

★ **Robin Hood** 1991   104 mins (cert PG)
Patrick Bergin as Robin, *Uma Thurman* as Marian in a drably
disappointing version which seems much of the time to be
sending itself up.

★★★ **Robin Hood: Prince of Thieves** 1991   143 mins (cert PG)
Kevin Costner's earnest folk hero is totally overshadowed by *Alan
Rickman*'s gloriously hammy Sheriff of Nottingham.

★★ **Robocop** 1987   103 mins (cert 18)
Peter Weller as a cop who dies in the course of duty and is then
transformed into a cyborg – but one who wants revenge on
his killers.

★★ **Robocop 2** 1990   102 mins (cert 18)
Weak sequel in which a wicked corporation and a drug dealer
want to kill Robo with their own bigger, better cyborg. *Peter
Weller* and *Nancy Allen* are back from the original.

★★ **Robocop 3** 1994   105 mins (cert 15)
Robert Burke takes over as the Cyborg cop, this time helping the
homeless organise resistance against the company that made
them so.

★★ **The Rocketeer** 1991   120 mins (cert PG)
Amiable, 1930s spoof in which a unique flying machine brings
adventures and danger for pilot hero. *Bill Campbell* and *Jennifer
Connolly* star.

★★★ **Rocky** 1976   119 mins (cert PG)
Raw energy emanates from *Sylvester Stallone*'s portrayal of
small-time fighter given a shot at the title. Best of the series.

★★ **Rocky 2** 1979   119 mins (cert PG)
Adequate sequel continues much along lines of original. But by
now we've seen it all before.

★★ **Rocky 3** 1982   99 mins (cert PG)
And we see it all again as Rocky loses title to *Mr T* and goes for
the re-match.

★ **Rocky 4** 1985   91 mins (cert PG)
Utter nonsense as Rocky avenges his friend's death and fights
for world peace against Russian champ *Dolph Lundgren*.

ACTION/ADVENTURE

★ **Rocky 5** 1990   104 mins (cert PG)
Not that you'd notice, but the champ has suffered brain damage; worse, he's lost all his money. But by now nobody cares.

★★★ **Romancing the Stone** 1984   105 mins (cert PG)
Romantic adventure. Novelist *Kathleen Turner* involved with *Michael Douglas* in search for kidnapped sister in South America. Fast, enjoyable and a lot of fun.

★★ **Romeo Is Bleeding** 1994   123 mins (cert 18)
Gary Oldman as a crooked cop meeting his match in the form of seductive prisoner *Lena Olin*. A dark and rather nasty thriller.

★ **Romper Stomper** 1992   91 mins (cert 18)
Vicious drama about Australian skinheads and racism. Alienating but energetic and sometimes thought-provoking.

★★ **Rumble Fish** 1983   94 mins (cert 18)
Intense, over-stylised drama of alienated teenager *Matt Dillon* manipulated by older brother *Mickey Rourke*.

★★★ **The Sea Hawk** 1940   122 mins (cert U)
Errol Flynn cuts a dashing blade as Sir Francis Drake. *Flora Robson* plays Elizabeth I. Good, swashbuckling stuff.

★ **Shanghai Surprise** 1986   97 mins (cert 15)
Pretty dire romantic adventure featuring *Madonna* and her then husband *Sean Penn*. Feeble plot, feeble performances.

★★ **Shining Through** 1992   132 mins (cert 15)
So bad it's funny. *Melanie Griffith* as a spy in Germany during WWII. *Michael Douglas* is the woefully negligent intelligence officer who sent her there. Hilariously absurd.

★★★ **Sneakers** 1992   125 mins (cert 12)
Great caper movie with starry cast, wonderful gadgetry and clever plot. *Robert Redford* and *River Phoenix* lead the good guys; *Ben Kingsley* is the baddy out to rule the world.

★★ **Sniper** 1992   98 mins (cert 15)
US army snipers *Tom Berenger* and *Billy Zane*, on a killing mission in hostile jungle, bicker their way tediously through the bush.

★★★ **The Sound Barrier** 1952   118 mins (cert U)
Soaring cinematography, solid performances by *Ralph Richardson* and *Ann Todd*, plus David Lean's direction distinguish this tale of the men who tested the early jet planes.

★★★ **South Central** 1992   99 mins (cert 15)
Black gang culture explored in a sincere and thoughtful study of the dangers of life in the ghetto.

★★★★ **Southern Comfort** 1981   106 mins (cert 18)
Intense, survival-of-the-fittest yarn based on National Guardsmen caught in guerrilla warfare in the Louisiana swamps. Terrific atmosphere and taut direction by Walter Hill.

★★★ **Spartacus** 1960   196 mins (cert PG)
Spectacular story of the slave, *Kirk Douglas*, who led a rebellion against Rome. Good support from the likes of *Laurence Olivier*, *Tony Curtis* and *Peter Ustinov*.

★★ **The Specialist** 1994   102 mins (cert 18)
Sylvester Stallone is the explosives specialist, *Sharon Stone* the client who hires him to avenge her parents, murdered by *Eric Roberts*. Very spectacular but quite soulless.

★★★★ **Speed** 1994   115 mins (cert 15)
Palm-sweating excitement as a bus bearing a bomb careers along Californian freeways. *Dennis Hopper* placed the bomb; only brave cop *Keanu Reeves* can save the passengers with the help of *Sandra Bullock* driving the bus. Brilliant special effects and set action pieces.

★ **Spymaker: The Secret Life of Ian Fleming** 1990   100 mins (cert 15)
Weak, fictionalised biography of the creator of James Bond. Nice touch, though, to cast Sean Connery's son, *Jason Connery*, in the title role.

★★★ **The Spy Who Loved Me** 1977   125 mins (cert PG)
One of the best Bond movies pits *Roger Moore* and *Barbara Bach* against indestructible adversary, Jaws – *Richard Kiel*.

★★★★ **Stalag 17** 1953   120 mins (cert PG)
Brilliant blend of drama, excitement and wit in Billy Wilder's tale of Americans in a German POW camp. Probably *William Holden*'s best performance.

ACTION/ADVENTURE

★★★ **Streets of Fire** 1984   94 mins (cert 15)
Prettier to look at than listen to. Rock 'n' roll fantasy with *Michael Pare* fighting to free girlfriend *Diane Lane* from kidnappers.

★★★ **Striking Distance** 1994   113 mins (cert 15)
A killer's on the loose and river patrol cop *Bruce Willis* thinks it's a member of the force. But can he even trust his partner, *Sarah Jessica Parker*? Lots of violent action.

★★ **Super Mario Brothers** 1992   105 mins (cert PG)
You've played the video game – now see the movie. Not that it's up to much, alas. *Bob Hoskins* and *John Leguizamo* are the two Brooklyn plumbers plunged into a parallel world to save *Samantha Mathis*.

★★★ **The Taking of Pelham 123** 1974   104 mins (cert 15)
Robert Shaw hijacks a New York subway train, holding the passengers to ransom. *Walter Matthau* has a tension-packed hour to free them.

★★★★ **A Tale of Two Cities** 1935   121 mins (cert U)
Lavish version of Charles Dickens' classic story of the French Revolution. *Ronald Colman* and *Elizabeth Allan* lead.

★★ **Tango and Cash** 1989   104 mins (cert 15)
Mediocre action movie about two policemen, *Kurt Russell* and *Sylvester Stallone*, at loggerheads over different attitudes to their profession.

★★ **Teenage Mutant Ninja Turtles** 1990   93 mins (cert PG)
Four mutated turtles – Leonardo, Donatello, Raphael and Michelangelo – fight New York crimewave from their home in the sewers. So-so mix of action and comedy.

★★ **Teenage Mutant Ninja Turtles II** 1991   87 mins (cert PG)
Pizza-loving dudes return to wage war on toxic waste. Young viewers should find it as pleasing – or not – as the first.

★★ **Teenage Mutant Ninja Turtles III** 1992   95 mins (cert PG)
Mixture as before as the overgrown terrapins go back in time to ancient Japan to rescue April, *Paige Turco*.

★★★★ **The Ten Commandments** 1956   219 mins (cert U)
Cecil B DeMille's biblical epic. Cast of thousands. *Charlton Heston* as Moses, *Yul Brynner* as Pharaoh.

***** **Thelma and Louise** 1991   130 mins (cert 15)
A smashing movie. Great photography, superb direction by Ridley Scott and outstanding performances by *Geena Davis* and *Susan Sarandon* as two rebellious women having a ball on the run for murder.

**** **The Three Musketeers** 1973   107 mins (cert U)
Entertaining, tongue-in-cheek version of the romantic swashbuckler with *Oliver Reed, Richard Chamberlain, Michael York, Raquel Welch, Charlton Heston* and *Faye Dunaway*.

* **The Three Musketeers** 1993   106 mins (cert PG)
Kiefer Sutherland, Charlie Sheen and *Chris O'Donnell* buckle badly rather than swash in this unnecessary and inept remake.

*** **Three Ninja Kids** 1992   85 mins (cert PG)
Three kids are taught the martial arts by Oriental grandad and use them to help their FBI agent father foil evil arms importers.

*** **Thunderball** 1965   132 mins (cert PG)
The fourth in the Bond series and still good value. *Sean Connery* as 007, *Adolfo Celi* the evil Largo. Connery did it all again in the remake, 'Never Say Never Again'.

**** **To Have and Have Not** 1944   100 mins (cert 15)
A sort of Howard Hawkes version of 'Casablanca'. *Humphrey Bogart* reluctantly embroiled with French Resistance while wooing *Lauren Bacall*.

*** **Top Gun** 1986   110 mins (cert 15)
Young naval pilot *Tom Cruise* conducts passionate love affair with *Kelly McGillis* against backdrop of incredible flying sequences.

*** **Tora! Tora! Tora!** 1970   144 mins (cert U)
Tense action movie portraying the events leading up to the attack on Pearl Harbor from both American and Japanese points of view.

*** **The Towering Inferno** 1974   165 mins (cert 15)
Contrived disaster movie, enhanced by good effects and expensive cast: *Paul Newman, Steve McQueen, Fred Astaire, Faye Dunaway*, et al.

★★★ **A Town Like Alice** 1956   117 mins (cert U)
Powerful story of female POWs in Malaysia, headed by *Virginia McKenna* and helped by the man from Alice Springs, *Peter Finch*. Nicely romantic.

★★★ **Toy Soldiers** 1991   112 mins (cert 15)
Problem preppies – *Sean Astin*, et al – show astonishing ingenuity when their school is hijacked by terrorists. Enjoyable, though much suspension of disbelief required.

★★★ **Trespass** 1992   101 mins (cert 18)
Two white firemen, *Bill Paxton* and *William Sadler*, hunting for treasure in a disused warehouse run into a drugs gang – *Ice T* and *Ice Cube* among them – with violent results.

★★★ **True Lies** 1994   99 mins (cert 12)
Arnold Schwarzenegger as a sort of James Bond, whose wife *Jamie Lee Curtis* thinks he's just a computer salesman, takes on a bunch of megalomaniac villains. James Cameron directed, reportedly with a budget of $120 million – the largest ever. Without question the special effects are the best thing in the film.

★★★★ **True Romance** 1993   119 mins (cert 18)
Quentin Tarantino wrote, Tony Scott directed. *Christian Slater* and *Patricia Arquette* as newlyweds who kill her pimp, find cocaine and travel to LA to sell it in the course of their honeymoon. Witty and extremely violent thriller.

★★★★ **Twelve O'Clock High** 1949   132 mins (cert U)
Great performances by *Gregory Peck* and *Dean Jagger* in taut absorbing story of American bomber crews based in England during WWII.

★★ **Under Siege** 1992   103 mins (cert 15)
Sea cook *Steven Seagal* single-handedly rescues his battleship from potential world-destroyer *Tommy Lee Jones*. Action from Seagal, acting class from Jones.

★★★★ **The Untouchables** 1987   119 mins (cert 15)
Prohibition Chicago's the setting for FBI agent Elliot Ness, *Kevin Costner*, to bring down Al Capone, *Robert De Niro*, with the help of Irish cop *Sean Connery*. Taut Brian De Palma thriller.

★★★ **A View to a Kill** 1985   121 mins (cert PG)
Roger Moore as Bond, *Christopher Walken* as the villain, seeking to corner the world's microchip supply.

★★★★ **Viva Zapata!** 1952   112 mins (cert PG)
Marlon Brando gives outstanding portrayal of the legendary Mexican revolutionary who rose to the presidency.

★★★ **War and Peace** 1956   208 mins (cert U)
Simplified King Vidor version of Tolstoy's epic. *Audrey Hepburn*, *Henry Fonda* and *John Mills* star. Spectacular battle scenes.

★★★ **The Wild One** 1954   79 mins (cert PG)
The original biker movie, which was once banned in Britain. Misunderstood *Marlon Brando* and gang run riot in town.

★ **Wings of the Apache** 1990   89 mins (cert 15)
A poor man's 'Top Gun'. Helicopters instead of planes and *Nicolas Cage* and *Sean Young* instead of Tom Cruise and Kelly McGillis.

★★★ **The Wooden Horse** 1950   101 mins (cert U)
Solid British wartime escape drama with *Leo Genn* and *David Tomlinson*.

★★★★ **The Young Lions** 1958   167 mins (cert PG)
A blond *Marlon Brando* takes some getting used to but this is a gripping WWII story told from both the German and American points of view.

★★ **You Only Live Twice** 1967   108 mins (cert PG)
Sean Connery in typical fast, jokey, James Bond caper. *Donald Pleasence* as the evil Blofeld.

★★★★ **Zulu** 1964   133 mins (cert PG)
Stanley Baker and *Michael Caine* at the battle of Rourke's Drift during the Zulu wars. Superb battle scenes.

★★★ **Zulu Dawn** 1979   115 mins (cert PG)
A prequel to the above, with *Burt Lancaster* and *Peter O'Toole*, centring on the battle that immediately preceded that of Rourke's Drift.

COMEDY

★★★★ **Ace Ventura: Pet Detective** 1993   82 mins (cert 12)
Jim Carrey, he of the rubber face, plays a private eye employed to find a missing dolphin. *Sean Young* is the police chief who's more than she seems. Daft but hilarious.

★★★★ **Adam's Rib** 1949   100 mins (cert U)
Katharine Hepburn and *Spencer Tracy* work beautifully together as husband and wife lawyers on opposite sides of the same case.

★★ **Adventures in Babysitting** 1987   99 mins (cert 15)
Elizabeth Shue's babysitting stint goes crazily wrong on a wild night out in Chicago. Amiable comedy/thriller.

★★ **The Adventures of Baron Munchausen** 1989   126 mins (cert PG)
Terry Gilliam's ambitious, uneven, sometimes dazzling tale of the 18th-century Prussian fantasist (a rather miscast *John Neville*). The parts are much better than the whole.

★★★ **The Adventures of Priscilla, Queen of the Desert** 1994   104 mins (cert 15)
Priscilla's a bus taking two drag queens and transexual *Terence Stamp* though the homophobic Australian outback to a gig in Alice Springs. Unusual and sometimes very funny.

★★★ **After Hours** 1985   97 mins (cert 15)
Martin Scorsese's dark, funny comedy. Lonely *Griffin Dunne*'s date with *Rosanna Arquette* turns into a nightmare in hostile Manhattan.

★★ **Airheads** 1994   92 mins (cert 15)
Dimwitted comedy about three thick headbangers who accidently take a radio station hostage as they try to get their demo tape played on air.

★★★★ **Airplane!** 1980   98 mins (cert 12)
Hilarious skit on the 'Airport' disaster movies which made a star of *Leslie Nielsen*. *Lloyd Bridges* is terrific, too.

★★★ **Airplane II: The Sequel** 1982   84 mins (cert 12)
Much the same as 'Airplane!', only not quite so good. Notable cameo though from *William Shatner*, aka Captain Kirk.

★★★ **Alice** 1991 105 mins (cert 12)
Surreal moral comedy by Woody Allen. Rich, bored housewife *Mia Farrow* finds the meaning of life from magical Chinese herbs.

★★★ **All of Me** 1984 91 mins (cert 15)
Lily Tomlin shares *Steve Martin*'s body in screwball comedy with a fair share of slapstick laughs.

★★★ **American Graffiti** 1973 110 mins (cert PG)
Director George Lucas' nostalgic look at 1960s USA. Great rock 'n' roll soundtrack and impressive cast.

★★★ **And Now for Something Completely Different** 1972 88 mins (cert PG)
Collection of Monty Python's TV best including that family favourite 'The Dead Parrot' sketch.

★★★★ **Annie Hall** 1977 93 mins (cert 15)
Woody Allen's brilliant, Oscar-winning romantic comedy about a neurotic Jewish comedian's troubled affair with a disorganised WASP – *Diane Keaton* at her scattiest.

★★★★ **The Apartment** 1960 125 mins (cert PG)
Jack Lemmon and *Shirley MacLaine* shine in Billy Wilder's sharp satire of inter-office relationships.

★★★★ **Arsenic and Old Lace** 1944 118 mins (cert PG)
Cary Grant at his effortless best trying to stop two elderly ladies poisoning lonely old men. Time-honoured classic that creaks hardly at all in its old age.

★★★ **Arthur** 1981 97 mins (cert 15)
Dudley Moore as an alcoholic and unhappy millionaire risking his inheritance for the woman he loves, *Liza Minnelli*. Daft but fun. *John Gielgud*, as the butler, steals the show.

★ **Arthur II: On the Rocks** 1988 110 mins (cert PG)
Deeply feeble sequel in which Arthur does lose his inheritance and strives to get it back.

★★ **Baby Boom** 1987 110 mins (cert PG)
Diane Keaton plays a yuppie who inherits a baby and finds fulfilment. Charming and best of the baby movies that flooded the screen around that time.

★★★ **Baby It's You** 1982   101 mins (cert 15)
Rosanna Arquette leads a neat cast in John Sayles' amusing look at love and life in 1960s New Jersey.

★★★ **Bad Behaviour** 1993   100 mins (cert 15)
Comedy/drama about a London Irish household coping with all manner of disasters. *Stephen Rea* and *Sinead Cusack* head a very accomplished cast.

★★★ **Bananas** 1971   81 mins (cert 15)
Whacky, rather uneven caper from *Woody Allen* who finds himself caught up in a South American revolution and becomes a reluctant rebel leader. Fine sprinkling of splendid Allen gags.

★★★ **Barefoot in the Park** 1967   109 mins (cert PG)
Neil Simon's engaging play of struggling, squabbling, Manhattan newly-weds, *Jane Fonda* and *Robert Redford*, coping with in-laws, neighbours and the problems of a fifth-floor flat.

★★★ **Barton Fink** 1991   116 mins (cert 15)
Surreal comedy from the Coen Brothers about Hollywood, writer's block and a serial killer. With *John Turturro* and *John Goodman*.

★★★ **Beetlejuice** 1988   92 mins (cert 15)
Comic caper of ghosts, *Alec Baldwin* and *Geena Davis*, trying to exorcise modernist family from home with help of whacky Betelgeuse, *Michael Keaton*.

★★ **Betsy's Wedding** 1990   94 mins (cert 15)
Alan Alda's mannered comedy revolves around the preparations for his daughter *Molly Ringwald*'s big day. Amiable but very predictable.

★★ **The Big Picture** 1989   100 mins (cert 15)
Engaging satire with *Kevin Bacon* as a promising filmmaker corrupted by Hollywood where integrity may (just) buy the groceries but not the Porsche and the house in Beverly Hills.

★★★ **Biloxi Blues** 1988   100 mins (cert 15)
Neil Simon's delightful observations of the lives of raw recruits in a wartime training camp. *Matthew Broderick* stars as the innocent called to arms.

★★ **Bird on a Wire** 1990   111 mins (cert 12)
Acceptable action/comedy pairs ex-lovers, *Mel Gibson* and *Goldie Hawn*, running from killers. The stars are better than the plot.

★★★★ **Blazing Saddles** 1974   93 mins (cert 15)
Mel Brooks' hilarious Western spoof with *Gene Wilder*. Includes the celebrated farting scene after a bean supper.

★★★ **Bob Roberts** 1992   104 mins (cert 15)
Tim Robbins wrote, directed, sang and starred in this clever political satire as a hypocritical right-wing political candidate in America. Numerous cameos and lovely support performance from *Alan Rickman*.

★★ **Boomerang** 1992   117 mins (cert 15)
Arrogant ladies' man *Eddie Murphy* overlooks nice *Halle Berry* and gets his comeuppance at the hands of beautiful new boss *Robin Givens*. The odd good gag and Murphy's okay.

★★★★★ **Bringing Up Baby** 1938   102 mins (cert U)
Howard Hawkes' inspired, classic comedy. Marvellous pairing of *Cary Grant* and *Katharine Hepburn* brought together by a missing leopard.

★★★ **Broadcast News** 1987   127 mins (cert 15)
William Hurt, *Holly Hunter* and *Albert Brooks* in a sharp, funny satire of the TV news industry.

★★★★ **Broadway Danny Rose** 1984   86 mins (cert PG)
Woody Allen as Broadway agent involved with third-rate variety acts and Mafia moll *Mia Farrow*. Delightful.

★★ **Cadillac Man** 1990   98 mins (cert 15)
Car salesman *Robin Williams* is held hostage by *Tim Robbins* in a comedy that starts well but fades fast.

★ **California Man** 1992   88 mins (cert PG)
Sean Astin unearths Neanderthal man in his back yard and causes a comic stir when he takes him to school. Hopelessly moronic stuff.

★★★★ **California Suite** 1978   103 mins (cert 15)
Four separate but intertwined stories of guests at the Beverly Hills Hotel at Oscar time. Sharp, funny script by Neil Simon. Great cast. *Maggie Smith* superb.

★ **Carry On Columbus** 1992   91 mins (cert PG)
Latest and possibly worst of the 39 films in the series. Even a reasonable cast can do little with the deeply naff script.

★★★ **Carry On Up the Khyber** 1968   88 mins (cert PG)
One of the best of series with typical lavatorial humour and familiar, well-loved original cast. (Numerous other 'Carry On's available on video have their moments. 'Carry On Cleo' is easily the best of them; 'Carry On England' is best avoided.)

★★ **The Chase** 1993   89 mins (cert 15)
Charlie Sheen as escaped – but innocent – convict taking a millionaire's daughter hostage to ensure safe passage. *Kristy Swanson*, the hostage, falls in love with her captor. Sheen's natural aptitude for comedy is not used to its best here.

★ **Chasers** 1994   110 mins (cert 15)
Don't give up the day job, *Dennis Hopper*, if this is your best directorial effort. Silly, clichéd tale of two naval policemen – *William McNamara* and *Tom Berenger* – escorting felon *Erika Eleniak* to the airport.

★★ **A Chorus of Disapproval** 1988   99 mins (cert PG)
Michael Winner's movie adaptation of Alan Ayckbourn's shrewd, funny play falls flat and wastes an excellent cast headed by *Jeremy Irons* and *Anthony Hopkins*.

★★★ **City Lights** 1931   87 mins (cert U)
Charlie Chaplin's sweet but hugely sentimental classic about his love for blind flower seller.

★★★ **City Slickers** 1991   114 mins (cert 12)
Witty, charming story in which *Billy Crystal*, *Bruno Kirby* and *Daniel Stern* work out mid-life crisis on modern cattle drive. *Jack Palance* won supporting Oscar as the herd boss.

★ **City Slickers II: The Legend of Curly's Gold** 1994   115 mins (cert 12)
Dismal sequel resurrects *Jack Palance*, who died in the original, as his own twin brother. Weak jokes and feeble plot drown even *Billy Crystal*'s comic talent. *Jon Lovitz*, who replaced Bruno Kirby, is wasted.

★★★ **Clockwise** 1986   96 mins (cert PG)
Madcap vehicle for *John Cleese*, desperately trying to get to Norwich in time for a headmasters convention.

★★ **Comfort and Joy** 1984   106 mins (cert PG)
Bill Forsyth's quirky story of ice cream wars in Glasgow. *Bill Paterson* is splendid as disc jockey who inadvertently becomes involved.

★★ **Company Business** 1991   98 mins (cert 15)
Three generations of a family attempt a robbery planned by grandfather, *Sean Connery*. Even an excellent cast (*Dustin Hoffman* and *Matthew Broderick* also star) can't make it work.

★★ **The Concierge** 1993   95 mins (cert PG)
Michael J Fox as the Mr Fix-It concierge of a Manhattan hotel who can solve everyone's problems but his own. Fox makes the script appear better than it is.

★★★ **Cool Runnings** 1993   99 mins (cert PG)
Charming story based on truth about a Jamaican bobsled team in the Olympics. Penultimate film for *John Candy*, who's delightful as the team's coach.

★★ **Cousins** 1989   113 mins (cert 15)
Ted Danson and *Isabella Rossellini* as lovers and cousins in family comedy. Inferior American remake of French 'Cousin, Cousine'.

★★ **Crazy People** 1990   92 mins (cert 15)
Dudley Moore finds *Darryl Hannah* and sanity in a lunatic asylum. Silly but sometimes agreeable.

★★★★ **Crimes and Misdemeanours** 1989   104 mins (cert 15)
Woody Allen's bold, skilful blending and bringing together of two separate stories involving comedy, murder and adultery.

★★★ **Crossing Delancey** 1988   96 mins (cert PG)
Wistful tale with some charm of a romance and arranged marriage in the Jewish community of downtown New York.

★★★ **Dave** 1993   110 mins (cert 12)
Kevin Kline impersonates president when incumbent has a stroke but can he fool the nation, not to mention the first lady, *Sigourney Weaver*? Very pleasing comedy with a tip or two to offer any national leader.

★★★ **A Day at the Races** 1937   109 mins (cert U)
Typical *Marx Brothers* vehicle graced by *Maureen O'Hara*. Perfunctory story; brothers on top form.

★★ **Deadly Advice** 1994   91 mins (cert 15)
Repressed spinster *Jane Horrocks* kills her mother, *Brenda Fricker*, after being urged on by the ghosts of dead murderers. Not much to laugh about. Even the talented Horrocks can make little of a weak script.

★★★ **Dead Men Don't Wear Plaid** 1982   88 mins (cert PG)
Clever editing sees private eye *Steve Martin* meeting late Hollywood greats in pleasant film noir pastiche.

★★ **Death Becomes Her** 1992   104 mins (cert PG)
Breathtaking special effects can't help the stupid plot. *Goldie Hawn* and *Meryl Streep* demand immortalizing drug – no matter what harm befalls their bodies. *Bruce Willis* is the object of their affections.

★★★★ **Desperately Seeking Susan** 1985   104 mins (cert 15)
Excellent comedy of mistaken identities between kooky *Rosanna Arquette* and streetwise *Madonna* in her best film role to date.

★★★ **Dirty Rotten Scoundrels** 1988   110 mins (cert PG)
Good knockabout fun with *Steve Martin* and *Michael Caine* as conmen working the French Riviera.

★★ **The Distinguished Gentleman** 1992   114 mins (cert 15)
Conman *Eddie Murphy* runs for congress and when there quickly cleans up some of the shady deals in Washington. Funny and romantic satire of American politics.

★★ **Down and Out in Beverly Hills** 1986   103 mins (cert 15)
Comic adventures prompted when tramp *Nick Nolte* tries to commit suicide in *Richard Dreyfuss* and *Bette Midler*'s pool.

★★★ **Dragnet** 1987   106 mins (cert PG)
Amusing parody of TV police shows with *Tom Hanks* and *Dan Aykroyd* as the hapless cops. Starts better than it finishes since momentum tends to wane.

★★★ **The Dream Team** 1989   113 mins (cert 15)
Hilarious adventures of four mental patients – *Michael Keaton*, *Christopher Lloyd*, *Peter Boyle* and *Stephen Furst* – at large in downtown New York.

★★★★ **Dr Strangelove** 1964   93 mins (cert 15)
Triple role for *Peter Sellers* in Stanley Kubrick's deep black satire about crazy US General launching nuclear attack on Russia.

★ **Earth Girls Are Easy** 1989   100 mins (cert PG)
Vibrant colours and songs do little to help feeble comedy of
three licentious aliens invading home of valley girl *Geena Davis*.

★★ **18 Again!** 1988   100 mins (cert PG)
Aged *George Burns* and grandson Charlie Schlatter swap bodies
with feeble results.

★★ **Erik the Viking** 1989   102 mins (cert 12)
Monty Python's *Terry Jones* directed this scrappy, sometimes
funny story of Norsemen setting off to save the world. Usual
crew plus *Tim Robbins*.

★★★ **Every Which Way But Loose** 1978   114 mins (cert 12)
Lightweight comedy with plenty of knockabout action pairing
Clint Eastwood as gallant clod and an orang-utan as his smarter
companion.

★★ **Fatal Instinct** 1994   86 mins (cert 15)
Carl Reiner's spoof on all those loony, murderous women films
with *Armand Assante*, *Sherilyn Fenn* and *Sean Young*. Fun in parts.

★★ **Father of the Bride** 1992   105 mins (cert PG)
Unnecessary remake of the Spencer Tracey/Elizabeth Taylor
movie. *Steve Martin* too lightweight and too much the comedian
to be convincing.

★★ **The Favour** 1994   96 mins (cert 15)
Harley Jane Kuzak, happily married to *Bill Pullman*, becomes
obsessed with her high school boyfriend *Ken Whal* and gets her
friend *Elizabeth McGovern* to try him out. Mediocre stuff.

★★★ **Fear of a Black Hat** 1994   87 mins (cert 15)
Untidy but wickedly funny spoof about a black rapping band –
Niggaz With Hats – who produce such albums as 'Granny Says
Kick Your Ass' and 'Straight Outta Da Butt'.

★★ **Filofax** 1990   108 mins (cert 12)
Convict *James Belushi* finds *Charles Grodin*'s filofax and takes over
his life. Has its moments but not enough of them.

★★★★ **A Fish Called Wanda** 1988   108 mins (cert 15)
Hilarious romantic caper. *John Cleese* and *Jamie Lee Curtis* as
barrister and crook in love. *Kevin Kline* steals the movie as her
dim, jealous suitor.

★★★★★ **Forrest Gump** 1994   140 mins (cert PG)
Special effects hit new heights as *Tom Hanks* plays the simple hero who, one way or another, is present at every important event of the past three decades. Don't miss it, it's a gem.

★★★ **The Fortune Cookie** 1966   125 mins (cert U)
Substandard Billy Wilder comedy in which *Jack Lemmon* and *Walter Matthau* try to pull off an insurance scam.

★★★★ **Four Weddings and a Funeral** 1994   112 mins (cert 15)
Actually it's four weddings etc plus two people who are just right for each other – *Hugh Grant* and *Andie MacDowell* – though they can't always see it. Encapsulates British charm. Hugely enjoyable.

★★★★ **The Freshman** 1990   103 mins (cert PG)
College student *Matthew Broderick* falls in with mobster *Marlon Brando*, here gloriously parodying his 'Godfather' role. A very funny and offbeat comedy.

★★ **Frozen Assets** 1993   95 mins (cert 12)
Romantic cryogenics comedy. Manager of sperm bank ensures a plentiful supply by running an outrageous virility contest. With *Shelley Long* and *Corbin Bernsen*.

★★★★ **The General** 1927   80 mins (cert U)
The best of *Buster Keaton*'s stunt-filled romps, set during the American Civil War. Keaton in search of his stolen train – and his sweetheart.

★★★ **Ghengis Cohn** 1993   111 mins (cert PG)
Jewish comedian *Anthony Sher*, killed at Auschwitz, returns to haunt SS officers and convert them to Judaism. *Robert Lindsay* as the chief-of-police learning to love kosher food in a novel, engaging story.

★★★★ **Ghost** 1990   126 mins (cert 12)
Hugely popular comedy/drama sees murdered *Patrick Swayze* returning to protect his threatened lover, *Demi Moore*. *Whoopi Goldberg* as medium lifts tone delightfully.

★★ **The Gods Must Be Crazy** 1981   108 mins (cert 15)
Three stories amalgamate in eccentric slapstick from South Africa which has developed cult following.

★★★★★ **The Gold Rush** 1925   72 mins (cert U)
The Klondike 1898 provides the setting for *Charlie Chaplin*'s important silent classic in which he eats his own boots and laces and performs the dance of the bread rolls.

★★★ **Good Morning Vietnam** 1987   121 mins (cert 15)
Fine performance by *Robin Williams* as irreverent DJ cheering the troops in Vietnam. Basic plot's a bit thin, though.

★★ **Greedy** 1994   113 mins (cert 12)
Kirk Douglas is an unpleasant millionaire who hires a beautiful nurse, *Maryam D'Abo*. Favourite nephew *Michael J Fox* is called in to ensure Douglas's money doesn't leave the family. Vaguely romantic, vaguely amusing.

★★★ **Green Card** 1990   107 mins (cert 12)
Romantic comedy featuring *Gérard Depardieu* and *Andie MacDowell* in a marriage of convenience and a divorce of courtship.

★★★★★ **Gregory's Girl** 1980   91 mins (cert PG)
Superb direction by Bill Forsyth and an outstanding debut by *John Gordon Sinclair*. A comic jewel that should appear in anyone's top ten favourites.

★★★★ **Groundhog Day** 1993   103 mins (cert PG)
Bill Murray finds himself living the same day over and over and over again – until he gets it right. Very funny and thought-provoking.

★ **Grumpy Old Men** 1994   89 mins (cert 12)
Walter Matthau and *Jack Lemmon* as grouchy old neighbours who squabble over pretty widow *Ann-Margret*. Unsatisfying comedy, poorly written.

★★★★ **Guess Who's Coming to Dinner** 1967   112 mins (cert PG)
Spencer Tracy and *Katharine Hepburn* forced to come to terms with inter-racial marriage of daughter *Katharine Houghton* to *Sidney Poitier*. Tracy's last film.

★★ **Hairspray** 1988   88 mins (cert PG)
John Waters' nostalgic, comic satire of the style and fashions of the dance-crazed 1960s.

★★★★ **Hannah and Her Sisters** 1986   107 mins (cert 15)
Woody Allen's best plot to date concentrates on the fortunes of three sisters – *Mia Farrow*, *Barbara Hershey* and *Dianne Wiest* – and *Michael Caine*, who won an Oscar.

★★★★ **Harvey** 1950   104 mins (cert U)
Sheer delight about an endearing drunk, *James Stewart*, whose relatives want him committed due to his friendship with a six-foot, invisible rabbit called Harvey.

★★★★ **Hear My Song** 1991   103 mins (cert 15)
Delightful, heart-warming tale of nightclub owner trying to find noted, tax-dodging Irish tenor Josef Locke and bring him to Liverpool for a concert. *Adrian Dunbar* and *Ned Beatty* excel.

★★ **The Heartbreak Kid** 1972   106 mins (cert PG)
Charles Grodin tires of wife on honeymoon where he falls for *Cybill Shepherd* in poignant, bittersweet Neil Simon comedy of embarrassment.

★★ **Heart Condition** 1990   100 mins (cert 15)
Racist cop *Bob Hoskins* is given the heart of dead black lawyer *Denzel Washington*, who returns to haunt him, help him and change him.

★★ **High Anxiety** 1977   94 mins (cert 15)
Disappointing, sporadically funny attempt by *Mel Brooks* to do to Hitchcock what he'd done to the Western in 'Blazing Saddles'.

★★★ **High Hopes** 1988   110 mins (cert 15)
Mike Leigh's biting condemnation of Thatcherite London, yuppiedom and the like. A strong ensemble cast extracts the full humour and satire from the sharp dialogue.

★★★ **Honeymoon in Vegas** 1993   95 mins (cert 12)
Nicolas Cage loses fiancée, *Sarah Jessica Parker*, in card game to wealthy *James Caan*. Best and funniest of the crop of films treating women as commodities. Lovely running gag about Elvis impersonators.

★★★★ **Hope and Glory** 1987   113 mins (cert 15)
John Boorman's delightful, nostalgic and autobiographical story of life as a small boy during WWII.

★ **Hostile Hostages** 1994   92 mins (cert 15)
Dennis Leary takes a sparring couple hostage at Christmas and has a miserable time when the entire family turns up and just bickers. A comedy only in name which was 'The Ref' in US.

★★ **Hot Shots** 1991   85 mins (cert 12)
Charlie Sheen and *Lloyd Bridges* attempt to do to 'Top Gun' what 'Airplane!' did to 'Airport'. Nice try, doesn't quite work; the sequel gets nearer the mark.

★★★ **Hot Shots Part Deux** 1992   89 mins (cert 12)
'Rambo' spoof, though many more films come in for the typical treatment. *Charlie Sheen* and *Lloyd Bridges* funnier than before.

★★★ **Housesitter** 1992   102 mins (cert PG)
Frenetic comedy in which *Goldie Hawn* poses as *Steve Martin*'s wife after a one-night stand with him. Moving into his unoccupied new home she becomes the bane of his life. Hawn overly kooky and Martin's talents stifled.

★★ **How to Get Ahead in Advertising** 1989   104 mins (cert 15)
More satirical than funny comedy about marketing man, *Richard E Grant*, with a talking boil on his neck.

★★★ **The Hudsucker Proxy** 1994   121 mins (cert PG)
Charming, Capra-esque pastiche of 1930s comedies. *Tim Robbins* is the boy from the postroom who rises and falls within the Hudsucker company. *Jennifer Jason Leigh* is superb as the hard-nosed reporter on his case.

★★★ **Husbands and Wives** 1992   108 mins (cert 15)
Marital strife as *Sydney Pollack* and *Judy Davis* announce their separation leaving second couple, *Woody Allen* and *Mia Farrow*, to re-examine the shaky foundations of their own marriage.

★★ **I Love You to Death** 1990   98 mins (cert 15)
True, comic story about a wife, *Tracy Ullman*, who botched numerous attempts to murder her cheating husband, *Kevin Kline*. *River Phoenix*, *William Hurt* and *Joan Plowright* also star.

★★★ **I'm Alright Jack** 1959   104 mins (cert U)
Funny spoof on the British work ethic. *Peter Sellers* and *Ian Carmichael* head excellent cast.

★★★ **I'm Gonna Git You, Sucka** 1988   89 mins (cert 15)
Hip, witty parody of 1970s Blaxploitation movies, written and directed by its star *Keenen Ivory Wayans*.

★★★ **The Importance of Being Ernest** 1952   95 mins (cert U)
Edith Evans' delivery of the line 'A handbag' immortalized this delightful adaptation of Oscar Wilde's comic play.

★★ **Indiscreet** 1958   100 mins (cert PG)
Typically enjoyable *Cary Grant* romantic comedy. *Ingrid Bergman* as the woman he can't forget.

★★ **Innocent Blood** 1993   113 mins (cert 15)
Vampire story with a difference. *Anne Parillaud* as the fanged predator, fancying Italian and biting into neck of Mob boss *Robert Loggia*, bites off more than she can chew in funny, rather quirky, bloodbath.

★★★ **It Could Happen to You** 1994   94 mins (cert PG)
Cop *Nicolas Cage* shares proceeds of winning lottery ticket with waitress *Bridget Fonda*. His wife, *Rosie Perez*, is furious and life will never be the same again. Good, romantic fun.

★★★★★ **It Happened One Night** 1934   105 mins (cert U)
Frank Capra's glorious romantic comedy. Marvellous pairing of reporter *Clark Gable* and runaway heiress *Claudette Colbert* won all the major Oscars that year.

★★★★ **The Jerk** 1979   94 mins (cert 15)
Steve Martin in first leading role as naive white boy leaving his adoptive black family and joining a circus. Hilarious.

★★ **Joe Versus the Volcano** 1990   102 mins (cert PG)
Lightweight but very enjoyable fantasy about a hypochondriac, *Tom Hanks*, conned into making himself a human sacrifice. *Meg Ryan* provides an amusing diversion in three different roles.

★★ **Just Like a Woman** 1992   106 mins (cert 15)
Divorcee *Julie Walters* falls in love with lodger *Adrian Pasdar*, only to discover he's a transvestite. Not so much a comedy, more a poignant tale of small lives not conforming to the norm.

★★ **Just One of the Girls** 1992   98 mins (cert 15)
Corey Haim poses as female to avoid class bully but falls in love with the girl who befriends him – a far cry from 'Tootsie', I fear.

★★★★★ **Kind Hearts and Coronets** 1949   106 mins (cert U)
Marvellous Ealing black comedy in which *Alec Guinness* plays all eight members of an aristocratic family murdered by title-hunting *Dennis Price*.

★★ **King Ralph** 1991   95 mins (cert PG)
Daft, witless farce has Las Vegas cabaret artist *John Goodman* ascending to British throne.

★★★★ **The Ladykillers** 1955   97 mins (cert U)
Ealing caper of highest class. Gang of crooks – *Alec Guinness*, *Peter Sellers*, et al – thwarted by a sweet little old lady, beautifully played by *Katie Johnson*.

★★★ **LA Story** 1990   95 mins (cert 15)
Amiable *Steve Martin* comedy about love and life in smog-ridden city. Some, but not enough, excellent moments.

★★★★ **The Lavender Hill Mob** 1951   78 mins (cert U)
Classic Ealing stuff. *Alec Guinness* plans the perfect robbery, aided and abetted by *Stanley Holloway* and *Sid James*.

★★★★ **A League of Their Own** 1992   128 mins (cert PG)
Very funny look at women's baseball during WWII. *Geena Davis* is excellent as the star player, *Tom Hanks* equally good as her team's drunken manager. *Madonna* not bad either.

★★ **Leap of Faith** 1992   108 mins (cert PG)
Curious *Steve Martin* vehicle in which he plays a cynical, bogus travelling evangelist whose troupe fetches up, with unexpected results, in a small American town. At its best when Martin's doing his stuff.

★★★ **Lenny: Live and Unleashed** 1989   94 mins (cert 15)
Lenny Henry's one-man show. Very funny in parts, particularly his brilliant take-off of Steve Martin.

★★ **Leon the Pig Farmer** 1992   104 mins (cert 15)
Emotional chaos ensues when a Jewish boy, *Mark Frankel*, discovers his real father's a Yorkshire pork farmer. *Brian Glover*, *Connie Booth*, *Janet Suzman* and *Gina Bellman* complete the cast of an engaging low-budget movie.

★★★ **Letter to Brezhnev** 1985   94 mins (cert 15)
Likeable Liverpudlian comedy about two girls, *Alexandra Pigg* and *Margi Clark*, seeking aid of Soviet president in their romance with Russian soldiers.

★★★★ **Life Is Sweet** 1990   102 mins (cert 15)
So is this smashing, funny delight from Mike Leigh. A slice of suburban family life which is not to be missed. *Jane Horrocks* shines as the bulimic daughter of the household.

★★ **Lightning Jack** 1994   97 mins (cert PG)
Legend in his own lunchtime Jack Kane – *Paul Hogan* – thinks himself (erroneously) a terrifying outlaw of the Wild West. He and mute Ben Doyle – *Cuba Gooding Jr* – somehow become most wanted men. Funny in places, a little silly in others, but gently amusing.

★★ **Like Father Like Son** 1987   98 mins (cert PG)
Dudley Moore's contribution to the life-swap movies that proliferated around that time. He changes places with his 16-year-old son, *Kirk Cameron*, in an engaging enough tale.

★★★ **The Little Shop of Horrors** 1986   94 mins (cert PG)
Mixed genres of horror, comedy and music spark mixed reactions to Frank Oz's movie. *Rick Moranis*, *Steve Martin* and *Bill Murray* among the cast.

★★★★ **Look Who's Talking** 1989   96 mins (cert 12)
Original comedy of a baby's eye-view of the world (voiced by *Bruce Willis*). *Kirstie Alley* as single mother, *John Travolta* the cab-driving baby-sitter and *George Segal* the father.

★ **Look Who's Talking Too** 1990   81 mins (cert 12)
Baby Mikey gets a sister (voiced by *Roseanne Barr*) in witless, uncharming sequel.

★★★ **Look Who's Talking Now** 1994   95 mins (cert 12)
This time it's the dogs – *Danny DeVito*, a mongrel, and *Diane Keaton*, a pampered poodle – who look on as *Kirstie Alley* and *John Travolta* come close to divorce. Much better than the second though still not as good as the first of the trilogy.

★★★ **Lost in Yonkers** 1994   103 mins (cert 12)
Neil Simon's delightful tale of two children staying with weird relations during the 1950s. Good performances from *Mercedes Ruehl* and *Richard Dreyfuss*.

★★★ **Love and Death** 1975   85 mins (cert PG)
One of *Woody Allen*'s best. Sharp skit on Russian literature and various movies. *Diane Keaton* co-stars.

★★ **Love and Human Remains** 1994   100 mins (cert 18)
Comedy about two friends and their mutual serial killer acquaintance.

★★★ **Love at First Bite** 1979   96 mins (cert 15)
Pleasing spoof of Dracula movies with *George Hamilton* as suave 20th-century Count with a lust for blood and *Susan Saint James* his happy victim.

★★ **Made in America** 1993   111 mins (cert 12)
Whoopi Goldberg finds the surrogate father of her daughter is a white, second-hand car salesman, *Ted Danson*. Frenetic, fairly funny comedy of errors.

★ **Madhouse** 1990   90 mins (cert 15)
Silly family farce, full of racial and sexual stereotypes, about guests who never leave. Redeemed somewhat by presence of *Kirstie Alley*.

★★★ **Major League** 1989   107 mins (cert 15)
Bitchy woman owner plots the downfall of an already no-hoper baseball team. Players *Tom Berenger*, *Charlie Sheen*, etc, are out to thwart her. Light-hearted fun.

★★★ **Major League II** 1994   93 mins (cert 12)
Wherein the Cleveland Indians are in trouble again. As funny as the original. All the old cast, except Wesley Snipes, are back and there's a smashing cameo from *Randy Quaid* as an increasingly disillusioned fan.

★★★★ **Manhattan** 1979   96 mins (cert 15)
Woody Allen's satirical black-and-white comedy of life and love in his beloved New York. *Diane Keaton* and *Mariel Hemingway* are the objects of Allen's desire.

★★★ **The Man in the White Suit** 1951   85 mins (cert U)
Alec Guinness plays a scientist who's invented everlasting cloth. Big business wants formula destroyed in delightful Ealing comedy.

★ **Man Trouble** 1992　　　　　　　　　　　　100 mins (cert 15)
Silly slapstick as *Ellen Barkin* hires a guard dog from trainer, *Jack Nicholson*, and both become embroiled in a chase to find her kidnapped sister. It all falls pretty wide of the humorous mark.

★★★★★ **The Man with Two Brains** 1983　　　　　　93 mins (cert 15)
Steve Martin's funniest comedy. He plays a brilliant brain surgeon seduced by conniving vamp, *Kathleen Turner*.

★★★ **The Mask** 1994　　　　　　　　　　　　　100 mins (cert 15)
Jim Carrey is excellent as the mild-mannered nerd transformed into a grinning superman when he dons a magic mask. Daft but enjoyable plot; brilliant special effects.

★★ **Matinee** 1992　　　　　　　　　　　　　　99 mins (cert PG)
The film within the film works better than the outer trappings. But *John Goodman* is fine as a Sixties schlock horror movie maker. Overall the comedy is decidedly uneven.

★★ **Memoirs of an Invisible Man** 1992　　　　　99 mins (cert PG)
Decidedly soppy comedy remake by John Carpenter of the Claude Rains classic with *Chevy Chase* in the title role, *Darryl Hannah* as the love interest.

★★★★ **Mermaids** 1990　　　　　　　　　　　　111 mins (cert 15)
Terrific romantic comedy featuring *Cher* as the single mother unable to settle down, *Winona Ryder* her troublesome daughter, and *Bob Hoskins* the new man in her life. Great swinging Sixties soundtrack.

★★★ **Metropolitan** 1990　　　　　　　　　　　98 mins (cert 15)
Sharply original comedy that neatly satirizes the world of young, uppercrust New York yuppies.

★★ **Micki + Maude** 1984　　　　　　　　　　118 mins (cert PG)
Dudley Moore amusing as bigamist trying to placate his two wives, *Amy Irving* and *Ann Reinking*.

★★★ **Midnight Run** 1988　　　　　　　　　　126 mins (cert 15)
Comedy/action/adventure matches bounty hunter *Robert De Niro* against white-collar fugitive *Charles Grodin*, whose performance steals the film.

★★★ **Midnight Sting** 1992   98 mins (cert 15)
Conman *James Woods*, released from prison, heads for a town ruled by *Bruce Dern* to carry out a boxing scam involving *Louis Gossett Jr*. Clever and nicely entertaining.

★★★ **A Midsummer Night's Sex Comedy** 1982   98 mins (cert 15)
Woody Allen's wryly amusing look at sexual interaction of three couples on a weekend holiday.

★ **Monkey Trouble** 1994   97 mins (cert U)
Organ grinder *Harvey Keitel* plans to use his monkey to carry out a heist. But the ape runs away to the home of a troubled young girl, *Thora Birch*. Funny? No, the monkey's the best thing in it.

★★★★ **Monty Python and the Holy Grail** 1973   90 mins (cert 15)
Comic crew's wickedly funny send-up of the Arthurian legend. A kind of very upmarket 'Carry On Arthur'.

★★★★ **Monty Python's Life of Brian** 1979   93 mins (cert 15)
Hugely controversial and achingly funny send-up of organised religion in which Brian is mistaken for the Messiah. Easily the best of all the Python movies.

★★ **Monty Python's The Meaning of Life** 1983   90 mins (cert 15)
Monty Python's irreverent, uneven series of sketches exploring various facets of life and death. Occasionally hilarious but not often enough.

★★ **Mr Baseball** 1993   104 mins (cert 15)
Tom Selleck, past his sell-by-date on the pitch, is transferred to a Japanese team. Comic look at the personality and cultural clashes which ensue.

★★★★ **Mr Deeds Goes to Town** 1936   118 mins (cert U)
Frank Capra's immaculate social comedy wherein *Gary Cooper* inherits a fortune and finds his sanity disputed when he tries to give it away.

★★ **Mr Saturday Night** 1992   119 mins (cert 15)
Billy Crystal's rather depressing comedy about the life of a comedian and his brother through the rise and fall of their act. Neither of them ages convincingly – the makeup just gets heavier and whiter.

★★★ **Mrs Doubtfire** 1993   121 mins (cert 12)
Divorced *Robin Williams* disguises himself as a nanny to be near his children. As a woman he's fine; as a man he's far too sentimental. *Pierce Brosnan* nearly steals the film.

★★★ **Mr Wonderful** 1993   98 mins (cert 15)
Matt Dillon wants to rid himself of alimony payments so tries to fix up ex-wife *Anabella Sciorra* with a husband. Truly romantic tale by 'Truly, Madly, Deeply' director, Anthony Minghella.

★★★★ **Much Ado About Nothing** 1993   110 mins (cert 15)
Glorious and most accessible adaptation of Shakespeare's comedy with *Emma Thompson* and director *Kenneth Branagh* as Beatrice and Benedick, ably supported by *Denzel Washington*, *Keanu Reeves*, *Michael Keaton* and *Richard Briers*.

★★ **Murder by Death** 1976   94 mins (cert PG)
Neil Simon's spoof of murder mysteries provides passable comic vehicle for *Peter Sellers*, *Maggie Smith* and *David Niven*.

★★★ **My Blue Heaven** 1990   96 mins (cert PG)
Sometimes very funny story of a mobster, *Steve Martin*, who goes into the witness protection programme with the help of FBI agent *Rick Moranis*.

★★ **My Cousin Vinny** 1992   119 mins (cert 15)
Courtroom comedy with *Joe Pesci* as inept lawyer defending cousin, *Ralph Macchio*, on murder charge. Good start, good end, flabby in the middle.

★★ **My Father the Hero** 1994   86 mins (cert PG)
Mildly amusing, though contrived remake of a French film about a father who takes his daughter on holiday where she blossoms into a young woman. *Gérard Depardieu* brings a touch of class as the father.

★★★★ **My Favourite Year** 1982   92 mins (cert PG)
Peter O'Toole walks off with this funny, touching tale of a boozy, has-been actor – a kind of washed-up Errol Flynn – making his come-back on a live TV show.

★★ **My Stepmother Is an Alien** 1988   107 mins (cert 15)
Scientist *Dan Aykroyd* gets involved in comic capers when he marries extra-terrestrial, *Kim Basinger*. Has its moments.

★★★★ **Naked** 1993   126 mins (cert 18)
Mike Leigh's blackest comedy to date examines the brutishness of modern Britain with savage humour. *David Thewlis'* performance is a tour-de-force.

★★★★ **The Naked Gun** 1988   85 mins (cert 15)
Hilarious police spoof starring *Leslie Nielsen* and *Priscilla Presley*, who proves herself a surprisingly good comedienne. By the makers of 'Airplane!'

★★★ **The Naked Gun 2½** 1991   81 mins (cert 12)
Nearly as funny as original. *Leslie Nielsen*'s back to save the world from toxic waste, aided and abetted by *Priscilla Presley*.

★★★★ **The Naked Gun 33⅓** 1994   83 mins (cert 12)
All the old cast but new jokes as *Leslie Nielsen* has to save – and in the process nearly destroys – the Oscar ceremony. Could be the funniest of the three.

★★★ **Naked in New York** 1994   93 mins (cert 15)
Eric Stoltz relates his eccentric life during college. Good one for playing spot the star since the likes of *Kathleen Turner*, *Tony Curtis*, *Quentin Crisp*, *Timothy Dalton* and others pop up.

★★★★ **Nashville** 1975   159 mins (cert PG)
Robert Altman's sly, witty comedy/drama which brings a score of disparate characters together at a country music concert. Great stuff.

★★ **The National Health** 1973   97 mins (cert U)
Jim Dale and *Lynn Redgrave* star in acerbic black comedy about the British health service.

★★★ **National Lampoon's Animal House** 1978   104 mins (cert 15)
Sex, drugs and rock 'n' roll are the targets of this hit-and-miss American college farce with *John Belushi* at his grossest and probably funniest. First of the National Lampoon series.

★★ **National Lampoon's Christmas Vacation** 1989   97 mins (cert PG)
Chevy Chase and *Beverly D'Angelo* on their third holiday – this time spent at home. Uninvited relations cause havoc as they pop in during the festive season.

★★ **National Lampoon's European Vacation** 1985   94 mins (cert 15)
The Griswolds descend on Europe and England with frenetic results. Hit-and-miss comedy, though *Eric Idle* scores a bullseye as polite British cyclist.

★★ **National Lampoon's Loaded Weapon** 1993   83 mins (cert PG)
Emilio Estevez and *Samuel Jackson* in a send-up of the 'Lethal Weapon' movies. Some of it's not bad but the mickey-taking formula is fast running out of steam.

★★★ **National Lampoon's Vacation** 1983   98 mins (cert 15)
First and best of the series about the hapless Griswold, *Chevy Chase*, and his unfortunate wife, *Beverly D'Angelo*. Amusing fiasco of a holiday as they travel across America en famille for a visit to Walleyworld.

★★★★ **A Night at the Opera** 1935   90 mins (cert U)
Possibly the best-loved film from the *Marx Brothers*, though 'Duck Soup' is better.

★★★ **9 to 5** 1980   110 mins (cert 15)
Cast – *Jane Fonda*, *Lily Tomlin* and *Dolly Parton* – better than plot in office-based satire. Has its moments though.

★★★★★ **Ninotchka** 1939   110 mins (cert U)
Greta Garbo's most joyous performance as hard-nosed Russian envoy succumbing to love and the lure of capitalism.

★★★ **Nuns on the Run** 1990   95 mins (cert 12)
Pleasing British farce with *Robbie Coltrane* and *Eric Idle* posing as nuns to avoid hitmen.

★★★★ **Nuts in May** 1984   100 mins (cert 12)
Hilarious, slice-of-life comedy by Mike Leigh about a right-on, 'green' couple taking a camping holiday.

★★★★ **The Odd Couple** 1968   105 mins (cert 12)
Jack Lemmon and *Walter Matthau* are splendidly funny as two incompatible men sharing a flat in Neil Simon's comedy.

★★ **Oscar** 1991   110 mins (cert PG)
Farcical plot revolving around marriage plans of Mafia boss's daughter. *Sylvester Stallone* reveals surprisingly light touch. Rather sweet if you like that sort of thing.

★★ **Other People's Money** 1991　　　　　　　101 mins (cert 15)
Ruthless Wall Street tycoon, *Danny DeVito*, defied by
honourable, old-fashioned *Gregory Peck*. Fast and amusing.

★★★ **Outrageous Fortune** 1987　　　　　　　100 mins (cert 15)
Ill-matched *Bette Midler* and *Shelley Long* join forces to find the
man who deceived them both, in agreeable, raucous adventure.

★★ **Overboard** 1987　　　　　　　　　　　112 mins (cert PG)
Amnesia after falling off her yacht causes bitchy heiress *Goldie
Hawn* to rough it as housekeeper to *Kurt Russell* and his kids in
light romantic comedy.

★★★ **Parenthood** 1989　　　　　　　　　　124 mins (cert 12)
Touching, funny insights into problems of parenthood in one
large family. *Steve Martin* heads splendid cast.

★★★★ **Passport to Pimlico** 1949　　　　　　　84 mins (cert U)
Wonderful Ealing comedy in which a London borough declares
independence when an ancient Royal Charter is unearthed.

★★ **Peggy Sue Got Married** 1986　　　　　　103 mins (cert 15)
'Back to the Future' yarn. Disillusioned *Kathleen Turner* is given
the chance to return to high school and change her life.

★★ **Peter's Friends** 1992　　　　　　　　　101 mins (cert 15)
Similar to 'The Big Chill' since it involves reunion of old college
friends some years down the line. Alternately amusing and
touching. *Kenneth Branagh* stars and directs a strong cast.

★★★★ **The Philadelphia Story** 1940　　　　　112 mins (cert U)
This charming film provided the basis for 'High Society'.
Katharine Hepburn has to cope with an ex-husband, *Cary Grant*,
and an amorous reporter, *James Stewart*, on the day before
her wedding.

★★★ **The Pink Panther** 1964　　　　　　　113 mins (cert 15)
David Niven, the suave cat-burglar pursued by bungling sûreté
Inspector Clouseau. *Peter Sellers* is hilarious in his first outing as
the inept copper.

★ **The Pink Panther Strikes Again** 1976　　103 mins (cert U)
The fifth of the Panther films – *Sellers*, *Herbert Lom*, *Burt Kwouk*,
et al, in the search for a kidnapped scientist. (The previous four
are all better.)

★ **Planes, Trains and Automobiles** 1987   93 mins (cert 15)
Surprisingly unfunny comedy of problems encountered by *Steve Martin* trying to get home for Thanksgiving. *John Candy* does little to help.

★★★★ **The Player** 1992   124 mins (cert 15)
Marvellously witty satire on Hollywood as big-shot script commissioner, *Tim Robbins*, becomes embroiled in murder. Count the cameo appearances – more than 60 of them.

★★★ **Play It Again, Sam** 1972   86 mins (cert 15)
Woody Allen on top form as writer coached by ghost of *Humphrey Bogart* in efforts to win *Diane Keaton* – some clever editing employed.

★★★ **Plaza Suite** 1971   114 mins (cert PG)
Three funny Neil Simon playlets all linked by same suite in New York's Plaza Hotel.

★★ **Police Academy** 1984   95 mins (cert 18)
Farcical romp set in police training camp where misfit recruits need licking into shape. Six sequels reprise the gags less effectively.

★★ **The Pope Must Die** 1991   97 mins (cert 15)
Up-and-down comedy of errors. *Robbie Coltrane* is mistakenly appointed head of the Vatican.

★★ **The Pope of Greenwich Village** 1984   120 mins (cert 15)
Sharply observed study of New York hustler, *Mickey Rourke*, reluctantly involved with cousin, *Eric Roberts*, in mad schemes.

★★★★ **Pretty Woman** 1990   120 mins (cert 15)
Irresistible fairytale of hooker, *Julia Roberts*, falling in love with wealthy businessman client, *Richard Gere*. Still Roberts' best performance.

★★★ **The Prime of Miss Jean Brodie** 1969   116 mins (cert 15)
Maggie Smith as avant-garde schoolmistress steering her charges towards womanhood is both funny and touching.

★★★ **A Private Function** 1985   94 mins (cert 15)
Funny, sometimes cruel, comedy set in food-rationed, post-war England with *Michael Palin* and *Maggie Smith*.

★★★ **The Private Life of Sherlock Holmes** 1970 125 mins (cert PG)
Billy Wilder's affectionate look at hitherto unknown aspects of the great detective's career. With *Robert Stevens* and *Colin Blakely*.

★★★ **Private's Progress** 1956 102 mins (cert U)
Good humoured army farce with *Ian Carmichael* as a national serviceman duped by thieves. *Terry-Thomas* and *Richard Attenborough* in support.

★★ **Pump Up the Volume** 1990 102 mins (cert 15)
Teenage movie with *Christian Slater* as a high school kid by day and a pirate radio DJ by night.

★★ **Punchline** 1988 122 mins (cert 15)
Oddly glum tale about comedy. Stand-up comic, *Tom Hanks*, teaches housewife *Sally Field* how to make people laugh.

★★★★ **The Purple Rose of Cairo** 1985 82 mins (cert PG)
Delightful Woody Allen comedy with *Mia Farrow* as down-trodden housewife whose hero, *Jeff Daniels*, steps out of movie screen and sweeps her away.

★★★ **Quick Change** 1990 89 mins (cert 15)
The bank raid's easy. It's the getting out of NY that proves tricky for *Bill Murray* and gang. Appealing and funny.

★★★ **Radio Days** 1987 85 mins (cert PG)
Woody Allen's nostalgic, always amusing reminiscences of boyhood in 1950s Queens, New York.

★★★★ **Raining Stones** 1993 90 mins (cert 15)
Blistering Ken Loach satire on life in recession-hit North of England. It should make you laugh and make you angry. Excellent performances do justice to fine script.

★★ **Raising Arizona** 1987 94 mins (cert 15)
Childless couple, *Nicolas Cage* and *Holly Hunter*, plan to steal one of quintuplets. Untidy comedy. Pre-credit sequence the best.

★★★ **Renaissance Man** 1994 129 mins (cert 12)
Advertising exec *Danny DeVito* loses his job and is sent to teach English in a military camp. A rude awakening for the little fellow as well as his students. Funny and touching.

★★ **Repo Man** 1984   92 mins (cert 18)
Veteran car-repossessor *Harry Dean Stanton* shows rookie *Emilio Estevez* how to do it. Offbeat satire.

★★★ **Risky Business** 1983   98 mins (cert 18)
Teenager *Tom Cruise* turns his absent parents' home into a brothel in an imaginative coming-of-age comedy.

★ **Robin Hood: Men in Tights** 1993   105 mins (cert U)
Mel Brooks' disappointing send up of Kevin Costner's 'Robin Hood: Prince of Thieves'. Why send up what wasn't a very good film in the first place?

★★★ **The Rocky Horror Picture Show** 1975   95 mins (cert 15)
An innocent couple take refuge in a house packed with weirdos in this camp but funny send-up of horror pix. *Tim Curry* and *Susan Sarandon* lead.

★★ **Room Service** 1938   78 mins (cert U)
Marx Brothers as destitute producers holed up in a hotel room. Okay but not one of their best.

★★ **Rosencrantz and Guildenstern Are Dead** 1990   117 mins (cert PG)
Tom Stoppard directs lively screen version of his own play. *Tim Roth* and *Gary Oldman* as hapless, untrustworthy and ill-fated friends.

★★★ **Roxanne** 1987   107 mins (cert PG)
Steve Martin's funny, modern-day version of 'Cyrano de Bergerac' set around a fire station. *Darryl Hannah* is the latter-day Roxanne.

★★★ **Ruthless People** 1986   94 mins (cert 18)
Bette Midler is so spoiled that when she's kidnapped, husband *Danny DeVito* refuses to pay the ransom. Great comic performance by Midler.

★★ **Sabrina Fair** 1954   113 mins (cert U)
So-so romantic comedy from Billy Wilder with a miscast *Humphrey Bogart* falling for chauffeur's daughter, *Audrey Hepburn*.

★★ **Scenes from a Mall** 1991   88 mins (cert 15)
Disappointing Paul Mazursky comedy starring *Woody Allen* in which an anniversary shopping trip brings out startling marital revelations between Allen and wife, *Bette Midler*.

★★ **Scrooged** 1988   101 mins (cert PG)
Contemporary, comic version of Dickens' 'A Christmas Carol'.
Bill Murray finds festive spirit with the help of three hip ghosts.
Not great, not terrible.

★★★ **The Secret Life of Walter Mitty** 1947   110 mins (cert U)
Whimsical charmer with *Danny Kaye* as the timid Mitty – based
on James Thurber character – who daydreams of being a hero.
Virginia Mayo as love interest.

★★ **See No Evil, Hear No Evil** 1990   107 mins (cert 15)
Silly comedy in which a blind *Richard Pryor* and deaf *Gene Wilder*
gets together to clear up the murder of which they're wrongly
suspected.

★★★ **Serial Mom** 1994   93 mins (cert 18)
Fine comic performance from *Kathleen Turner* as the perfect
suburban mom – until she gets annoyed, whereupon she wastes
anyone who upsets her. John Waters directed.

★★★★ **The Seven Year Itch** 1955   105 mins (cert 12)
Tom Ewell is the middle-aged man attracted, during his wife's
absence, to the blonde upstairs, *Marilyn Monroe*. Lovely Billy
Wilder comedy, notable for the famous skirt-lifting scene.

★★ **Shadows and Fog** 1992   89 mins (cert 15)
Black-and-white pre-war Europe examined by *Woody Allen*. *Mia
Farrow*, *Madonna*, *John Malkovich*, *Jodie Foster*, etc., appear. Not
one of Allen's best.

★★ **Shag** 1988   98 mins (cert 15)
Four high school students head for the beach for a shag. No, not
that – this shag is a dance. *Phoebe Cates*, *Scott Caffrey* and *Bridget
Fonda* head a likeable cast.

★★★ **She's Gotta Have It** 1986   84 mins (cert 18)
Spike Lee's highly promising first feature examines the pros and
cons of being a liberated modern woman. *Tracy Camilla Johns* is
the girl choosing between three lovers.

★★ **She's Having a Baby** 1988   106 mins (cert 15)
A bland John Hughes comedy with *Kevin Bacon* as the newly-wed
having second thoughts about marriage to *Elizabeth McGovern*
and his impending fatherhood.

★★ **Sibling Rivalry** 1990   88 mins (cert 15)
Nice comic idea, shame about the script. Repressed housewife *Kirstie Alley* has brief affair with stranger who not only dies but turns out to be her husband's long lost brother.

★★★ **Sister Act** 1992   100 mins (cert PG)
Whoopi Goldberg plays a nightclub singer hiding from the Mob in a convent – like hiding a raven in a dovecote. Mother superior *Maggie Smith* lets her join the choir with delightful results.

★★ **Sister Act 2: Back in the Habit** 1994   95 mins (cert PG)
The sight of *Whoopi Goldberg* as a nightclub singer back in the nun's habit is past its sell-by-date the second time around. Even so, it's just about the best joke the sequel offers.

★★★★★ **Sleeper** 1973   88 mins (cert 15)
Lovely stuff from *Woody Allen* as a man deep-frozen for 200 years who awakes in a world where alcohol and smoking are good for you.

★★★★ **Sleepless in Seattle** 1993   95 mins (cert PG)
Feel-good romantic comedy in which *Meg Ryan* hears widower *Tom Hanks* talking on the radio and falls in love. Charming.

★★★★ **The Snapper** 1992   91 mins (cert 15)
A sharply spicy Roddy Doyle story about the effects of unmarried pregnancy on an Irish family. Delightful cast well-directed by Stephen Frears.

★★★ **Soapdish** 1991   96 mins (cert 12)
Offbeat comedy following the off-camera lives of a soap opera cast, including *Sally Field* and *Kevin Kline*.

★★★ **Soft Top, Hard Shoulder** 1993   95 mins (cert 15)
Gently engaging comedy about *Peter Capaldi*'s accident-prone attempt to get himself to Glasgow in time for his father's 60th birthday.

★★★ **So I Married an Axe Murderer** 1993   95 mins (cert 12)
Mike Myers suspects the woman of his dreams is a notorious axe murderer. Patchy comedy much helped by amusing cameos from *Alan Arkin* and *Charles Grodin*.

★★★★★ **Some Like It Hot** 1959   122 mins (cert U)
Billy Wilder's classic comedy. *Jack Lemmon* and *Tony Curtis* pose as members of *Marilyn Monroe*'s all-female band to escape gangsters.

★★ **Son of the Pink Panther** 1994　　　　　　　89 mins (cert PG)
Nice idea which doesn't come off. Inspector Clousseau's long suffering boss *Herbert Lom* returns to show the policeman's son the ropes.

★★★★ **Splash** 1984　　　　　　　　　　　　110 mins (cert PG)
Deliciously funny fairytale set in modern-day New York where *Tom Hanks* unwittingly falls in love with a mermaid, *Darryl Hannah*.

★★ **Splitting Heirs** 1992　　　　　　　　　86 mins (cert 12)
Largely disappointing comedy of mistaken identity and lost inheritances by and starring *Eric Idle* with *Rick Moranis*, *Barbara Hershey* and *Catherine Zeta Jones*.

★★ **Staggered** 1994　　　　　　　　　　　95 mins (cert 15)
British comedy starring *Martin Clunes* struggling against the odds to reach his wedding on time. Far-fetched but it has its moments.

★★ **Stop! or My Mom Will Shoot** 1992　　　　87 mins (cert PG)
Comedy's not *Sylvester Stallone*'s strong point but as a cop backed up by his feisty mother, *Estelle Getty*, he has a certain charm.

★★★ **Straight Talk** 1992　　　　　　　　　91 mins (cert PG)
Small-town girl *Dolly Parton* lands a job as radio agony aunt in Chicago. Investigating journalist *James Woods* is intrigued. Delightful romantic comedy/drama.

★★★★ **Strictly Ballroom** 1992　　　　　　　91 mins (cert PG)
Surprisingly enjoyable romantic comedy set in the competitive world of Australian ballroom dancing. Fast, cheerful and very funny film.

★★★ **Suburban Commando** 1991　　　　　　90 mins (cert PG)
Wrestler *Hulk Hogan* stars as a fighter from another planet in a riotous farce which is much funnier and more satisfying than you'd expect.

★★★★ **The Sunshine Boys** 1975　　　　　　111 mins (cert U)
Hilarious Neil Simon comedy of an ageing, sparring showbiz duo, *Walter Matthau* and *George Burns*, reunited reluctantly for a big TV show.

★★ **Switch** 1992   103 mins (cert 15)

Murdered chauvinist returns with a man's mind but *Ellen Barkin*'s body. An uneasy comedy, light on laughs.

★★ **Switching Channels** 1988   105 mins (cert PG)

'The Front Page' now set in a modern TV news station. *Burt Reynolds*, *Kathleen Turner* and *Christopher Reeve* can't quite make it work.

★★★★★ **The Talk of the Town** 1942   118 mins (cert U)

Great romantic comedy. *Cary Grant* as an escaped convict hiding out in *Jean Arthur*'s home, rented by Supreme Court judge *Ronald Colman*.

★★ **The Tall Guy** 1989   92 mins (cert 15)

Jeff Goldblum plays the fall-guy to *Rowan Atkinson*'s comic until he meets nurse *Emma Thompson*. Pleasing movie; not as good as it should have been.

★★★★ **The Taming of the Shrew** 1967   122 mins (cert U)

Franco Zeffirelli's zesty, colourful version of Shakespeare's sex-war comedy featuring *Elizabeth Taylor* and *Richard Burton*.

★★★ **Tango** 1993   88 mins (cert 15)

Comedy from 'Hairdresser's Husband' director Patrice Leconte. Womanizing husband tries to murder his unfaithful wife who's had enough of his infidelity.

★★★ **Things Change** 1988   100 mins (cert PG)

Shoemaker *Don Ameche* agrees to take the rap for a Mafia killer. As a reward, *Joe Mantegna* takes him on a lavish fling before he gives himself up. Moving and funny.

★★ **This Is My Life** 1992   94 mins (cert 12)

Nora Ephron's tale of two sisters growing up in the shadow of their showbiz mother, *Julie Kavner*. Amiable but uneventful.

★★★★ **This Is Spinal Tap** 1984   82 mins (cert 15)

Wicked parody of rock bands and music documentaries. Narrated and directed by *Rob Reiner*.

★★★ **Three Men and a Baby** 1987   102 mins (cert PG)

Lively comedy about three confirmed bachelors – *Ted Danson*, *Tom Selleck* and *Steve Guttenberg* – whose lives are disrupted when a baby girl is left on their doorstep.

★ **Three Men and a Little Lady** 1990   104 mins (cert PG)
Crass sequel sees the boys trying to stop young Mary being
taken to England by her mother, *Nancy Travis*.

★★★ **Three of Hearts** 1993   105 mins (cert 18)
Offbeat and quite funny romantic comedy in which two
lesbians, *Kelly Lynch* and *Sherilyn Fenn*, use and abuse male
escort *William Baldwin*.

★★★ **Threesome** 1994   98 mins (cert 15)
Sexual awakenings as two boys and a girl share rooms at college.
Nice performances from an attractive trio: *Stuart Baldwin*, *Lara
Flynn Boyle* and *Josh Charles*, sympathetic as the homosexual roomie.

★★ **Throw Momma from the Train** 1987   88 mins (cert 15)
Thin comedy in which *Danny DeVito* and *Billy Crystal* exchange
murders. (Hitchcock did it straight and much better with
'Strangers on a Train'.)

★★★★ **The Time Bandits** 1981   116 mins (cert 15)
Ralph Richardson and six dwarfs escort a young boy through time
in a hilarious romp amply spiced with guest stars. *Ian Holm*
marvellous as tiny Napoleon.

★★★ **Tin Men** 1987   112 mins (cert 15)
Danny DeVito and *Richard Dreyfuss* paired as loser and hustler,
brought together by a car crash in a warmly amusing tale.

★★★★ **The Titfield Thunderbolt** 1953   84 mins (cert U)
Unadulterated fun from Ealing. Group of villagers, led by *Stanley
Holloway* and *Sid James*, fighting to keep their beloved railway.

★★★★★ **To Be or Not To Be** 1942   99 mins (cert PG)
Jack Benny and *Carole Lombard* lead this delightful Ernst Lubitsch
farce of a group of actors posing as Nazis in war-torn Poland.
Glorious bad taste.

★★ **To Be or Not To Be** 1983   107 mins (cert PG)
A quite unnecessary remake; much cruder, much less funny.
The stars this time are *Mel Brooks* and *Anne Bancroft*.

★ **To Die For** 1994   104 mins (cert 15)
To call it a comedy is giving it the benefit of the doubt since this
amateurish British movie starts as a drama about homosexuals
and AIDS and develops into a jokey piece with ghosts.

★★★★ **Tom Jones** 1963   128 mins (cert PG)
Sprightly version of Henry Fielding's 18th-century novel about a young man's bawdy experiences. *Albert Finney* excellent in title role.

★★ **Too Hot to Handle** 1991   117 mins (cert 15)
Alec Baldwin and *Kim Basinger* as the star-crossed lovers in this romantic comedy set in 1950s. The couple fell in love and subsequently married in real life – ahhh.

★★★★ **Tootsie** 1982   116 mins (cert PG)
Outstanding performance by *Dustin Hoffman* as an actor who passes himself off as a woman in order to get work. Sparkling comedy.

★★ **Top Secret!** 1984   90 mins (cert 15)
Spy spoof from the 'Airplane!' team. *Val Kilmer* is a pop star accidentally involved with Nazis on a tour of Eastern Europe.

★★ **Toys** 1993   121 mins (cert PG)
Robin Williams as eccentric heir to toy factory threatened by uncle, *Michael Gambon*, who wants to turn it into a weapons factory. Visually outstanding but weak and disjointed story.

★★★ **Trading Places** 1988   119 mins (cert 15)
Down-and-out *Eddie Murphy* and spoilt rich kid *Dan Aykroyd* are manipulated into swapping lives. Great fun, marred by soppy climax on train.

★★ **True Identity** 1991   95 mins (cert 15)
Lenny Henry as an actor hunted by the Mob disguises himself as, among other things, a white man. Great make-up but Henry much better than the script.

★★ **Twins** 1988   112 mins (cert PG)
Reasonably comic adventures ensue when unlikely twins, *Danny DeVito* and *Arnold Schwarzenegger* – separated at birth – are reunited.

★ **Uncle Buck** 1989   100 mins (cert 12)
John Candy, the slobbish relative of the title, babysitting his brother's brattish kids. Feeble comedy of little substance.

★★ **Used People** 1992   115 mins (cert 15)
Romantic comedy wherein Jewish widow *Shirley MacLaine* finds love the second time around with an Italian, *Marcello Mastroianni*.

★★ **Vampire's Kiss** 1989   103 mins (cert 18)
Horror spoof which falls apart as literary agent *Nicolas Cage* imagines he's a vampire after lusty *Jennifer Beals* bites him.

★★ **Vice Versa** 1988   98 mins (cert PG)
Judge Reinhold and son, *Fred Savage*, swap bodies in thin, but well-played, role-reversal comedy.

★★★ **War Games** 1983   113 mins (cert PG)
Computer whizzkid *Matthew Broderick* creates enjoyable havoc when he taps into American defence programme.

★★★★ **The War of the Roses** 1989   111 mins (cert 15)
Achingly funny black comedy about marriage turning sour. *Kathleen Turner* and *Michael Douglas* as warring partners. No one contemplating marriage – or divorce – should miss it.

★★ **Wayne's World** 1992   95 mins (cert PG)
A lesser, more streetwise 'Bill and Ted'. *Mike Myers* and *Dana Carvey*, hosts of a cult TV show broadcast from a basement, are exploited by *Rob Lowe*. The occasional flash of comedy.

★★★ **Wayne's World 2** 1994   100 mins (cert PG)
A rare occasion of the sequel being better than the original. Here dastardly *Christopher Walken* has designs on Wayne's girlfriend, *Tia Carrere*.

★★★ **Welcome Home, Roxy Carmichael** 1990   95 mins (cert 12)
Enigmatic comedy about a lonely young girl, *Winona Ryder*, adapting to adoption and relationships.

★★★ **What About Bob?** 1991   110 mins (cert PG)
Psychiatrist *Richard Dreyfuss* is driven mad when his neurotic patient, *Bill Murray*, follows him on a family holiday. Very funny.

★★★★ **Whatever Happened to Baby Jane?** 1962   132 mins (cert 18)
Wild, over-the-top black comedy of two sisters tormenting one another. Magnificently hammy performances by a demented *Bette Davis* and a crippled *Joan Crawford*.

★★★★ **What's Up Doc?** 1972   94 mins (cert U)
Great comedy of errors based on a mix-up of mismatched couples. *Ryan O'Neal* and *Barbra Streisand* lead.

★★★★ **When Harry Met Sally** 1989   95 mins (cert 15)
Billy Crystal and *Meg Ryan* put paid to the theory that men and women can have a platonic relationship in this delightful tale, featuring THAT fake orgasm scene.

★★★★★ **Whisky Galore** 1949   82 mins (cert U)
Rich, classic Ealing comedy about a small Scottish community stealing cache of whisky from wartime shipwreck.

★★★ **White Men Can't Jump** 1992   112 mins (cert 15)
Wesley Snipes and *Woody Harrelson* as a pair of basketball hustlers in a nicely offbeat comedy. (In Europe the film was called 'White Men Can't Get It Up'.)

★★★ **Widows Peak** 1993   97 mins (cert PG)
An Irish community is disrupted by the arrival of a glamorous beauty. Good cast including *Joan Plowright*, *Jim Broadbent* and *Mia Farrow* plus some pretty scenery.

★ **Wild West** 1993   85 mins (cert 15)
Ragged comedy/drama about young Asians in South London trying to break away from poverty trap through music.

★★ **Wilt** 1988   91 mins (cert 15)
A blow-up doll causes comic problems for detective *Mel Smith* and murder suspect, *Griff Rhys-Jones*.

★★★ **Wish You Were Here** 1987   92 mins (cert 15)
Bittersweet seaside comedy about a young girl's sexual growing-up in wartime Britain. Remarkable performance by a young *Emily Lloyd*.

★★★ **The Witches of Eastwick** 1987   118 mins (cert 18)
Three beautiful women – *Cher*, *Susan Sarandon* and *Michelle Pfeiffer* – seduced by the devilish *Jack Nicholson*. Good fun.

★★ **Withnail & I** 1987   105 mins (cert 15)
1960s-based British comedy. Unemployed actors, *Richard E Grant* and *Paul McGann*, leave life of drink and drugs in London for disastrous country holiday.

★★★ **Working Girl** 1988   113 mins (cert 15)
Sophisticated comedy of errors. *Melanie Griffith* is an upwardly-mobile secretary, *Sigourney Weaver* her ruthless boss. *Harrison Ford* provides the love interest.

★★★ **Young Frankenstein** 1974   106 mins (cert 15)
Funny, farcical parody of Hollywood horror movies by Mel Brooks. *Gene Wilder* as the mad scientist, *Madeleine Kahn* his fiancée who becomes the monster's wife.

★★★ **Zelig** 1983   79 mins (cert PG)
Woody Allen as ubiquitous human chameleon who hob-nobs with Hitler and others. Great editing and marvellous trick photography.

DRAMA

★ **Above the Rim** 1995   96 mins (cert 15)
Over-simplistic urban drama about a young, black basketball player who hopes his skills will help him escape the crime and poverty of the streets.

★★★ **Accident** 1967   105 mins (cert PG)
Dirk Bogarde as Oxford tutor in study of events leading to death of a girl student. Sharp, cerebral script by Harold Pinter. Joseph Losey directed.

★★ **Accidental Hero** 1992   116 mins (cert 15)
Dustin Hoffman saves plane crash survivors but hobo *Andy Garcia* claims the reward – and the admiration of TV journalist *Geena Davis*. Should have been better.

★★ **Accidental Tourist** 1988   121 mins (cert PG)
William Hurt as a travel writer whose emotional journey through divorce makes for bleak drama lightened by *Geena Davis'* comic touch.

★★★★ **The Accused** 1988   110 mins (cert 18)
Brilliantly executed rape drama. Victim, Oscar-winner *Jodie Foster*, and lawyer *Kelly McGillis* fight for justice.

★★ **After Darkness** 1985   109 mins (cert 15)
Dangerous study of schizophrenia in which a man tries to cure his brother with perilous results. *John Hurt* and *Julian Sands* star.

★★★ **The Age of Innocence** 1993   125 mins (cert 15)
Martin Scorsese's adaptation of Edith Wharton's novel about 19th-century New York. *Daniel Day-Lewis* is the man torn between *Michelle Pfeiffer* and his fiancée *Winona Ryder*. Beautifully made, though very light on passion.

★★★ **Agnes of God** 1985   98 mins (cert 15)
Jane Fonda, *Anne Bancroft* and *Meg Tilly* in a poignant, affecting story of a nun suspected of killing her baby.

★★★ **Alice Doesn't Live Here Any More** 1975   108 mins (cert 15)
Ellen Burstyn as the widow coming to terms with her own life after the death of her husband in Martin Scorsese's tender, thoughtful movie.

★★★★★ **All About Eve** 1950 138 mins (cert U)
A volatile actress, *Bette Davis*, fastens her seatbelt for a bumpy ride when she befriends *Anne Baxter*'s insinuating Eve. Brilliant drama of the old school.

★★★★ **All the President's Men** 1976 138 mins (cert 15)
Compelling account of how Washington Post journalists, *Dustin Hoffman* and *Robert Redford*, exposed the Watergate scandal. Gripping stuff.

★★★ **All This and Heaven Too** 1940 143 mins (cert U)
Ill-fated romance between French nobleman, *Charles Boyer*, and governess, *Bette Davis*. Weepy melodrama.

★★★ **Always** 1985 123 mins (cert PG)
Spielberg's charming romance of the old school sees *Richard Dreyfuss* as ghostly guardian angel to old flame *Holly Hunter*.

★★★★ **Amadeus** 1984 158 mins (cert PG)
Oscar-winning examination of rivalry between envious court composer Salieri, *F Murray Abraham*, and scatological young upstart Mozart, *Tom Hulce*.

★★ **American Heart** 1993 114 mins (cert 15)
Paroled convict *Jeff Bridges* and teenage son *Edward Furlong* fight the odds in a doomed search for a better future. Well-played but bleak drama.

★★★ **And the Band Played On** 1993 122 mins (cert 15)
A star-studded cast including *Richard Gere* and *Matthew Modine* appear in this story about the fight to identify the AIDS virus.

★★ **Angie** 1993 108 mins (cert 15)
Geena Davis is a single mother who can't form a relationship with her child until she's found her own mother – a woman not seen for years. Sentimental and downbeat.

★★★ **Anna Karenina** 1948 123 mins (cert 12)
Vivien Leigh takes the title role of Tolstoy's tragic tale about a woman blindly in love with a Russian officer.

★★★ **Another Country** 1984 90 mins (cert 15)
Beautiful and touching story about a future spy's boyhood. (Guy Burgess was the inspiration.) *Rupert Everett* and *Colin Firth* excel as the rebellious public school boys.

★★ **Assassin of the Tsar** 1991　　　　　　　　　　104 mins (cert 12)
Good performance by *Malcolm McDowell* as a schizophrenic who claims he murdered the Russian Tsar in 1881. Rather unconvincing script, though.

★★★ **Atlantic City** 1981　　　　　　　　　　　　105 mins (cert 15)
Louis Malle's wickedly observant character study of winners and losers in America's famous gambling resort. Probably *Burt Lancaster*'s best performance.

★★ **Aunt Julia and the Scriptwriter** 1991　　　　107 mins (cert 12)
Budding radio writer *Keanu Reeves* falls for his aunt, *Barbara Hershey*, in 1950s New Orleans. *Peter Falk* takes the acting honours in a film that should have been better.

★★★★ **Awakenings** 1990　　　　　　　　　　　121 mins (cert 12)
Outstanding performances mark this traumatic true tale of a doctor, *Robin Williams*, helping encephalitic patients – notably *Robert De Niro* as his guinea pig.

★ **The Baby of Macon** 1993　　　　　　　　　　120 mins (cert 18)
Peter Greenaway abandons the thin storyline of a Christ-like child in favour of imagery. Visually spectacular but self-indulgent and deeply pretentious.

★★★ **Backbeat** 1994　　　　　　　　　　　　　96 mins (cert 15)
The story of the fifth Beatle, Stuart Sutcliffe, who left the band and then died before they struck it rich. *Stephen Dorff* is impressive as one of the world's unluckiest men.

★★★ **The Bad and the Beautiful** 1952　　　　　　118 mins (cert PG)
Great performances by *Kirk Douglas* as ruthless Hollywood producer and *Lana Turner* as a victimized star.

★★★ **Badlands** 1973　　　　　　　　　　　　　94 mins (cert 18)
Disturbing account of the notorious Starkweather–Fugate spate of killings in 1950s America – led by *Martin Sheen* and *Sissy Spacek*. Terrence Malick's first and best film, which now enjoys a cult following.

★★★ **Bad Lieutenant** 1992　　　　　　　　　　96 mins (cert 18)
Abel Ferrara's chilling study of the decline and fall of a corrupt cop. Harrowing and deeply disturbing but illuminated by a brilliant performance in the title role from *Harvey Keitel*.

★★★ **The Ballad of Little Jo** 1993   115 mins (cert 15)
A woman in the Old West finds the only way to survive is as a man. *Suzy Amis* is very effective as Jo with the occasional scene-stealing performance from *Ian McKellern*.

★★★ **Barry Lyndon** 1975   187 mins (cert PG)
Breathtaking photography in Stanley Kubrick's lengthy, variable version of Thackerey's story about the adventures of an 18th-century Irish rogue. *Ryan O'Neal* not quite up to the title role.

★★ **Beaches** 1988   124 mins (cert 15)
Unashamedly over-sentimental tale of love and loss between childhood friends *Bette Midler* and *Barbara Hershey*.

★★★ **The Belly of an Architect** 1987   118 mins (cert 15)
Peter Greenaway's great to look at but enigmatic tale of a dying architect, *Brian Dennehy*, in Rome. Dennehy lends impressive human warmth to a cool story.

★★★ **Benny and Joon** 1993   95 mins (cert PG)
Aidan Quinn looks after daffy sister *Mary Stuart Masterson* until *Johnny Depp* moves in. Marching to a different drummer, he and Masterson fall in love. Whimsical drama with a touch of magic in more ways than one.

★★★★ **The Best Years of Our Lives** 1946   159 mins (cert U)
Poignant account of three US soldiers returning to civilian life after the end of WWII. *Frederic March*, *Myrna Loy* and *Dana Andrews* star. William Wyler directs.

★ **The Big Blue** 1988   119 mins (cert 15)
Water-logged tale of insurance investigator, *Rosanna Arquette*, trailing her boyfriend around diving competitions. Luc Besson directed but why did he bother?

★★★★ **The Big Chill** 1983   103 mins (cert 15)
Intelligent direction by Lawrence Kasdan of an absorbing story of college friends reuniting in mid-life. With *Tom Berenger*, *Glenn Close*, *Jeff Goldblum* and *William Hurt*. Kevin Costner was in it, too, but his entire role ended on the cutting-room floor.

★★ **Billy Bathgate** 1991   107 mins (cert 15)
Young lad yearns to join ranks of *Dustin Hoffman*'s mob in 1930s overlong gangster story. *Bruce Willis* and *Nicole Kidman* co-star. Hoffman not menacing enough as Dutch Schultz.

★★★ **Billy Liar** 1963   98 mins (cert PG)
Tom Courtenay plays a day dreamer escaping from dreary life in a smashing adaptation of Keith Waterhouse's novel of Walter Mittyism and gritty north country drama.

★★★ **Birdy** 1984   120 mins (cert 15)
Vietnam-traumatized *Matthew Modine* yearns to fly. *Nicolas Cage* is the friend determined to help him in Alan Parker's thoughtful study of the effects of war.

★★★★ **Black Narcissus** 1946   98 mins (cert U)
Deborah Kerr and young *Jean Simmons* in Powell/Pressburger story of the emotional and sexual problems facing a group of nuns in the Himalayas.

★★★ **Bodies Rest and Motion** 1993   96 mins (cert 15)
Offbeat tale of romance and relationships with interesting, attractive young cast – *Bridget Fonda*, *Tim Roth*, *Eric Stoltz*, *Phoebe Cates*. Fonda shines as the one who eventually finds freedom.

★★★ **The Bodyguard** 1992   130 mins (cert 15)
Diva *Whitney Houston*, pestered by death threats, further complicates her life by employing an attractive bodyguard, *Kevin Costner*. Romantic goings-on are thus inevitable. Undemanding and enjoyable. (Houston provides the pleasing soundtrack.)

★★★ **Born on the Fourth of July** 1989   151 mins (cert 18)
Tom Cruise superb as embittered, crippled army veteran in Oliver Stone's Oscar-winning Vietnam movie, part two of his war trilogy that began with 'Platoon'.

★ **Boxing Helena** 1993   107 mins (cert 18)
Unintentionally funny story of obsessed doctor *Julian Sands* imprisoning the object of his desire, *Sherilyn Fenn*, by removing her arms and legs. It cost Kim Basinger $6 million when she walked away from this turkey. Money well spent.

★★★ **Boyz N the Hood** 1991   111 mins (cert 15)
Black teenagers struggle to survive in drug-ridden South Central LA. Bleak but leaving room for hope. Notable debut by director John Singleton.

★★★ **Breakfast at Tiffany's** 1961   115 mins (cert PG)
Touching love story involving cute call-girl *Audrey Hepburn* and writer *George Peppard*. Excellent score includes 'Moon River'.

★★★ **The Breakfast Club** 1984   93 mins (cert 15)
John Hughes' comic teen flick set in school detention class. Brat Pack cast headed by *Emilio Estevez* and *Molly Ringwald*.

★★★★ **Brideshead Revisited** 1981   664 mins (cert 15)
The award-winning ITV series now available on video and a must for any household.

★★★ **Brief Encounter** 1945   86 mins (cert PG)
Dated but still charming David Lean classic telling of doomed love affair between *Trevor Howard* and *Celia Johnson*.

★★ **Bright Lights, Big City** 1988   104 mins (cert 18)
Michael J Fox as the kid who comes to New York to find success and is caught up in a life of drugs, sex and alcohol.

★★★ **A Bronx Tale** 1994   120 mins (cert 18)
Robert De Niro's accomplished debut as a director with a gently absorbing tale of a young Bronx boy's friendship with the local Mafia honcho.

★★★ **The Browning Version** 1994   97 mins (cert 15)
Remake of the 1951 film with *Albert Finney* as retiring school master who realises his life and marriage to *Greta Scacchi* are a sham. Beautiful to look at and fine performances enhance an otherwise slender tale.

★★★ **Bugsy** 1991   135 mins (cert 18)
Warren Beatty plays the hood who 'invented' Las Vegas as a gambling resort. Overlong but good performances.

★★★ **Bull Durham** 1988   108 mins (cert 15)
Kevin Costner and *Susan Sarandon* try to nurture the talents of promising baseballer *Tim Robbins*. Neat, underrated story.

★★★ **Bus Stop** 1956   96 mins (cert U)
Comedy/drama about a rodeo star, *Don Murray*, pursuing sexy showgirl, *Marilyn Monroe*, in one of her best roles.

★★★ **Buster** 1988   103 mins (cert 15)
Phil Collins more than adequately portrays the Great Train Robber but *Julie Walters* shines as Buster's wife.

★★ **The Butcher's Wife** 1991   105 mins (cert 12)
Sporadic laughs in romantic story about a clairvoyant, *Demi Moore*, who moves in and changes the neighbourhood.

★★★ **The Caine Mutiny** 1954   125 mins (cert U)
Two naval officers court-martialled for mutiny against paranoid captain. *Humphrey Bogart* leads excellent cast.

★★★ **Cal** 1984   102 mins (cert 15)
Exceptional drama of an Irish teenager, *John Lynch*, trying to sever ties with IRA and falling for *Helen Mirren*.

★★★ **The Candidate** 1972   110 mins (cert PG)
Sharply cynical look at American politics. *Robert Redford* runs for the Senate on integrity ticket only because he thinks he can't win.

★★★ **Carve Her Name with Pride** 1958   119 mins (cert U)
Moving WWII biopic of young British widow, *Virginia McKenna*, enlisted as spy to help French resistance. Marvellous tale of heroism.

★★★★★ **Casablanca** 1942   102 mins (cert U)
Quite simply one of the great movie romances, set in Morocco with *Humphrey Bogart* and *Ingrid Bergman*, not to mention *Claude Rains*.

★★ **Catch 22** 1970   122 mins (cert 15)
Alan Arkin leads good cast in Mike Nichols' disappointing attempt to bring Joseph Heller's brilliant anti-war novel to the screen.

★★★ **Cat on a Hot Tin Roof** 1958   108 mins (cert 15)
Sparring couple, *Elizabeth Taylor* and *Paul Newman*, in goodish adaptation of Tennessee Williams' scorching melodrama. *Burl Ives* great as Big Daddy.

★★ **Cat on a Hot Tin Roof** 1976   100 mins (cert 15)
Fairish TV adaptation of the above. *Laurence Olivier* fine in Burl Ives role; *Natalie Wood* OK as Taylor-substitute.

★★ **The Cement Garden** 1993   105 mins (cert 18)
Ian McEwan's downbeat tale of incest between strange siblings after their parents die. Rather glum vehicle for *Sinead Cusack* and *Charlotte Gainsborough*.

★★ **The Cemetery Club** 1993   102 mins (cert 12)
Three widows searching for love again. *Olympia Dukakis*, *Ellen Burstyn* and *Diane Ladd* all rather better than the story.

★★★ **Chaplin** 1992   144 mins (cert 12)
Richard Attenborough's solid biopic of the little comic greatly enhanced by the title performance from *Robert Downey Jr*. Fine support from *Anthony Hopkins*, *James Woods*, *Dan Aykroyd* and *Kevin Kline*.

★★★★ **Chariots of Fire** 1981   121 mins (cert U)
Oscar-winning and absorbing story of two British sprinters and their successful bid for gold medals in 1924 Olympics.

★★ **Children of a Lesser God** 1986   119 mins (cert 15)
Touching love affair between a teacher, *William Hurt*, and his deaf student, *Marlee Matlin*.

★★★★★ **Citizen Kane** 1941   119 mins (cert U)
One of the best films ever made. *Orson Welles* was a mere 24 when he directed and starred in it. Everyone should see it.

★★ **City of Joy** 1991   135 mins (cert 12)
Calcutta slums form backdrop of intelligent but over-earnest drama with *Patrick Swayze* and *Pauline Collins*. A good try.

★★ **The Client** 1994   123 mins (cert 15)
A John Grisham thriller with *Susan Sarandon* as the lawyer trying to help a young boy beset by both the Mafia and the FBI. *Tommy Lee Jones*, as the DA, and Sarandon are good but the story lacks suspense.

★★ **Close My Eyes** 1991   107 mins (cert 18)
Sibling incest forms basis of unusual English drama lightened by presence of *Alan Rickman*.

★★ **Cocktail** 1988   104 mins (cert 15)
Tom Cruise tends bar, services women and juggles a very good cocktail too in a pretty pointless romantic drama.

★★ **The Color of Money** 1986   119 mins (cert 15)
So-so sequel to 'The Hustler' pairs sex symbols *Tom Cruise* and *Paul Newman* in battle of green baize. Oscar for Newman, though he deserved it more for the first film.

★★ **The Color Purple** 1985   152 mins (cert 15)
Spielberg's lavish, unconvincing story of a young black woman's hard life and times in American south. *Whoopi Goldberg* stars along with *Danny Glover* and *Oprah Winfrey*.

★★★ **Colors** 1988   116 mins (cert 18)
An ageing cop, *Robert Duvall*, and his young partner, *Sean Penn*, take on the urban gangs of LA in a meandering story that works rather well.

★★ **The Company of Wolves** 1984   95 mins (cert 15)
Freudian but unsatisfying adult version of Little Red Riding Hood. Good sets and costumes.

★★★★ **The Cook, the Thief, His Wife and Her Lover** 1989   120 mins (cert 18)
Peter Greenaway's visually astonishing black comedy set in restaurant owned by greedy gang boss, *Michael Gambon*. Horrifying as well as funny.

★★★★ **Cool Hand Luke** 1967   126 mins (cert 15)
Convict *Paul Newman* as individual fighting penal system. Similar in theme (and compares favourably) to 'One Flew Over the Cuckoo's Nest'.

★★ **Corrina, Corrina** 1994   116 mins (cert PG)
Whoopi Goldberg as the nanny helping single husband *Ray Liotta* care for his young daughter. Romance is sweet, though humour could be better.

★★★ **The Cotton Club** 1984   128 mins (cert 15)
Francis Coppola's flawed but vivid drama centred on famous Harlem nightclub and rise of the Mafia.

★★★ **Cry Freedom** 1987   158 mins (cert PG)
Richard Attenborough's fiercely anti-apartheid drama tells of the friendship between South African journalist Donald Woods, *Kevin Kline*, and black activist Steve Biko, *Denzel Washington*.

★★★ **The Crying Game** 1992   112 mins (cert 18)
IRA hitman, *Stephen Rea*, escapes the cause by going to London where he meets mysterious *Jaye Davidson* – more twists than a corkscrew will keep you guessing from start to finish. Fascinating stuff.

★★★ **A Cry in the Dark** 1988   121 mins (cert 15)
Based on the 'Dingo Baby' case in Australia. *Meryl Streep* is exceptional as mother wrongly accused of infanticide.

★ **Dad** 1989   118 mins (cert PG)
Slushy father and son reconciliation drama with *Jack Lemmon* seriously miscast as irascible father to *Ted Danson*.

★★★ **Dance with a Stranger** 1985   102 mins (cert 15)
Fine British reconstruction of events leading to hanging of Ruth Ellis. Brilliant portrayal of murderess by *Miranda Richardson*. *Rupert Everett* is her lover.

★ **Dangerous Game** 1994   108 mins (cert 18)
Shoddy indictment of the film industry and the infidelities of those working within it. *Harvey Keitel*, a director, sleeps with an actress, *Madonna*, who in turn sleeps with co-star *James Russo*. No involvement since each character is totally unsympathetic.

★★★★ **Dangerous Liaisons** 1988   120 mins (cert 15)
Sexual games and corruption in 18th-century France, starring *Glenn Close*, *John Malkovich* and *Michelle Pfeiffer* in excellent Stephen Frears film.

★★ **A Dangerous Woman** 1993   97 mins (cert 18)
Brave performance from *Debra Winger* as ESN woman whose sexuality is awakened by itinerant worker *Gabriel Byrne*. *Barbara Hershey* finishes off fine cast as Winger's wealthy aunt, who spoils her fun.

★★★ **Darling** 1965   122 mins (cert 15)
Very stylish, very Sixties story of a young fashion model, Oscar-winning *Julie Christie*, and the men – *Dirk Bogarde*, *Laurence Harvey* – she uses to help her climb the social ladder.

★ **Daughters of the Dust** 1993   113 mins (cert PG)
Set amongst the Gullah people in the early 1900s who lived off the coast of Georgia. An African-American family headed by 88-year-old matriarch gathers for their last evening before they leave the island for the mainland.

★★★ **The Day of the Jackal** 1973   142 mins (cert 15)
Suspenseful but inevitably predictable political drama sees *Edward Fox* as assassin gunning for French president Charles de Gaulle.

★★★ **Days of Heaven** 1978   95 mins (cert PG)
Ménage-à-trois among the mid-west wheatfields in 1916. With *Richard Gere*, *Brooke Adams* and *Sam Shepard*. Box office flop at the time but brilliantly directed by Terrence Malik.

★★★ **Dazed and Confused** 1994   95 mins (cert 18)
Bunch of college kids, drunk and stoned, cruise the streets looking for a party. Much to enjoy but it's not quite the 'American Graffiti' of the Nineties.

★★★★ **The Dead** 1987   83 mins (cert U)
Superb adaptation by John Huston (his last film) of James Joyce story. *Anjelica Huston* heads a terrific – and otherwise Irish – cast.

★★★★ **Dead Poets Society** 1989   129 mins (cert PG)
Peter Weir's moving, thoughtful drama of unorthodox teacher *Robin Williams* and his effect, for good and ill, on his pupils.

★★★ **Death in Venice** 1971   128 mins (cert 15)
Visconti's slow, beautiful version of Thomas Mann novel with *Dirk Bogarde* as dying artist obsessed with young boy.

★★★★ **The Deer Hunter** 1978   183 mins (cert 18)
Powerful, painful, Oscar-winning story of young Pittsburgh workers before, during and after Vietnam war. *Robert De Niro* and *Meryl Streep* head a strong cast.

★★★ **Diner** 1982   110 mins (cert 15)
Thoughtful, funny, inconsequential tale of a group of friends (including *Ellen Barkin* and *Mickey Rourke*) hanging out in a Baltimore café in the late 1950s.

★★★ **Distant Voices, Still Lives** 1988   85 mins (cert 15)
Haunting, stylized memories of a working-class family and its births, deaths and marriages in post-war England.

★★★ **The Doctor** 1992   123 mins (cert 12)
Surgeon *William Hurt* reviews flippant attitude to medical profession when he finds himself on other end of scalpel. *Elizabeth McGovern* as fellow cancer sufferer.

★★★★ **Doctor Zhivago** 1965   192 mins (cert 15)
David Lean's lush treatment of *Julie Christie* and *Omar Shariff*'s ill-starred romance during Russian Revolution.

★★★★ **Dog Day Afternoon** 1975　　　　　　　　130 mins (cert 15)
Al Pacino terrific as loser who robs bank so lover can have sex-change op. The raid – but not the film – goes disastrously wrong.

★★ **The Doors** 1991　　　　　　　　141 mins (cert 18)
Oliver Stone's interesting but overlong version of the life of Jim Morrison, *Val Kilmer*, and those around him, including *Meg Ryan*.

★★ **Do the Right Thing** 1989　　　　　　　　120 mins (cert 18)
Spike Lee confronts racial issues in part-comedy, part-drama slice of life during a day in the life of a Brooklyn community.

★★★ **The Dresser** 1983　　　　　　　　118 mins (cert PG)
Touching tale of actor-manager *Albert Finney*, his assistant *Tom Courtenay*, and their mutual reliance on one another.

★★★ **Driving Miss Daisy** 1989　　　　　　　　99 mins (cert U)
Pleasant, beautifully-played examination of unlikely friendship between testy old southern belle, *Jessica Tandy*, and her black chauffeur, *Morgan Freeman*. *Dan Aykroyd* provides lighter moments.

★★★ **A Dry White Season** 1989　　　　　　　　101 mins (cert 15)
South African apartheid forms axis on which this absorbing tale rotates. Cameo from *Marlon Brando* adds depth.

★★★ **East of Eden** 1955　　　　　　　　119 mins (cert PG)
John Steinbeck's powerful story of two brothers' rivalry for father's love. *James Dean*, in debut, exploded onto screen as the prodigal son.

★★★ **Easy Rider** 1969　　　　　　　　115 mins (cert PG)
Great, even mould-breaking in its time, but now rather dated Sixties road movie featuring *Peter Fonda*, *Jack Nicholson* and *Dennis Hopper*.

★★★ **Educating Rita** 1983　　　　　　　　110 mins (cert 15)
Delightful, touching tale about Liverpudlian hairdresser, *Julie Walters*, taking Open University degree under tutorship of *Michael Caine*.

★★★ **Eight Men Out** 1984　　　　　　　　120 mins (cert PG)
Charlie Sheen and *John Cusack* in absorbing story of Chicago White Sox baseball team who threw the World Series in 1919.

★★ **Eight Seconds** 1994   107 mins (cert PG)
True story of a champion rodeo rider. *Luke Perry* is the cowboy who could hang on to a bull's mane like grim death. Well enough made but on this evidence rodeo is not a spectator sport.

★★★ **84 Charing Cross Road** 1987   97 mins (cert U)
Anne Bancroft and *Anthony Hopkins* charm as a book buyer and book seller corresponding across the Atlantic.

★★★ **The Electric Horseman** 1979   120 mins (cert PG)
Ex-rodeo star, *Robert Redford*, steals thoroughbred horse to save them both from the scrap heap. Journalist *Jane Fonda* gives chase in this satire on big business.

★★ **Elenya** 1992   88 mins (cert PG)
Quiet tale of lonely Welsh girl befriending an injured German parachutist during WWII. Better suited to TV where you could take a coffee break during the slower parts.

★★★ **The Elephant Man** 1980   124 mins (cert PG)
David Lynch's sentimentalized version of the life of disfigured John Merrick expertly played by *John Hurt*.

★★ **The Emerald Forest** 1985   113 mins (cert 15)
Ecological drama based on true story of man's ten-year struggle to recover kidnapped son from Amazon jungle. John Boorman directed.

★★★ **Empire of the Sun** 1987   153 mins (cert PG)
Glossy but overlong Spielberg adaptation of J G Ballard's boyhood in Japanese POW camp in WWII.

★★★ **Enchanted April** 1991   95 mins (cert U)
Four Edwardian ladies – *Miranda Richardson*, *Joan Plowright*, *Josie Lawrence* and *Polly Walker* – take a holiday in Italy where their lives turn around. Charming and unusual.

★★ **The End of the Golden Weather** 1992   103 mins (cert 12)
Young New Zealand boy believes miracles can happen – and finds they do – as he befriends a backward neighbour during a perfect summer of 1930s childhood.

★★ **An Enemy of the People** 1977   107 mins (cert 15)
Sincere but misguided attempt by bearded *Steve McQueen* to bring Ibsen classic to screen.

★★★★ **An Englishman Abroad** 1985   60 mins (cert PG)
Utterly delightful account of how actress *Carol Browne* (playing herself) met spy/traitor Guy Burgess, *Alan Bates*, in Moscow.

★★★ **The Entertainer** 1960   96 mins (cert 18)
Laurence Olivier superb as shabby, third-rate music hall star in fine adaptation of John Osborne play.

★★ **Equinox** 1992   110 mins (cert 15)
Two brothers – a mechanic and a hoodlum – reunited by an inheritance in a thoughtful but sometimes dull story about the search for identity. *Matthew Modine* stars.

★★★ **The Fabulous Baker Boys** 1989   113 mins (cert 15)
Sultry cabaret singer *Michelle Pfeiffer* stirs up hidden emotions in the brothers, *Beau* and *Jeff Bridges*, whose act she joins. Highly accomplished study of the humbler reaches of show business.

★★★ **The Falcon and the Snowman** 1985   131 mins (cert 15)
Well-made true story of two wealthy Americans, *Sean Penn* and *Timothy Hutton*, who sold state secrets to the Russians.

★★ **Fallen Angels** 1993   90 mins (cert 15)
Tom Cruise and *Tom Hanks* are among a number of many famous faces in front of and behind the camera in this series of short crime stories – ranging from fair to dull – released on two videos.

★★ **The Fallen Idol** 1948   94 mins (cert 12)
Young boy worships servant accused of murdering wife in skilful adaptation of Graham Greene story.

★★★★ **Falling Down** 1993   115 mins (cert 18)
Michael Douglas as (fairly) ordinary Joe who snaps and rebels against a hostile Los Angeles and goes on a violent rampage. Splendidly topical and un-politically correct. *Robert Duvall* great as the policeman who tracks Douglas down.

★★ **Far and Away** 1992   140 mins (cert 12)
Poor Irish lad, *Tom Cruise*, and haughty noble woman, *Nicole Kidman*, run away to seek mixed fate and fortune in America. A lengthy melodrama that amounts to little.

★★ **Far From the Madding Crowd** 1967   175 mins (cert U)
Beautiful photography by Nicolas Roeg, skilful direction from John Schlesinger, and sharp acting from *Julie Christie* and *Alan Bates* in underrated version of Thomas Hardy novel.

★★★★ **Fearless** 1994   121 mins (cert 15)
Imaginative, thought-provoking story of a man, *Jeff Bridges*, who re-examines himself and life after surviving a fatal aircrash. *Rosie Perez* is also good as another survivor whom he befriends and comforts.

★★★★ **A Few Good Men** 1992   138 mins (cert 15)
Cracking courtroom drama as *Tom Cruise* proves more than a plea bargaining lawyer when appointed to defend two Marines court-martialled on a murder charge. *Jack Nicholson* is the Marine colonel, *Kevin Bacon* the prosecutor.

★★ **The Field** 1990   112 mins (cert 12)
Irishman's obsession with a piece of land leads to tragedy in this florid drama. *Richard Harris* stars as a kind of Irish King Lear. (King O'Leary?)

★★★ **The Fisher King** 1991   137 mins (cert 15)
Heartwarming 'bit of everything' story sees disillusioned DJ *Jeff Bridges* shown value of life by down-and-out *Robin Williams* in Terry Gilliam's delightful fantasy.

★★★ **Flesh and Bone** 1994   126 mins (cert 15)
A dark tale of a man, *Dennis Quaid*, who falls in love with a woman, *Meg Ryan*, who, it transpires, is the only survivor of a family his father murdered. Too much coincidence to be entirely convincing but well-played.

★★ **The Fool** 1990   137 mins (cert U)
Victorian drama starring *Derek Jacobi* as a clerk with amazing double life. First-rate British cast can't quite surmount an unconvincing story.

★★★ **Forever Young** 1992   102 mins (cert PG)
Frozen 1940s pilot, *Mel Gibson*, defrosted 50 years later and searching for his lost love in a romantic weepie.

★★★ **For Queen and Country** 1988   105 mins (cert 15)
Outstanding portrayal by *Denzel Washington* of a black soldier's mistreatment following demobilization from British army.

★★ **For the Boys** 1991 140 mins (cert 15)
Bette Midler and *James Caan* star as couple of musicians entertaining US troops through three wars. Overblown and disappointing.

★★★ **1492: The Conquest of Paradise** 1992 155 mins (cert 15)
Beautiful, but rather dull and very long account of what happened after Columbus, *Gérard Depardieu*, stumbled upon the Americas. Good cast including *Sigourney Weaver* and *Armand Assante*.

★★★ **Frances** 1982 139 mins (cert 15)
Outstanding portrayal by *Jessica Lange* of the tragic 1930s actress, Frances Farmer, who was virtually driven into madness.

★★★ **Frankie and Johnny** 1991 117 mins (cert 15)
Bittersweet comedy set in a NY greasy spoon where romance blossoms between lonely hearts *Michelle Pfeiffer* and *Al Pacino*. Trouble is both are too attractive to be so lonely.

★★★ **The French Lieutenant's Woman** 1981 123 mins (cert 15)
Thoughtful adaptation of John Fowles' period novel with *Jeremy Irons* and *Meryl Streep* as both 18th-century soldier and the object of his desire and 20th-century lovers.

★★★★ **Fried Green Tomatoes at the Whistle Stop Café** 1991 130 mins (cert 12)
Jessica Tandy relates tale of two young women, *Mary Stuart Masterson* and *Mary Louise Parker*, in America's deep south to *Kathy Bates* and changes her life. Looks great. Most pleasing.

★★ **The Front** 1976 95 mins (cert 15)
America's notorious Communist witch hunt forms the premise for this sharp, witty drama. *Woody Allen* as frontman for banned scriptwriters.

★★★★ **Gandhi** 1982 188 mins (cert PG)
Epic, Oscar-winning spectacular from Richard Attenborough about the life and death of the Indian leader. *Ben Kingsley* heads a superb cast as Gandhi.

★★ **Giant** 1956 201 mins (cert PG)
Overlong but stylish family saga about rise of Texas oil barons, starring *Elizabeth Taylor*, *James Dean* and *Rock Hudson*.

★★★ **Glengarry Glen Ross** 1992   100 mins (cert 15)
Powerful character-led drama by David Mamet. Full of nail-biting tension as real estate salesmen, notably *Jack Lemmon* and *Al Pacino*, are given a week to meet their targets. *Alec Baldwin* dynamic in cameo role.

★★ **Gloria** 1980   123 mins (cert PG)
Gena Rowlands gives a lovely performance in title role of tough, savvy housewife protecting orphan boy from Mafia.

★★★★★ **Gone With the Wind** 1939   220 mins (cert U)
The classic, all-encompassing saga of the American Civil War, about which everyone gives a damn. *Vivien Leigh* and *Clark Gable* head the splendid cast.

★★★★ **Goodbye Mr Chips** 1939   114 mins (cert U)
Robert Donat's magnificent portrayal of a retiring school master who has devoted his life to his boys.

★★★ **Gorillas in the Mist** 1988   129 mins (cert 15)
Biopic about Diane Fossey, who was murdered for trying to save gorillas. Sensitively played by *Sigourney Weaver*.

★★★★ **The Graduate** 1967   105 mins (cert 15)
Dustin Hoffman in unforgettable account of graduate's journey to adulthood (and adultery) via an affair with girlfriend's mother, *Anne Bancroft*.

★★★ **Grand Canyon** 1992   134 mins (cert 15)
Steve Martin, *Kevin Kline* and *Danny Glover* lead well-written social drama about problems of living in modern, violent LA.

★★★★ **Grand Hotel** 1932   115 mins (cert U)
Berlin hotel provides backdrop for excellent character study of guests: *Greta Garbo*, *Joan Crawford*, *John* and *Lionel Barrymore*. Often copied but the format works best here.

★★★★ **The Grapes of Wrath** 1940   128 mins (cert PG)
Compelling Steinbeck tale of workers' migration to California during the Depression. Beautifully acted by *Henry Fonda*.

★ **Great Balls of Fire!** 1989   107 mins (cert 15)
Dennis Quaid is always watchable as the legendary rocker Jerry Lee Lewis but the script and direction continually let him down.

★★ **The Grifters** 1990   119 mins (cert 18)
Dark story about a thieving mother, *Anjelica Huston*, and her
conman son, *John Cusack*, never quite finds its feet.

★★ **Guilty by Suspicion** 1991   105 mins (cert 15)
Rather heavy-handed account of the Hollywood victims of the
1950s Un-American Activities Committee. *Robert De Niro* as
chief suspect.

★★★ **Hamlet** 1948   142 mins (cert U)
Masterly performance in the title role by *Laurence Oliver*, who
also directed. Great supporting cast.

★★★ **Hamlet** 1991   133 mins (cert U)
Franco Zeffirelli's lucid, highly accessible version of William
Shakespeare's tragedy. *Mel Gibson* excels as the prince.

★★ **A Handful of Dust** 1988   118 mins (cert PG)
Harrowing story from Evelyn Waugh about aristocrats seeking
fulfilment. Pretty to look at, disturbing to watch.

★★ **The Handmaid's Tale** 1990   104 mins (cert 18)
Natasha Richardson rebels against her role of child-bearer in a
repressive society of the future. Disappointing adaptation.

★ **Hangin' with the Homeboys** 1991   90 mins (cert 15)
Odd adventures of mixed ethnic trio on a big night out in
Manhattan. Messy but affecting.

★ **Havana** 1990   145 mins (cert 15)
Cuban politics form basis of rather drab 'Casablanca' rip-off.
Robert Redford, *Raul Julia* and *Alan Arkin* all deserve better.

★★ **Heartburn** 1986   109 mins (cert 15)
Formidable cast, *Meryl Streep* and *Jack Nicholson*, try to cope with
marital problems but result disappoints.

★★ **Heat and Dust** 1983   130 mins (cert 15)
Merchant Ivory story of two Englishwomen, *Greta Scacchi* and
Julie Christie, from two eras immersed in mystery and romance
of India.

★★★ **Heathers** 1989   103 mins (cert 18)
Christian Slater and *Winona Ryder* sparkle in this sharp black
comedy about adolescence and high school politics.

★★ **Heaven and Earth** 1994   134 mins (cert 15)
Final part of Oliver Stone's Vietnam trilogy in which a young village woman marries an American GI, *Tommy Lee Jones*, and leaves her war-torn homeland for America. Heavy, laboured and grim.

★★ **Henry and June** 1990   136 mins (cert 18)
Earnest and strangely dull version of Henry Miller's lusty relationship with Anais Nin. With *Fred Ward*, *Maria De Medeiros* and *Uma Thurman*.

★★★★ **Henry V** 1944   137 mins (cert U)
Laurence Olivier's stirring, colourful pageant ideally suited to its time and the nation's celebration of coming victory.

★★★★ **Henry V** 1989   135 mins (cert PG)
Kenneth Branagh's superb, gritty contrast to Olivier's version. Olivier's troops were the guards, Branagh's the SAS.

★★ **Hoffa** 1992   140 mins (cert 15)
Jack Nicholson as the dubious 1950s union boss who may or may not have had close dealings with the Mafia and who disappeared mysteriously. *Danny DeVito* is his sidekick and director in a film that never quite works.

★★ **A Home of Our Own** 1993   100 mins (cert PG)
Kathy Bates as the single mother of a large, unruly brood which turns a derelict shack into a home with help from the local community. Good idea but unengaging characters make it hard to get involved.

★ **Homer and Eddie** 1990   99 mins (cert 15)
Bleakish hotch-potch plot about an escaped mental patient, *Whoopi Goldberg*, offering help to brain-damaged *James Belushi*.

★★★ **House of the Spirits** 1994   125 mins (cert 15)
A nice adaptation of Isabel Allende's family saga about a mystic and her marriage. *Meryl Streep*, *Jeremy Irons*, *Glenn Close* and *Winona Ryder* do more than justice to the tale.

★★★★ **Howards End** 1992   140 mins (cert PG)
Anthony Hopkins and Oscar-winner *Emma Thompson* lead in this beautifully-played, gorgeous-looking version of E M Forster's novel.

★★★★ **The Hunchback of Notre Dame** 1939   115 mins (cert PG)
The portrayal of the bell-ringing cripple by *Charles Laughton* is a tour-de-force. Remarkably touching.

★★★★ **The Hustler** 1961   135 mins (cert 18)
Paul Newman at his best as a hungry young pool shark taking on the formidable Minnesota Fats, *Jackie Gleason*. Riveting and almost unbearably tense.

★★★★ **If . . .** 1969   111 mins (cert 15)
Savage – if dated – satire on the British school and class system. Surreal violence originally earned it an 'X' (18) certificate.

★★ **Indian Runner** 1991   126 mins (cert 15)
Sean Penn's glum, but not unimpressive, directorial debut about two brothers on opposite sides of the law.

★★★ **Inherit the Wind** 1960   127 mins (cert U)
Scathing examination of 1925 prosecution of American teacher propounding Darwinian theories. *Spencer Tracy* immaculate as defence attorney.

★ **The Inner Circle** 1992   134 mins (cert 15)
Tom Hulce as Stalin's cinema projectionist surviving (just about) the terrors of the regime. First film ever to go inside the KGB headquarters – even if it was just the lobby.

★★★ **Innocent Moves** 1994   105 mins (cert PG)
True story of a child chess prodigy oppressed by his parents' expectations. *Joe Mantegna* is the father in this engaging tale.

★★★ **The Inn of the Sixth Happiness** 1958   159 mins (cert U)
Touching biography of missionary Gladys Aylwood, played by *Ingrid Bergman*, who trekked through war-torn China with refugee children.

★★★ **Intersection** 1993   107 mins (cert 15)
Classic eternal triangle set on a collision course in romantic drama with *Sharon Stone* and *Richard Gere*. *Lolita Davidovich* plays the mistress.

★★★★★ **In the Name of the Father** 1993   135 mins (cert 15)
Overwhelming performance by *Daniel Day-Lewis* as one of the wrongfully imprisoned 'Guildford Four'. Righteously angry, wickedly funny and a superb piece of filmmaking.

★★ **Ironweed** 1987   144 mins (cert 15)
Depression-based, and depressing, drama about a couple of
alcoholic down-and-outs: *Meryl Streep* and *Jack Nicholson*.

★★ **Jacknife** 1989   98 mins (cert 15)
Post-Vietnam war trauma confronted in well-acted drama.
Robert De Niro, *Kathy Baker* and *Ed Harris* do the business.

★★ **Jack the Bear** 1993   98 mins (cert 12)
Danny DeVito as a single father trying to raise two young sons.
Trouble comes when the youngest is kidnapped by local weirdo.
Uncomfortable balance of humour and horror leaves a nasty
taste in the mouth. Ill-paced direction by DeVito.

★★★ **Jane Eyre** 1944   96 mins (cert PG)
Joan Fontaine plays Charlotte Brontë's eponymous heroine who
falls for her employer – the enigmatic Mr Rochester, played
superbly by *Orson Welles*.

★★★★ **JFK** 1992   190 mins (cert 15)
Don't let the length deter you. Oliver Stone's fascinating
examination of who killed the president is flawed but riveting.
Kevin Costner heads stellar cast.

★★ **Johnny Suede** 1991   97 mins (cert 15)
Set in 1950s with *Brad Pitt* inspired to pursue career as musician
after a pair of blue suede shoes fall on his head. Quirky story
dealing with complexities of romance.

★★ **Josh and SAM** 1993   98 mins (cert 12)
Two boys torn between their parents find themselves alone, on
the open road, as they flee the trauma of divorce.

★★ **The Joy Luck Club** 1994   134 mins (cert 15)
Personal histories of a group of Chinese women in America
unfold as one of them prepares to meet the sisters she never
knew she had. Overblown and over-sentimental but strong
performances amply compensate.

★★ **Juice** 1992   91 mins (cert 15)
Rites-of-passage story about a group of teenagers discovering
whether they have the guts (the juice) to survive on the streets
of Harlem. Tough parable about the dangers of violence.
Stylishly shot.

★★★ **Julia** 1977   116 mins (cert PG)
Fine acting by *Jane Fonda* as Lillian Hellman, *Vanessa Redgrave* as Julia, in a distinguished story of a woman's ill-fated involvement with European resistance.

★★★ **Julius Caesar** 1953   121 mins (cert U)
Fine adaptation and great cast, notably *Marlon Brando* as Mark Anthony, in spectacular version of Shakespeare's play.

★★ **Jungle Fever** 1991   132 mins (cert 18)
Spike Lee's sharp, angry look at black/white relationships and bigotry on both sides. With *Wesley Snipes* and *Annabella Sciorra*.

★★★ **The Killing Fields** 1984   142 mins (cert 15)
Roland Joffe's sensitive account of a news reporter's harrowing experience during Cambodian war packs a hefty punch.

★★ **Killing Zoe** 1994   94 mins (cert 18)
A lesser 'Reservoir Dogs' in which *Eric Stoltz* gets involved in a Parisian bank robbery that goes wrong.

★★★ **King of the Hill** 1993   114 mins (cert 12)
'sex, lies and videotape' director Steven Soderbergh does the business again with this delicious tale of a young boy escaping poverty and loneliness in his dream world.

★★★★ **Kiss of the Spider Woman** 1985   119 mins (cert 15)
Thoughtful, sensitive tale about understanding. *William Hurt* plays the gay, *Raul Julia* the political activist sharing prison cell.

★★★★ **Kramer vs Kramer** 1979   105 mins (cert PG)
Warm-hearted drama of divorced couple, *Meryl Streep* and *Dustin Hoffman*, fighting for custody of their son.

★★★★ **Ladybird, Ladybird** 1994   80 mins (cert 18)
Brilliant but distressing story of a woman whose children were taken away from her by over-zealous social workers. Newcomer *Chrissie Rock* gives startling performance. Fine direction by Ken Loach.

★ **Lake Consequence** 1993   121 mins (cert 18)
So dull it's as erotic as a limp lettuce. Former model *Joan Severance* abandons responsibilities and morals for a weekend of lust with *Billy Zane* and co.

★★★ **The Last Days of Chez Nous** 1990   97 mins (cert 15)
Director Gillian Armstrong's complex tale of the mixed-up
relationships in a Sydney household headed by middle-aged
writer *Lisa Harrow* and her French husband, *Bruno Ganz*.

★★★★ **The Last Detail** 1973   108 mins (cert 18)
Navy veterans *Jack Nicholson* and *Otis Young* escort kleptomaniac
recruit *Randy Quaid* to the brig in this snappy comedy/drama.

★★★ **The Last Emperor** 1987   162 mins (cert 15)
Bernardo Bertolucci's Oscar-winning dramatization of the life
of China's last imperial ruler. Vivid and colourful but over-
earnest and overlong.

★★ **Last Exit to Brooklyn** 1989   102 mins (cert 18)
Vaguely repellent adaptation of Hubert Selby's notorious slice-
of-life novel set in Brooklyn's seedier, more violent streets.

★★★★ **The Last Picture Show** 1971   118 mins (cert 15)
Nostalgic look at growing up in small Texas town in the 1950s.
Stars *Timothy Bottoms*, *Jeff Bridges* and *Cybill Shepherd*. Great
soundtrack.

★★★ **Last Tango in Paris** 1973   129 mins (cert 18)
Butter never tasted the same after Bertolucci's erotic, not to
mention explicit, drama starring *Marlon Brando* and *Maria
Schneider*. Infamous in its time.

★★★ **The Last Temptation of Christ** 1988   164 mins (cert 18)
Martin Scorsese's controversial and thought-provoking drama
about Jesus' self doubts. Disturbing but, despite vociferous
critics, definitely not blasphemous.

★★★ **Lenny** 1974   111 mins (cert 18)
Dustin Hoffman stars in this Hollywood biopic of controversial
comedian Lenny Bruce. First-class performance by *Valerie
Perrine* as his stripper wife.

★★★ **Let Him Have It** 1991   115 mins (cert 15)
Disturbing account of the Chris Craig/Derek Bentley murder
trial and the latter's subsequent scandalous execution.

★★★★ **A Letter to Three Wives** 1949   102 mins (cert U)
Rich portrayal of three women's reactions to a letter from the
town tramp who's run off with one of their husbands.

★ **Light Sleeper** 1991   103 mins (cert 15)
Susan Sarandon and *Willem Dafoe* lead this thriller set in the seedy world of drug-running.

★★★★ **The Lion in Winter** 1968   134 mins (cert 15)
Atmospheric account of power struggle between Henry II, *Peter O'Toole*, and his queen, Eleanor, *Katharine Hepburn*. Splendid performances and atmosphere.

★★★ **Little Buddha** 1994   135 mins (cert PG)
Bertolucci's Buddhism for beginners. The story of how Buddha, *Keanu Reeves*, came to be is interwoven with a modern tale. Reeves makes an interesting, if not altogether successful choice but the scenery is pretty.

★★★★ **Little Dorrit** 1988   360 mins (cert U)
A superb six-hour production of Dickens' social drama with *Alec Guinness* as the Marshalsea prison inmate. Great cast. Usually shown in two parts.

★★★ **Little Man Tate** 1991   99 mins (cert PG)
Jodie Foster directs and stars as the inadequate mother of an eight-year-old genius who is pulled between her and his teacher, *Dianne Wiest*.

★★★★ **Little Women** 1933   115 mins (cert U)
George Cukor's version of Louisa M Alcott's tale of family life, centring on the fortunes of the four daughters. *Katharine Hepburn* stars. Remade – less well and with *June Allyson* – in 1949 and, for TV, in 1978.

★★★ **Lolita** 1962   152 mins (cert 18)
Stanley Kubrick's rich, dark version of Vladimir Nabokov's story of the infamous nymphet. *Sue Lyon* as Lolita, *James Mason* her middle-aged victim.

★★★★ **The Loneliness of the Long Distance Runner** 1962   104 mins (cert 15)
Tom Courtenay first-rate as young rebel selected to represent his reform school in a race. *Michael Redgrave* co-stars.

★★★ **The Lonely Passion of Judith Hearne** 1987   110 mins (cert 15)
Lonely Irish spinster, *Maggie Smith*, finds repressed feelings stirred by charming American, *Bob Hoskins*. Marvellous performance by Smith.

DRAMA ■

★★★ **The Long Day Closes** 1991 85 mins (cert 12)
Continuing Terence Davies' autobiographical series after 'Distant Voices, Still Lives'. Leisurely, self-indulgent but oddly fascinating. Includes the longest close-up of a piece of carpet in cinema history.

★★ **Longtime Companion** 1990 99 mins (cert 15)
Tactful handling of the effect of AIDS on the homosexual community in New York.

★★★ **Look Back in Anger** 1958 115 mins (cert 18)
Richard Burton stars in screen version of John Osborne play that changed British theatre in the 1950s. Just about as good as Burton got in the movies.

★★ **The Lord of the Flies** 1990 95 mins (cert 15)
Aimed-at-America remake of Peter Brooks' 1963 version of William Golding's novel. Solid but pedestrian.

★★★ **Lorenzo's Oil** 1992 135 mins (cert 12)
Tour-de-force performance by *Susan Sarandon* as determined mother of AZT sufferer, who with husband *Nick Nolte* found a remedy for son's incurable disease. True story.

★★ **Love Field** 1993 101 mins (cert 15)
Deserved a cinema release. A quality tale of mixed race relationship in 1950s deep south USA between *Michelle Pfeiffer* and single father *Dennis Haysbert*.

★ **The Lover** 1992 115 mins (cert 18)
Jane March stars as a young girl growing up – rapidly – in Vietnam. An exploitative tale of East seduces West. Only remotely interesting question is: did March and *Tony Leung* REALLY do it?

★★ **Love Story** 1970 100 mins (cert PG)
Famous – or notorious? – sickly sweet story about a pair of young lovers, doomed *Ali MacGraw* and *Ryan O'Neal*, heading for tragedy.

★★★ **Love Streams** 1984 135 mins (cert 15)
Examination by *John Cassavetes* of a couple's relationship at a tough time in their lives. Cassavetes and *Gena Rowlands* are the couple. Thoughtful but not many laughs.

★★★ **Lucas** 1986 — 96 mins (cert 15)
Charming tale of love and romance between a 14-year-old boy and a 16-year-old girl and of how their relationship affects the people around them. An engaging movie.

★★ **Mac** 1993 — 117 mins (cert 12)
John Turturro's over-earnest but decent directorial debut with himself in the lead as a young builder extolling the now apparently moribund virtues of craftsmanship.

★★ **Macbeth** 1971 — 140 mins (cert 15)
Roman Polanski directs this violent but gripping version of Shakespeare's regal play, with *Jon Finch* and *Francesca Annis*.

★★★ **Madame Sousatzka** 1988 — 116 mins (cert 15)
Shirley MacLaine as an eccentric Russian piano teacher in London who is smitten with a desire to teach music – and the meaning of life – to a 15-year-old Indian boy.

★★★ **The Magic Box** 1951 — 118 mins (cert U)
Every noted British actor crops up in this fascinating biopic of William Friese-Greene, one of the inventors of the movies.

★★★ **Malcolm X** 1993 — 201 mins (cert 15)
An interminably long study of the black civil rights leader who embraced Islam and only at the end of his life renounced violence. *Denzel Washington* excellent in the title role. *Spike Lee* angry and indulgent in his direction.

★★ **The Mambo Kings** 1992 — 104 mins (cert 15)
Two lusty Latino brothers – played by *Armand Assante* and *Antonio Banderas* – arrive in New York from Cuba and introduce their own form of music and dance: mambo. Okay, but should have been better.

★★★★ **A Man for all Seasons** 1966 — 120 mins (cert U)
Absorbing account of Sir Thomas More's fateful refusal to betray the Church for his king, Henry II. *Paul Scofield* gives an outstanding performance.

★★★ **The Man in the Moon** 1991 — 99 mins (cert PG)
Sam Waterson and *Tess Harper* in a superior rites-of-passage story set in 1950s America. Love, tragedy and, for once, good strong roles for women.

★★★ **The Man Without a Face** 1993   114 mins (cert 12)
Reclusive *Mel Gibson*, scarred physically and emotionally by a car crash, offers help to young *Nick Stahl*. Impressive moral lesson about the way the unusual engenders suspicion and hostility.

★ **Map of the Human Heart** 1993   109 mins (cert 15)
Overpraised romantic drama spanning the formative years of two orphans, *Jason Scott Lee* and *Anne Parillaud*, first in the Arctic, then re-meeting in London during WWII.

★★★★★ **M·A·S·H** 1970   116 mins (cert 15)
This scathing story of a US military medical unit in Korean war spawned long-running TV series. *Donald Sutherland* and *Elliot Gould* as the charismatic doctors.

★★★ **Mask** 1985   120 mins (cert 15)
Eric Stoltz as the young lad disfigured by lionitis and *Cher* as his mother, determined to give him a normal life. Moving story based on fact.

★★ **Matewan** 1987   132 mins (cert 15)
John Sayles' thoughtful drama centring on the rebellion of the blacks imported to break West Virginian miners' strike in 1920.

★ **M Butterfly** 1994   96 mins (cert 15)
Remarkably dull considering it's based on a true story. *Jeremy Irons* plays a French diplomat who falls in love with an opera singer not realising 'she's' a man.

★★ **Medicine Man** 1992   105 mins (cert PG)
Sean Connery graces worthy but unconvincing ecological tale of doctor seeking cancer cure in rain forest. With *Lorraine Bracco*.

★★ **Meeting Venus** 1991   119 mins (cert 12)
Glenn Close stars as a diva in a David Puttnam/Istvan Szabo European co-production about love and language problems during an international production of Tannhauser.

★★ **Memphis** 1991   109 mins (cert 12)
Cybill Shepherd as member of kidnap gang who begins to feel sorry for their hostage.

★★ **Men Don't Leave** 1990   114 mins (cert 15)
Penniless widow *Jessica Lange* struggles to bring up two young sons alone. A touching, amusing soap opera, nicely played.

★★★ **A Midnight Clear** 1991   108 mins (cert 15)
Six GIs in the front line in 1944 learn what war is about. Young talented cast includes *Peter Berg*, *Kevin Dillon*, *Ethan Hawke* and *Arye Gross*. Strong, simple, anti-war movie.

★★★★ **Midnight Express** 1978   121 mins (cert 18)
Harrowing version of Billy Hayes' experiences in Turkish jail. Phenomenally powerful direction by Alan Parker.

★★★ **Millers Crossing** 1990   115 mins (cert 18)
Complex gangster movie of two Irish-American hoods, *Albert Finney* and *Gabriel Byrne*, at loggerheads over a woman.

★★ **The Misfits** 1961   124 mins (cert PG)
Marilyn Monroe and *Clark Gable* as a lonely, mismatched couple drawn to each other during mustang hunt in Nevada desert. Gable's last film.

★★ **Miss Firecracker** 1989   103 mins (cert PG)
Low-key comedy of Mississippi small-town life. *Holly Hunter* very good as lonely girl seeking love and self-esteem.

★★ **The Mission** 1983   125 mins (cert PG)
Roland Joffe's visually impressive but overly complex drama/tragedy about a Jesuit mission to the heart of South America. *Robert De Niro* and *Jeremy Irons* star.

★★★★ **Mississippi Burning** 1988   127 mins (cert 18)
Alan Parker's controversial but powerful account of the disappearance and murder of three 1960s civil rights workers in deep south USA.

★★ **Mississippi Masala** 1991   114 mins (cert 15)
Denzel Washington in story of love and bigotry between American blacks and expatriate Ugandan Asians.

★★ **Mo' Better Blues** 1990   129 mins (cert 15)
Spike Lee's surprisingly sentimental look at a jazz musician, *Denzel Washington*, forced to choose between his music and the women in his life.

★★ **The Moderns** 1988   126 mins (cert 15)
Keith Carradine as art forger in beautiful but bland look at the 1920s arty set in Paris.

★★ **The Molly Maguires** 1970   119 mins (cert PG)
Informer *Richard Harris* infiltrates secret 1870s group of Pennsylvanian miners, headed by *Sean Connery*, who use terrorism to seek better conditions. More worthy than exciting.

★★ **Mommie Dearest** 1981   124 mins (cert 15)
Faye Dunaway hams it up as Joan Crawford in a film based on the book by Crawford's daughter which exposed Joanie as a monster mum.

★★ **Mo' Money** 1991   90 mins (cert 15)
Comedy with a violent edge which spills over into humour about two brothers trying to rip off a gang of crooks. *Damon Wayans* and *Marlon Wayans* star.

★★★ **A Month in the Country** 1987   96 mins (cert PG)
Post-WWI drama about two scarred soldiers, *Colin Firth* and *Kenneth Branagh*, recovering from wartime horrors in Yorkshire village. So authentic you can smell the new-mown hay.

★★ **Mountains of the Moon** 1990   135 mins (cert 15)
Rival Victorian explorers, *Patrick Bergin* and *Iain Glen*, vie with each other to trace the source of the Nile. A slightly odd epic that doesn't quite add up.

★★ **Mr Jones** 1994   112 mins (cert 12)
A drama about mental illness is hard to believe when the central nutter is as savoury as *Richard Gere*. If all lunatics were as clean, wealthy and charming as this there'd be no need for community care.

★★★★ **Mrs Miniver** 1942   134 mins (cert U)
Greer Garson tries to keep body, soul and family together in face of encroaching WWII. Marvellous propaganda movie to encourage US involvement in war.

★★★★ **Mr Smith Goes to Washington** 1939   130 mins (cert U)
An innocent school teacher, *James Stewart*, finds nothing but corruption in US Senate and bravely fights to expose it in Capra's splendid, famous movie.

★★★★ **The Music Box** 1989   126 mins (cert 15)
Costa-Gavras' powerful, much underrated story of a lawyer, *Jessica Lange*, defending her father, *Armin Mueller-Stahl*, who is accused of wartime atrocities.

★★★ **My Beautiful Launderette** 1985   97 mins (cert 15)
Sensitive examination of racism in London's East End, as experienced by a young Pakistani and his gay white lover. First starring role for *Daniel Day-Lewis*.

★★★★ **My Left Foot** 1989   98 mins (cert PG)
Uplifting account of the life of Christy Brown, magnificently played by *Daniel Day-Lewis*, who, despite crippling cerebral palsy, became a celebrated writer.

★★ **My Own Private Idaho** 1991   105 mins (cert 18)
Two gay hustlers, *Keanu Reeves* and the late *River Phoenix*, go to Rome to find Phoenix's mother. A bizarre effort this, mixing fantasy and realism and with little apparent idea of where it's going.

★ **The Mystery of Edwin Drood** 1992   97 mins (cert 15)
Disappointing, anachronistic version of Dickens' unfinished novel. *Robert Powell* almost saves it but not quite.

★★★ **Mystic Pizza** 1988   104 mins (cert 15)
Sweetly appealing study of the hopes, dreams and amorous adventures of three young girls; co-stars *Julia Roberts* in an early role.

★★ **Naked Lunch** 1992   110 mins (cert 18)
Be warned – don't eat when watching this. Some of the effects are stomach-churning. Bold but unsuccessful attempt to film William Burrough's unfilmable book. *Peter Weller*, *Judy Davis* and *Julian Sands* try hard, though, under David Cronenberg's offbeat direction.

★★★ **The Natural** 1984   134 mins (cert PG)
Curious but watchable period piece with *Robert Redford* as an exceptionally – perhaps supernaturally – gifted baseball player.

★★★ **Network** 1976   120 mins (cert PG)
Sidney Lumet's effective satire of the TV world. *Peter Finch* won a posthumous Oscar in the starring role.

★★★ **New York Stories** 1989   125 mins (cert 15)
A trilogy of short films from Woody Allen (fine), Martin Scorsese (very good) and Francis Coppola (forget it).

★★★ **Nicholas and Alexandra** 1971   183 mins (cert PG)
Overblown epic depicting events leading to Russian Revolution and its effect on Tsar Nicholas, *Michael Jayston*, and family.

★★★ **Night on Earth** 1992   129 mins (cert 15)
Five stories based in five taxi cabs in five cities. Poignant, funny and bizarre featuring the likes of *Winona Ryder*, *Rosie Perez*, *Beatrice Dalle* and *Armin Mueller-Stahl*.

★★ **9½ Weeks** 1986   116 mins (cert 18)
Explicit sexual activity between *Mickey Rourke* and *Kim Basinger* but a tedious story takes the edge off erotica.

★★★ **No Highway** 1951   98 mins (cert U)
Halfway over the Atlantic the crew of a plane – designed by *James Stewart* – is told it's going to crash with *Marlene Dietrich* and *Glynis Johns* on board.

★★★ **Norma Rae** 1979   114 mins (cert PG)
Sally Field winning her first Oscar as the Southern mill worker organising a union. *Beau Bridges* as her husband.

★★★ **No Surrender** 1985   100 mins (cert 15)
Biting social satire set in a Northern nightclub where two sets of rival old folks come into riotous conflict.

★★ **Not Without My Daughter** 1991   115 mins (cert 12)
Sentimental but true story of an American mother, *Sally Field*, attempting to recover her daughter held in Iran by father *Alfred Molina*.

★★★★ **Now, Voyager** 1942   117 mins (cert PG)
A gloriously weepy melodrama with spinster *Bette Davis* embarking on anguished affair with married man *Paul Heinreid* during a cruise.

★★★★ **The Nun's Story** 1959   151 mins (cert U)
Audrey Hepburn as nun in the Belgian Congo rebelling against her vows. Beautifully acted with *Peter Finch*, *Edith Evans* and *Dame Peggy Ashcroft*.

★★★ **An Officer and a Gentleman** 1982   124 mins (cert 15)
Corny but well-acted story of love affair between officer-cadet, *Richard Gere*, and factory girl, *Debra Winger*.

★★★ **Of Mice and Men** 1992 110 mins (cert PG)
Beautiful remake of Steinbeck's touching tale. *Gary Sinise* (who also directed) is outstanding as George, the itinerant farm labourer trying to find work for himself and the simple Lennie, *John Malkovich*.

★★ **Old Gringo** 1989 119 mins (cert 15)
The Mexican revolution of 1910 is the setting for spinster, *Jane Fonda*, and her adventures with journalist, *Gregory Peck*, and revolutionary, *Jimmy Smits*.

★★★★ **Oliver Twist** 1948 116 mins (cert U)
Alec Guinness is brilliant as Fagin in the matchless David Lean version of Dickens' saga.

★★ **Once Around** 1991 110 mins (cert 15)
Italian-American family's life turned around when the daughter falls for an unsuitable suitor. With *Holly Hunter*, *Richard Dreyfuss*, *Danny Aiello* and *Laura San Giacomo*.

★★★★ **One Flew Over the Cuckoo's Nest** 1975 134 mins (cert 18)
Multi-Oscar winner by Milos Forman celebrates triumph of the individual over the system. *Jack Nicholson* excellent as are the rest of the cast.

★★★ **On Golden Pond** 1981 109 mins (cert PG)
Sentimental tale of family reconciliation made more poignant for featuring the estranged *Jane* and *Henry Fonda* – his last film – and *Katharine Hepburn*.

★★★ **Only Angels Have Wings** 1939 121 mins (cert U)
Cary Grant as boss of an airfreight company in the Andes where (continually) hazardous weather conditions and showgirl *Jean Arthur* create tension.

★★★★ **On the Waterfront** 1954 108 mins (cert PG)
Corruption amongst dock workers inspires ex-boxer *Marlon Brando* to fight against oppression in Elia Kazan's gripping film. Superb performances by all.

★★★ **Ordinary People** 1980 124 mins (cert 15)
A poignant tale of the effect of a boy's suicide on his family. With *Donald Sutherland* and *Mary Tyler Moore*. Robert Redford won the Oscar for his direction.

★★★ **Orlando** 1993   93 mins (cert PG)
Tilda Swinton stars as Virginia Woolf's androgynous heroine who lives 400 years. *Billy Zane* and *Quentin Crisp* in support. A little delight.

★★ **An Outcast of the Islands** 1951   102 mins (cert PG)
Study of moral decay. *Ralph Richardson* and *Trevor Howard* as hunter and hunted on Malayan island.

★★★ **Out of Africa** 1985   161 mins (cert PG)
Great cast – *Robert Redford* and *Meryl Streep* – great scenery, but mildly disappointing love story.

★★ **Painted Heart** 1994   112 mins (cert 15)
Offbeat and, despite the attempts at comedy, rather depressing tale about a builder with a secret, his painter and the builder's wife.

★★★ **The Paper** 1994   112 mins (cert 15)
Clichéd but amusing and satisfying tale of a day in the life of a newspaper man, *Michael Keaton*, who has a pregnant wife, *Marisa Tomei*, a boss with prostate trouble, *Robert Duvall*, and difficult colleagues, *Glenn Close* and *Randy Quaid*, not to mention a looming deadline for his scoop.

★★ **Paradise** 1992   111 mins (cert 12)
Melanie Griffith and *Don Johnson* as a married couple forced to confront their problems when young *Elijah Wood* comes to stay. Pretty but uninvolving.

★★ **Paris, Texas** 1984   150 mins (cert 15)
Wim Wenders' much-praised but ultimately unsatisfying Texan road movie. *Harry Dean Stanton* and *Nastassja Kinski* star.

★★★ **A Passage to India** 1984   163 mins (cert PG)
David Lean's sumptuous adaptation of E M Forster's drama of East-West culture clash in 1920s India. *Judy Davis* fine, but *Alec Guinness* miscast.

★★ **Passion Fish** 1993   135 mins (cert 15)
Story of burgeoning friendship between newly paralysed *Mary McDonnell* and home help *Alfre Woodard* with problems of her own. Pleasing story set against the beautiful backdrop of America's deep south.

★★★ **Philadelphia** 1993   110 mins (cert 12)
Tom Hanks won the Oscar for his portrayal of a lawyer dying of AIDS and fighting the unjust treatment of AIDS victims as he does so. A real weepy.

★★★ **The Piano** 1993   120 mins (cert 15)
Holly Hunter as the 19th-century mute mail-order bride shipped to New Zealand. *Harvey Keitel* co-stars in fascinating, unusual story of sexual passion.

★★★ **Picnic at Hanging Rock** 1975   112 mins (cert 18)
Gripping account of events leading to eerie disappearance of Australian schoolgirls and their teacher during school outing.

★★ **Places in the Heart** 1984   111 mins (cert PG)
Plucky *Sally Field* as a farmer's widow struggling during the Depression to keep her Texas farm.

★★ **The Playboys** 1992   108 mins (cert 12)
Albert Finney and travelling player *Aidan Quinn* vie for the hand of unmarried mother *Robin Wright* in a 1950s Irish village. Pleasing tale with good performances.

★★★ **Postcards from the Edge** 1991   104 mins (cert 15)
Hollywood portrayal of actress, *Meryl Streep*, the drug-addicted daughter of overshadowing famous mother, *Shirley MacLaine*. In parts very funny, in others a bit off the mark.

★★ **The Power of One** 1992   127 mins (cert 12)
Young lad growing up in South Africa in WWII. New slant on the race theme. Simplistic but pleasing.

★★★ **Prick Up Your Ears** 1987   110 mins (cert 18)
Gary Oldman very impressive as British playwright Joe Orton; *Alfred Molina* plays his lover who ultimately kills him.

★★ **Pride and Prejudice** 1940   116 mins (cert U)
This pleasing, though hardly faithful version of Jane Austen's delightful romance stars *Greer Garson* and *Laurence Olivier*.

★★ **The Prince of Tides** 1992   131 mins (cert 15)
Barbra Streisand's melodramatic love story. *Nick Nolte* is the man with a disturbed past; Streisand the psychiatrist making him confront it.

★★ **Proof** 1991   90 mins (cert 15)
Distrustful blind man uses photography to ensure people tell him the truth in strangely absorbing Australian story.

★★ **Prospero's Books** 1991   120 mins (cert 15)
Myriad of impressive visuals but style better than content in Peter Greenaway's version of 'The Tempest'.

★★ **Pumping Iron** 1977   85 mins (cert 12)
Only mentioned since it's amusing for an early sight of Mr Universe – *Arnold Schwarzenegger*. Bet he didn't demand a $15 million fee in those days.

★★★★ **Queen Christina** 1933   101 mins (cert U)
Probably *Greta Garbo*'s best dramatic role as Swedish queen relinquishing throne for love.

★★★ **The Quiet Man** 1952   131 mins (cert U)
Sentimental, romanticized vehicle for *John Wayne* as ex-boxer settling in Irish village full of usual stereotypes. Ludicrous fight sequence but pleasing nonetheless.

★ **The Rachel Papers** 1989   95 mins (cert 18)
Maladroit attempt at modern comedy of manners based on the Martin Amis novel.

★★★★ **Raging Bull** 1980   129 mins (cert 18)
Martin Scorsese's study of boxing champion Jake La Motta. Brilliant performance from *Robert De Niro* helps make this one of the best films of the 1980s.

★★★ **Rain Man** 1988   133 mins (cert 15)
Relationship of autistic savant, *Dustin Hoffman*, and initially ruthless brother, *Tom Cruise*. Two fine performances, especially by Cruise.

★★ **Rambling Rose** 1991   112 mins (cert 15)
Family life in 1930s disrupted by arrival of promiscuous child of nature, *Laura Dern*, in home of *Robert Duvall* and *Diane Ladd*.

★★★ **Reality Bites** 1994   99 mins (cert 12)
A bunch of twentysomethings – *Winona Ryder* and *Ethan Hawke* among them – find life after college difficult to accept. Observant and humorous script.

★★★ **Rebel Without a Cause** 1955   111 mins (cert PG)
James Dean's angry young man looks dated now but still bears emotional resonance of teenage alienation.

★★★ **Reds** 1981   196 mins (cert 15)
Warren Beatty's Oscar-winning directorial debut about American journalist's espousal of communism. Beatty and *Diane Keaton* star.

★★★★ **The Red Shoes** 1948   134 mins (cert U)
Powell and Pressburger's marvellous, innovative tale about the staging of a ballet and a young dancer, *Moira Shearer*, torn between two men.

★★ **Regarding Henry** 1991   107 mins (cert 12)
Harrison Ford in an unconvincing story about a ruthless lawyer whose attitude to family and work changes drastically after he's shot.

★★★★ **The Remains of the Day** 1993   138 mins (cert U)
Merchant Ivory stick faithfully to the book wherein class-conscious butler *Anthony Hopkins* reflects on his life of missed opportunities. Hopkins outstanding; well supported by *Emma Thompson*.

★★★ **Reversal of Fortune** 1990   111 mins (cert 15)
Impeccable performance by *Jeremy Irons* as Claus Von Bulow, accused of trying to murder his wealthy wife, *Glenn Close*. Based on a true story.

★★★★ **Richard III** 1955   161 mins (cert U)
Laurence Olivier's performance as Crookback scared generations of actors away from the role. Good, if stagy, production.

★★ **Rich in Love** 1993   105 mins (cert PG)
A nine-year-old girl tries to hold her family together when her mother walks out. *Albert Finney* is the deserted husband picking up pieces of his life. Gentle family drama set against spectacular back drop of deep south USA.

★★ **The River** 1984   122 mins (cert PG)
Mel Gibson and *Sissy Spacek* as Tennessee farmers who find their way of life is under threat. Intelligent, sombre drama.

★★ **A River Runs Through It** 1992   123 mins (cert PG)
Gentle, non-eventful tale of father *Tom Skerritt*'s relationship with his two very different sons, *Brad Pitt* and *Craig Sheffer*. *Robert Redford* narrates and directs.

★★★ **Robin and Marian** 1976   107 mins (cert PG)
Sean Connery and *Audrey Hepburn* as the now-ageing outlaws in a splendid period piece of such atmosphere you can smell it.

★★★ **The Rocking Horse Winner** 1950   90 mins (cert 15)
Unusual, moving D H Lawrence story of a small boy with the knack of picking racetrack winners. Fine performances.

★★★ **Roger & Me** 1989   91 mins (cert 15)
Michael Moore's extraordinary documentary exposes the despair of a Michigan town when General Motors moved out.

★★★ **Roman Holiday** 1953   118 mins (cert U)
Touching, tender romance between runaway princess *Audrey Hepburn* and journalist *Gregory Peck*.

★★★ **Romero** 1989   101 mins (cert 15)
Raul Julia stars in absorbing, though sometimes vague attempt to tell the story of the El Salvador archbishop/revolutionary who was assassinated in 1980.

★★★ **A Room With a View** 1985   115 mins (cert PG)
Beautiful adaptation of E M Forster's Italian-based tale of English manners. Photography and British cast superb.

★★ **Rosalie Goes Shopping** 1989   93 mins (cert 15)
Comic satire on Western consumerism. *Marianne Sagebrecht* is Rosalie, a bored housewife who mounts up a huge shopping bill on credit cards.

★★★ **Running on Empty** 1988   117 mins (cert 15)
Christine Lahti and *Judd Hirsch*, on the run for years from the FBI as wanted terrorists, find their safety threatened when their son, *River Phoenix*, is offered a music scholarship.

★★ **Rush** 1992   120 mins (cert 18)
Hard-hitting drama of narcotics cops, *Jennifer Jason Leigh* and *Jason Patric*, working undercover and becoming addicts themselves.

★★★ **Ryan's Daughter** 1970   206 mins (cert 15)
David Lean's overblown – but underrated – story of a young wife, *Sarah Miles*, and her love affair with a shell-shocked British soldier in a small Irish community.

★★★ **The Saint of Fort Washington** 1994   103 mins (cert 15)
Superb acting marks this downbeat story of the homeless. *Matt Dillon* is a schizophrenic who makes friends with hardened street-dweller *Danny Glover*.

★★★ **Salaam Bombay!** 1988   113 mins (cert 15)
Vivid characterization marks potent Indian tale of a young boy's struggle to survive on the streets of Bombay.

★★★ **Salvador** 1986   123 mins (cert 18)
Oliver Stone's powerful, sobering account of the experiences of journalist Richard Boyle – *James Woods* – in war-torn El Salvador.

★★ **Same Time Next Year** 1978   119 mins (cert 15)
Sweet story of a couple, *Ellen Burstyn* and *Alan Alda*, who meet for a brief adulterous affair every year for over 25 years. Low-key but charming.

★★★ **Saturday Night and Sunday Morning** 1960   89 mins (cert 15)
Albert Finney's first starring role as the angry young man in Alan Sillitoe's gritty, evocative study of working-class life.

★★★ **Scandal** 1989   114 mins (cert 18)
Absorbing examination of the Profumo Affair which brought down the British government in the 1960s. Lovely performances by *John Hurt*, *Joanne Whalley-Kilmer* and *Bridget Fonda*.

★★★ **Scent of a Woman** 1992   156 mins (cert 15)
Al Pacino is splendid as the blind war veteran who hires preppy *Chris O'Donnell* to be his eyes during one final, blow-out weekend in New York.

★★★★★ **Schindler's List** 1994   195 mins (cert 15)
Steven Spielberg's superb examination of the Holocaust. Shot in black and white, it stars *Liam Neeson* as the German who saved a number of Jews from the gas chambers. *Ralph Fiennes* is the SS officer who sent them there.

★★★★ **Second Best** 1994   112 mins (cert 12)
Marvellous performance by *William Hurt* as a lonely, loveless bachelor who adopts a disturbed 10-year-old boy. A familiar cast of English favourites including *Jane Horrocks* and *Keith Allen*.

★★★★ **Secret Honor** 1984   90 mins (cert 15)
Philip Baker Hall excels in this astonishing one-man show directed by Robert Altman and based on the alleged ravings of a suicidal Richard Nixon. Really chilling stuff.

★★ **The Secret of My Success** 1987   110 mins (cert PG)
Michael J Fox heads for the big city and finds corruption in the workplace, streets and bedroom.

★★★★ **sex, lies and videotape** 1989   100 mins (cert 18)
Astonishing directorial debut by Steven Soderbergh with story of small-town marital and extra-marital relationships. Fine cast headed by *James Spader* and *Andie MacDowell*.

★★★★ **Shadowlands** 1994   89 mins (cert PG)
Rich depiction of the romance between academic C S Lewis, *Anthony Hopkins*, and brash American divorcee *Debra Winger*. Beautifully shot, lovely performances and sensitive direction by Richard Attenborough.

★ **A Shadow of Doubt** 1994   120 mins (cert 15)
An 11-year-old accuses her father of sex abuse but the disbelief of her mother and friends leads to a family crisis.

★★★★ **Shawshank Redemption** 1995   120 mins (cert 18)
Brilliant prison drama with a superb performance from *Tim Robbins* as the respectable businessman accused of murdering his wife and serving two life sentences in foul, maximum security jail.

★★ **The Sheltering Sky** 1990   138 mins (cert 18)
Drab, period reconstruction of Paul Bowle's famous novel about a couple, *John Malkovich* and *Debra Winger*, discovering North Africa after WWII.

★★★★ **Shirley Valentine** 1989   109 mins (cert 15)
Delightful, gentle Willy Russell story with *Pauline Collins* as the bored Liverpudlian housewife who ups to a Greek island in search of romance.

★★★★ **The Shooting Party** 1984   96 mins (cert 15)
Deeply moving examination of class and culture centring on a weekend shooting party in 1913. *James Mason* brilliant in his penultimate role.

★★★ **Shopping** 1994   107 mins (cert 18)
An effective, albeit bleak English drama that depicts a near-future of bored youngsters and the increasing crime of ramraiding.

★★★★★ **Short Cuts** 1993   185 mins (cert 18)
Robert Altman takes the pick of Hollywood's actors and a bunch of stories and knits them all together in this gloriously inspired movie.

★★★ **Shout** 1991   85 mins (cert PG)
Quiet but appealing story about the effect of a music teacher – *John Travolta* – on a troubled teenager in reform school.

★★★ **Silas Marner** 1985   92 mins (cert PG)
Decent adaptation of the classic novel by George Eliot. *Ben Kingsley* is the miserly Marner, a weaver whose life is changed by an adopted child.

★★★ **Silkwood** 1983   131 mins (cert 15)
Meryl Streep as Karen Silkwood, who uncovered a dangerous secret at a nuclear plant and mysteriously died; *Cher* as her best friend. An important, disturbing film.

★★★ **Singles** 1992   99 mins (cert 12)
Group of late twentysomethings wanting to settle down and looking for Mr (or Ms) Right. With *Bridget Fonda*, *Matt Dillon*, *Kyra Sedgwick* and many others.

★★★ **Sirens** 1994   94 mins (cert 15)
Every scene as pretty as a picture in an Australian period drama-cum-comedy starring *Hugh Grant* as a prim clergyman and *Sam Neill* as a permissive artist. It also features (frequently naked) supermodel *Elle MacPherson*.

★★★★ **The Six Wives of Henry VIII** 1972   541 mins (cert PG)
Scintillating TV drama starring *Keith Michell*, excellent as the ambitious young king growing into a disillusioned, tyrannical monarch.

★★★ **Sleep with Me** 1994   98 mins (cert 15)
An amusing examination of relationships concentrating on a married couple, *Eric Stoltz* and *Meg Tilly*, and the best friend who threatens to come between them.

★★★ **Sommersby** 1992   112 mins (cert 15)
After the American Civil War *Richard Gere* returns home to wife *Jodie Foster* – but is he the man who went away? Moving story though the French version, 'Le Retour de Martin Guerre', is better.

★★★ **Sophie's Choice** 1982   151 mins (cert 15)
Meryl Streep gives a heartrending performance as the survivor of a Nazi concentration camp struggling to find happiness in America.

★★ **Stand and Deliver** 1987   104 mins (cert 15)
Gentle, based-on-fact drama of Hispanic headmaster adopting unorthodox methods to ensure his drug-pushing, gang-member pupils win qualifications.

★★★ **Stand By Me** 1986   87 mins (cert 15)
Affectionate, nostalgic glimpse of boyhood friendship in 1950s America, based on Stephen King's rites-of-passage story. *River Phoenix* splendid in the leading role.

★★ **Stanley and Iris** 1990   104 mins (cert 15)
Hard-up widow *Jane Fonda* finds love when teaching the dyslexic *Robert De Niro* to read. Sincerely meant but dullish stuff.

★★★ **Steel Magnolias** 1989   117 mins (cert 15)
Bittersweet comedy following the lives of female friends in a small Louisiana town. Nice acting from a cast that includes *Julia Roberts*, *Shirley MacLaine* and *Sally Field*.

★★ **Stella** 1989   114 mins (cert 15)
Presence of *Bette Midler*, sassy in the title role, almost saves sentimental story of a woman's lone fight to raise her daughter in a remake of 'Stella Dallas'. Almost.

★★★ **St Elmo's Fire** 1985   108 mins (cert 15)
Entertaining Brat Packers movie with *Emilio Estevez*, *Judd Nelson*, *Rob Lowe* and *Demi Moore* finding that life after college can be a bitch.

★★ **Stepping Out** 1991   105 mins (cert PG)
Liza Minnelli runs a tap-dance class of unfulfilled women and one man. All need the help and friendship the class provides. *Julie Walters* lightens tone.

★★ **Straight Out of Brooklyn** 1991   83 mins (cert 15)
A crime-ridden black area of NY is the setting for this bleak drama of a young lad in a downward spiral and unable to break out of social rut.

★★★ **Strapless** 1989   99 mins (cert 15)
David Hare directed his own story of an American doctor, *Blair Brown*, who marries on a whim but soon regrets it. Good performances by Brown and *Bridget Fonda*.

★★★★ **A Streetcar Named Desire** 1951   122 mins (cert 18)
Powerful Tennesse Williams melodrama. Great performances by Oscar-winning *Vivien Leigh*, *Kim Hunter*, *Karl Malden* and especially by *Marlon Brando* who, alone, missed an Oscar. Why?

★★★★★ **Sunset Boulevard** 1950   110 mins (cert PG)
Billy Wilder's subtly vicious indictment of Hollywood. *William Holden* as young writer tragically involved with has-been movie star *Gloria Swanson*.

★★ **Swing Kids** 1993   114 mins (cert 15)
Germany, 1939, and a group of kids who embrace the swing/jazz culture oppose the Nazis. Could have been fascinating but cops out. With *Robert Sean Leonard*, *Christian Bale* and *Kenneth Branagh* (who kept his name off the credits).

★★★ **Talk Radio** 1988   108 mins (cert 18)
Eric Bogosian as radio talk-show host whose controversial style wins notoriety and worse in Oliver Stone's grim, moral tale.

★★★★ **Taxi Driver** 1976   114 mins (cert 18)
Martin Scorsese's disturbing but brilliant view of ultra-violent New York seen through the eyes of a psychotic cabbie, *Robert De Niro*. Also stars a young *Jodie Foster*.

★★★ **Tender Mercies** 1983   90 mins (cert PG)
Poignant performance from *Robert Duvall* as a down-at-heel country singer rebuilding his life around young widow, *Tess Harper*, and her son.

★★★ **Terms of Endearment** 1983   132 mins (cert 15)
Sub-plot involving *Jack Nicholson* and *Shirley MacLaine* is funny but sentimentality of main plot where daughter, *Debra Winger*, is dying from cancer, sticks in the throat.

★★ **Texasville** 1990   126 mins (cert 15)
Disappointing follow-up to 'The Last Picture Show', resuming life stories of *Jeff Bridges*, *Cybill Shepherd*, *Timothy Bottoms* and *Randy Quaid* in the 1980s.

★★★★ **These Foolish Things** 1990   102 mins (cert PG)
Bertrand Tavernier's bittersweet story of the relationship between an ailing father, *Dirk Bogarde*, and his daughter, *Jane Birkin*. Beautifully played.

★★★★ **They Shoot Horses, Don't They?** 1969   129 mins (cert 15)
Bleak view of America during the Depression in a story of marathon dancing contests which sometimes lasted for weeks. *Jane Fonda* stars.

★★★★★ **The Third Man** 1949   100 mins (cert PG)
Carol Reed's superb thriller set in post-war Vienna with *Joseph Cotten* as the naive American searching for his mysterious friend, *Orson Welles*. A movie classic.

★★ **This Boy's Life** 1993   115 mins (cert PG)
Bland, yet hard-to-believe, coming-of-age story with a 'so what?' ending. *Robert De Niro* is the sadistic stepfather, *Ellen Barkin* the mother and *Leonardo DiCaprio* the boy.

★★★ **The Three Faces of Eve** 1957   91 mins (cert 15)
Powerful performance by *Joanne Woodward* as a schizophrenic with three diverse lives.

★★★ **To Kill a Mockingbird** 1962   129 mins (cert PG)
Rich drama based in deep south USA, concentrating upon the family of a lawyer, *Gregory Peck*, who defends a black man accused of rape.

★★ **Tom & Viv** 1994   99 mins (cert 15)
Dreary tale about T S Eliott and his schizophrenic wife. *Miranda Richardson*'s good as the mad woman but *Willem Dafoe*'s hardly credible as the poet.

★★★ **Torch Song Trilogy** 1988　　　　　　　　　　119 mins (cert 15)
Evocative and emotional comedy/drama told in three parts about a homosexual, *Harvey Fierstein*, coming to terms with his problems.

★★ **To Sir With Love** 1967　　　　　　　　　　　105 mins (cert PG)
Highly competent account of black school teacher, *Sidney Poitier*, earning respect and devotion of unruly pupils.

★★★★ **The Treasure of the Sierra Madre** 1948　　　126 mins (cert PG)
Classic moral drama about three gold prospectors – *Humphrey Bogart*, *Walter Huston* and *Tim Holt* – greedily fighting it out down Mexico way.

★★ **The Trial** 1993　　　　　　　　　　　　　　120 mins (cert 12)
Lengthy, all-too-faithful version of Kafka's surreal novel. *Kyle MacLachlan* is the man arrested for reasons he can never discover.

★★★★ **Truly, Madly, Deeply** 1991　　　　　　　　106 mins (cert PG)
Alternately touching and hilarious tale of coming to terms with grief. *Juliet Stevenson* is the woman trying to accept the death of her partner, *Alan Rickman*.

★★★★ **Twelve Angry Men** 1957　　　　　　　　　　95 mins (cert U)
Terrific courtroom drama focusing on the deliberations of a murder case jury. Cast headed by *Henry Fonda*. Brilliant directorial debut by Sidney Lumet.

★★★ **The Ugly American** 1962　　　　　　　　　　120 mins (cert U)
Far from ugly *Marlon Brando* plays ambassador – to Communist Asian country – whose mistakes threaten political and personal disaster.

★★★ **The Unbearable Lightness of Being** 1988　　　171 mins (cert 18)
Intelligent, absorbing character study, adapted from Milan Kundera's novel, of a doctor, *Daniel Day-Lewis*, reluctantly involved in political and sexual conflict.

★★★★ **Under Fire** 1983　　　　　　　　　　　　　128 mins (cert 15)
Nick Nolte and *Gene Hackman* as journalists on the front line of Nicaraguan rebellion in tense political thriller.

★★★ **Untamed Heart** 1993　　　　　　　　　　　102 mins (cert 15)
Busboy *Christian Slater* falls in love with waitress *Marisa Tomei*, but he has a weak heart. Not so this movie. Touching, in parts funny – thanks to *Rosie Perez* – and heart in the right place.

★★ **Valmont** 1989   137 mins (cert 15)
Milos Forman's version of Chodelos de Laclos' story of sex, corruption and decadence in 18th-century France. Suffers in comparison with 'Dangerous Liaisons'.

★★★ **The Verdict** 1982   128 mins (cert 15)
Disillusioned, dead-beat lawyer, *Paul Newman*, gets his act together to fight case of medical negligence. Splendidly directed by Sidney Lumet.

★★★ **Vincent and Theo** 1990   140 mins (cert 15)
Robert Altman's fine study of the relationship between Vincent Van Gogh and his brother. A convincing performance by *Tim Roth* as Vincent.

★★ **Vital Signs** 1990   103 mins (cert 15)
Pleasant enough attempt to do a sort of 'Doctor in the House' in contemporary America. Nice young cast boosted by the likes of *Jimmy Smits* and *William Devane*.

★★★ **Wall Street** 1987   124 mins (cert 15)
Oliver Stone's bleak indictment of greed and corruption among stock brokers. *Michael Douglas* and *Charlie Sheen* star.

★★★ **The Waterdance** 1992   107 mins (cert 15)
An entrancing story about a paraplegic hospital ward and the courage and humour displayed therein. *Eric Stoltz* and *Wesley Snipes* are two of the crippled inmates. A performance-led drama.

★★★ **What's Eating Gilbert Grape?** 1993   117 mins (cert 12)
Quirky, offbeat tale of smalltown life. *Johnny Depp* as a guy crumbling under the oppressive weight of his oddball family.

★★★ **What's Love Got To Do With It?** 1993   118 mins (cert 18)
Well-made biography of Tina Turner – played by *Angela Bassett*, though great lady herself provides the soundtrack. *Larry Fishburne* as the evil ex-husband, Ike.

★★ **When a Man Loves a Woman** 1994   126 mins (cert 15)
Why? would be a more apt question. *Meg Ryan* is the woman with everything – including most understanding husband *Andy Garcia* – who becomes an alcoholic. Garcia is good, Ryan is less so and it's difficult to care.

★★★ **Where Angels Fear to Tread** 1990   113 mins (cert PG)
This is not quite as pretty as Merchant Ivory usually manage with E M Forster adaptations. Nicely acted though by *Helena Bonham Carter*, *Judy Davis* and *Rupert Graves*.

★★★ **White Hunter, Black Heart** 1990   112 mins (cert PG)
Clint Eastwood as a director – a thinly-disguised John Huston – more obsessed with shooting an elephant than his movie. (Incidentally, the movie was 'The African Queen'.)

★★ **White Mischief** 1988   106 mins (cert 18)
Lusty sex and murder saga of expatriate community in Kenya with *Greta Scacchi*, *Charles Dance* and *Joss Ackland*.

★★★ **White Palace** 1990   105 mins (cert 18)
Sexy drama with *James Spader* as a yuppie widower falling for older, down-trodden waitress, *Susan Sarandon*.

★★★★ **Who's Afraid of Virginia Woolf?** 1966   131 mins (cert 18)
Elizabeth Taylor and *Richard Burton*, a perfect partnership, as academic couple in ferocious marital relationship.

★★ **Whose Life Is It Anyway?** 1981   118 mins (cert 15)
Richard Dreyfuss is fine as an artist, paralysed in an accident, fighting for his right to die but the film is too obviously stage-based.

★★★ **Wild at Heart** 1990   127 mins (cert 18)
... and weird on top. Ferocious, funny and kinky David Lynch tale with *Nicolas Cage* and *Laura Dern* as a bizarre couple on the run.

★★★★ **The Winslow Boy** 1950   117 mins (cert U)
Superb drama casts *Robert Donat* as barrister employed to clear name of *Cedric Hardwicke*'s son, no matter the cost to self or family.

★★ **With Honors** 1994   101 mins (cert PG)
Homeless *Joe Pesci* teaches life lessons to Harvard student *Brendan Fraser*, thereby proving that not everything can be learnt from a book. *Gore Vidal* makes a cameo appearance. All very worthy.

★★★ **A World Apart** 1988   110 mins (cert PG)
Highly charged drama set in South Africa. *Barbara Hershey*'s bitter struggle against apartheid as seen through the eyes of her daughter, *Jodhi May*.

★★ **Wrestling Ernest Hemingway** 1994   123 mins (cert 12)
A couple of cinema's original bad boys – *Richard Harris* and *Robert Duvall* – give spirited performances in this character-led drama concentrating on the relationship between two elderly, dissimilar men.

★ **Wuthering Heights** 1992   106 mins (cert U)
Oh dear. Do read the novel. Dull adaptation of one of the great books. *Ralph Fiennes* and *Juliette Binoche* woefully miscast as Heathcliffe and Cathy.

★★★ **Yanks** 1979   139 mins (cert 15)
Engaging story of Americans billeted in small-town England during WWII and the lives and loves they leave behind. *Richard Gere* leads.

★★★ **The Year of Living Dangerously** 1983   115 mins (cert PG)
Fine performances projected *Mel Gibson* and *Sigourney Weaver* to stardom as a couple investigating political crisis in Indonesia. *Linda Hunt* won Oscar as Gibson's (male) side-kick.

FAMILY

★★ **The Addams Family** 1991   99 mins (cert PG)
Ghoulish comic strip family brought to life Hollywood-style by *Anjelica Huston*, *Raul Julia* and *Christopher Lloyd* as Uncle Fester – who may or may not be an impostor.

★★★ **Addams Family Values** 1993   96 mins (cert PG)
Better than original with a stronger story and more effective jokes – every one a winner. *Christina Ricci* as Wednesday outshines the adult cast.

★★ **The Adventures of Huckleberry Finn** 1993   108 mins (cert PG)
Lush but uninspiring rendition of Mark Twain's adventure with *Robbie Coltrane* and *Jason Robards* notable as a couple of con artists.

★★★ **The Air Up There** 1994   91 mins (cert PG)
Kevin Bacon as a fraught basketball coach who goes to Africa in a wild attempt to sign up the player of his dreams. Delightful tale, nicely and affectionately played.

★★★★ **Aladdin** 1993   90 mins (cert U)
Disney's 31st animated feature film, based on Arabian Nights fable, became the highest grossing animated feature ever (until 'The Lion King'). *Robin Williams* is superb as the voice of the hip and happening genie.

★★★ **An American Tail** 1986   81 mins (cert U)
Steven Spielberg's animated fantasy of Russian mouse family emigrating to an America whose streets, they hope, are paved with cheese.

★★ **An American Tail II: Fievel Goes West** 1991   74 mins (cert U)
Further, though rather weaker adventures of the immigrant Mouskewitz family.

★★ **Arachnophobia** 1990   110 mins (cert PG)
Slick, Spielberg-produced, comic thriller about a small town overrun by killer spiders. Less scary than you might expect.

★★★ **The Aristocats** 1970   78 mins (cert U)
A feline family rescued from an evil butler who'd rather not see the cats inherit his mistress's fortune. Voices provided by the likes of *Phil Harris*, *Eva Gabor* and *Hermione Baddeley*.

★★ **Baby's Day Out** 1993   105 mins (cert PG)
A pampered toddler is snatched by incompetent kidnappers, headed by *Joe Mantegna*. Mayhem in the city ensues in over-sentimental John Hughes film.

★★★ **Baby: Secret of the Lost Legend** 1985   95 (cert U)
A group of palaeontologists discover a family of dinosaurs in Africa. Cute and technically impressive. Featuring *Sean Young*.

★★★★ **Bambi** 1942   69 mins (cert U)
Disney's telling of the little fawn growing up in the forest still has them weeping in the aisles and crying with joy at the end. Timeless classic.

★★ **The Bear** 1989   93 mins (cert PG)
Patronisingly anthropomorphic tale of an ursine family, but at the same time a beautifully filmed story of a cub and its fight for survival.

★★★★ **Beauty and the Beast** 1992   84 mins (cert U)
First animated feature ever nominated for Best Film Oscar – deservedly so. The Disney studio shows it can still produce excellent fairytale features better than anyone else.

★★ **Bedknobs and Broomsticks** 1971   117 mins (cert U)
Three children, plus kindly witch *Angela Lansbury* and a magic, flying bedstead, save Britain from invasion in 1940. Good special effects but otherwise disappointing.

★★★ **Beethoven** 1991   87 mins (cert U)
A St Bernard dog causes chaos for canine-hater *Charles Grodin* and family, and rounds up the bad guys. Grodin provides a sharp edge to cut the sugar.

★★ **Beethoven's 2nd** 1993   85 mins (cert U)
Beethoven finds himself a girlfriend and a family – but a latterday Cruella De Ville is after the pups. *Charles Grodin* steals the show again and the canines are appealing. Can't say the same for the story, though.

★★★ **Big** 1988   105 mins (cert PG)
Tom Hanks gives spirited performance as a twelve-year-old boy in an adult body and an adult world. The best of a bunch of life-swap movies that came out around that time – heaven knows why.

★★ **Bill and Ted's Bogus Journey** 1991   93 mins (cert PG)
The dudes travel through heaven and hell in an amusing sequel notable for jokes, special effects and *Bill Sadler*'s Grim Reaper.

★★★ **Bill and Ted's Excellent Adventure** 1989   89 mins (cert PG)
Keanu Reeves and *Alex Winter* as the cool but dim dudes given a history lesson via a time-machine phone box, so that, one day, they might save the world. Lively fun.

★★ **Blank Cheque** 1994   97 mins (cert 12)
Small boy, knocked off his bike by a villain, is accidentally given a blank cheque. But it's not blank for long – he fills it in for $1 million. Foreseeable and not terribly amusing capers ensue.

★★ **Buffy the Vampire Slayer** 1991   94 mins (cert 12)
Valley girl *Kristy Swanson* and loner *Luke Perry* clean up their neighbourhood, overrun by vampires led by *Rutger Hauer*. Highschool comic horror.

★★ **Captain America** 1990   97 mins (cert PG)
Comic book hero, *Matt Salinger*, patriotically sporting the stars and stripes, saves the US president from terrorists. Predictable.

★★ **Champions** 1992   104 mins (cert PG)
Emilio Estevez as hot-shot lawyer sentenced to community service training no-hope young ice hockey team. Lessons learned all round, not least by Estevez. (Called 'The Mighty Ducks' in USA.)

★★ **A Christmas Carol** 1984   100 mins (cert U)
Prettily restaged version of Dickens' tale. *George C Scott* as Scrooge is better than the rest of it.

★★★ **Cocoon** 1985   117 mins (cert PG)
Florida oldies find the fountain of youth, courtesy of visiting aliens, in warm, sentimental fable.

★★ **Cocoon: The Return** 1988   110 mins (cert PG)
Predictable sequel with the old folk returning to Earth for a visit. Great cast, shame about the script.

★ **Cool World** 1992   102 mins (cert 12)
Cartoon combining live and animated action about a cartoonist, *Gabriel Byrne*, who enters the fantasy world he's created but is followed out by his sexy heroine, *Kim Basinger*. Dire script.

★★ **Cop and a Half** 1993   93 mins (cert PG)
Cop and kid makes an amusing variation on buddy, buddy
theme thanks to straight playing by *Burt Reynolds* and the appeal
of young *Norman D Golden III* as witness and solver of crime.

★★★★ **Crocodile Dundee** 1986   98 mins (cert 15)
Surprisingly but deservedly successful yarn about outback
woodsman, *Paul Hogan*, uprooted to Manhattan. Great fun.

★★ **Crocodile Dundee II** 1988   111 mins (cert PG)
More violence, fewer jokes, as *Paul Hogan* leaves Manhattan and
returns to Oz to trap drug dealers.

★ **Curly Sue** 1991   102 mins (cert PG)
Slushy John Hughes comedy. Precocious little girl gets a mother
for Christmas but who cares?

★★★ **The Dark Crystal** 1983   93 mins (cert PG)
Muppets creator Jim Henson's dark, superbly animated fable of
good and evil.

★★★★ **David Copperfield** 1935   133 mins (cert U)
MGM's version of Dickens' masterpiece. *W C Fields* hilariously
playing a juggling Mr McCawber heads terrific cast.

★★ **Dennis** 1993   94 mins (cert PG)
Precocious child gives *Walter Matthau* a hard time. NOT to be
confused with Dennis the Menace. All very cutesy.

★★★ **Dick Tracy** 1990   103 mins (cert PG)
Warren Beatty's visually splendid version of gang-busting comic
book hero. *Madonna* co-stars, but *Al Pacino* steals the show.

★★★★ **Dumbo** 1941   90 mins (cert U)
Wealth of characters makes Disney's animation of a flying
elephant always worth watching.

★★★★ **Edward Scissorhands** 1990   105 mins (cert PG)
Johnny Depp as the man-made boy with blades for hands exposed
to 1950s small-town America. Lovely fantasy though marred by
harsh ending.

★★★ **Fantasia** 1940   135 mins (cert U)
Walt Disney's stunning, innovative blend of animation and
classical music. A minor work of art.

★★★ **Ferngully: The Last Rain Forest** 1993   76 mins (cert U)
Animated tale of forest folk fighting fiendish tree fellers. Strong on humour and ecology with voices supplied by *Robin Williams*, *Christian Slater* and *Samantha Mathis*.

★★★★★ **Field of Dreams** 1989   106 mins (cert PG)
Perfectly life-enhancing fantasy of farmer, *Kevin Costner*, told by a disembodied voice to build a baseball pitch among his crops so that late, great players may return. Magical.

★★ **The Flintstones** 1994   91 mins (cert U)
Cute effects, dim story. 34 script writers had a go at this feeble effort. *John Goodman* and *Rick Moranis* are okay as Fred and Barney. Otherwise Yabba Dabba Don't.

★ **Free Willy** 1994   107 mins (cert U)
Sentimental, hugely manipulative tale of relationship between troublesome kid and a caged killer whale. Unintentionally funny.

★★ **Getting Even with Dad** 1994   104 mins (cert PG)
Poorly written, badly executed tale of a crook, *Ted Danson*, and his estranged son, *Macaulay Culkin*. Weak characterisation and sentimental plot ruin a neat idea.

★★★ **The Golden Voyage of Sinbad** 1974   105 mins (cert U)
Colourful adaptation of Arabian Nights adventure. Special effects better than the acting.

★★★★★ **Great Expectations** 1946   100 mins (cert PG)
David Lean pays admirable homage to Dickens' classic story. *John Mills* as Pip, *Alec Guinness* as Herbert Pocket.

★★★ **The Great Mouse Detective** 1986   80 mins (cert U)
Engaging Disney animated cartoon with Sherlock Holmes as a mouse solving the mysterious disappearance of a toymaker.

★★★ **Gremlins** 1984   111 mins (cert 15)
Cute little creatures turn vicious if fed after midnight in adult children's story from the Spielberg stable.

★★ **Gremlins 2: The New Batch** 1990   107 mins (cert 12)
Special effects are an improvement on the original but the story's weaker.

★★ **Hocus Pocus** 1993   97 mins (cert PG)
Bette Midler, *Sarah Jessica Parker* and *Kathy Nijimy* play three witches who are reawakened after 300 years. They are offered immortality if they can eat the town's children before dawn. Lots of energy but little else.

★★★ **Home Alone** 1990   103 mins (cert PG)
Eight-year-old *Macaulay Culkin*, mistakenly left at home alone for Christmas, fights off burglars and discovers the value of family life. Overly sentimental but amusing.

★★ **Home Alone 2: Lost in New York** 1992   120 mins (cert PG)
Macaulay Culkin abandoned by his family at Christmas again! This time he's in the Big Apple and still facing hapless burglars *Joe Pesci* and *Daniel Stern*. Disturbingly violent and the humour and charm of the original are quite lost.

★ **Homeward Bound: The Incredible Journey** 1993   85 mins (cert U)
Awful remake of the Disney original. The two dogs and a cat crossing dangerous terrain to reach their human family are obnoxious due to the voice-overs from *Michael J Fox*, *Don Ameche* and *Sally Field*.

★ **Honey, I Blew Up the Kid** 1992   89 mins (cert U)
Dim sequel. *Rick Moranis* still tinkering with inventions that do strange things to his kids. This time he turns the new baby into a 100-foot, nappy nightmare.

★★★ **Honey, I Shrunk the Kids** 1989   93 mins (cert U)
Scientist, *Rick Moranis*, mistakenly shrinks his and neighbour's children to microscopic size. Family fun as kids fight for survival.

★★ **Hook** 1992   144 mins (cert U)
Lavish but hugely disapointing. *Robin Williams* as Peter Pan grown up returns to Never-Never Land and the Lost Boys. *Dustin Hoffman* is dastardly Captain Hook. Director Steven Spielberg overdoes everything.

★★★★★ **It's a Wonderful Life** 1946   129 mins (cert U)
And a wonderful film. A Frank Capra classic in which *James Stewart*, the would-be suicide, is shown by his guardian angel what life would be like without him. Just about as joyful as they come.

★★★ **Jason and the Argonauts** 1963   104 mins (cert U)
Ray Harryhausen's special effects dominate in this legendary adventure of search for the Golden Fleece. Great stuff.

★★★★ **The Jungle Book** 1967   78 mins (cert U)
Disney never bettered musically. Brilliant swinging numbers make this a true joy, though animated version bears little resemblance to Kipling's novel.

★★★★ **Jurassic Park** 1993   132 mins (cert PG)
Highest grossing film ever. *Richard Attenborough* in charge of a dinosaur park; *Jeff Goldblum*, *Laura Dern*, et al, the unlucky visitors. Marvellous effects and direction (by Steven Spielberg) when all hell breaks loose.

★★★ **Labyrinth** 1986   101 mins (cert U)
Pleasing Jim Henson fantasy in which teenager *Jennifer Connolly* must find her way through a menacing maze to save her little brother, kidnapped by goblins.

★★★★ **Lady and the Tramp** 1955   75 mins (cert U)
Timeless Disney delight. Animated adventures of well-bred spaniel and her raffish mongrel boyfriend.

★★ **The Little Mermaid** 1989   82 mins (cert U)
Disney's delightful – though much softened – adaptation of Hans Christian Anderson fairytale.

★★★ **The Little Princess** 1939   91 mins (cert U)
Shirley Temple (in colour for the first time) at her cutest as poor little rich girl cruelly mistreated at boarding school.

★★★★ **Local Hero** 1983   111 mins (cert PG)
Bill Forsyth's delightful examination of effect on Scottish coastal village when American tycoon wants to buy it and build an oil refinery there.

★★ **Mary Poppins** 1964   140 mins (cert U)
Disney's musical version of the no-nonsense, magical nanny. *Julie Andrews* somewhat miscast, *Dick Van Dyke* much more so as her improbable Cockney beau.

★★ **Mighty Ducks II** 1994   89 mins (cert 12)
Gordon Bombay – *Emilio Estevez* – reluctantly agrees to coach his old team to the Pee Wee Olympics but gets diverted by the commercial incentives. (The first 'Mighty Ducks' was released as 'Champions' in the UK.)

★★★ **Miracle on 34th Street** 1947   92 mins (cert U)
Enchanting fantasy of department store Santa put on trial to prove he really is Father Christmas. With *Maureen O'Hara* and *Edmund Gwenn*.

★★★★ **Miracle on 34th Street** 1994   100 mins (cert U)
John Hughes's version has all the magic of the original and *Richard Attenborough* looks cute as Santa Claus.

★★★★ **Moonstruck** 1987   102 mins (cert PG)
Enchanting romantic comedy set in Little Italy where *Cher* falls in love with fiancé's brother, *Nicolas Cage*. Mistake to miss this. It's life enhancing.

★★ **Mr Nanny** 1993   84 mins (cert PG)
Wrestler *Hulk Hogan* hired as nanny to protect the spoilt kids of threatened scientist *Austin Pendleton*. Pretty brutal in parts, amusing in others.

★★ **The Muppet Christmas Carol** 1992   85 mins (cert U)
Kermit as Tom Cratchitt, Miss Piggy in her dream role as his wife and *Michael Caine* as the miserly Scrooge. Nice one for all Muppet fans.

★ **My Girl** 1991   102 mins (cert PG)
Sentimental rites-of-passage stuff with *Dan Aykroyd*, *Macaulay Culkin* (getting his first screen kiss – Gosh!) and a woefully wasted *Jamie Lee Curtis*.

★★ **My Girl 2** 1994   98 mins (cert PG)
She of the title goes to LA to find out more about her late mother and becoming a young woman, while back home her stepmother *Jamie Lee Curtis* (wasted again) is having a baby.

★★★ **The Neverending Story** 1984   94 mins (cert U)
Children's adventure about a small boy entering the magical land in his story book. Good effects; not a bad yarn.

★★ **The Neverending Story 2** 1990   90 mins (cert U)
Plot's a little weak but the effects still impress in a further adventure set in Fantasia.

★ **The Neverending Story 3** 1994   93 mins (cert U)
The special effects are all there is as dragons, tree creatures and a six-foot talking rock enter the everyday world of small-town America.

★★★★ **The Nightmare Before Christmas** 1994   83 mins (cert U)
Animated story in which the head of Halloweentown visits Christmastown and hijacks the festive season. Impressive ideas that are well executed, though it may be a little frightening for the very young.

★ **North** 1994   87 mins (cert PG)
A small boy goes on a worldwide hunt to find the perfect parents. From Alaska to China he searches, intermittently helped by *Bruce Willis* as the Easter Bunny. Pretty duff, really.

★★ **Once Upon a Forest** 1993   68 mins (cert U)
Animated tale about a forest polluted by noxious gases and the subsequent attempts of a mouse, hedgehog and mole to save the day. *Michael Crawford* sings, but don't let that put you off.

★★ **On Christmas Eve** 1993   25 mins (cert U)
A magical animated Christmas story of a little girl who has written to Father Christmas – but with what results?

★★★ **Peter Pan** 1953   76 mins (cert U)
Disney animated feature of the classic J M Barrie story of the boy who never grows up.

★★★★★ **Pinocchio** 1940   80 mins (cert U)
Brilliant Disney animation about a wooden puppet who has to prove himself before he can become a real boy. A joy every time you watch it.

★★ **The Princess and the Goblin** 1993   98 mins (cert U)
Animated tale of princess who gets lost in forest, runs into goblins and is saved by a handsome miner's son. Voices provided by *Rik Mayall*, *Joss Ackland*, *Roy Kinnear*, *Claire Bloom* and *Molly Sugden*.

★★★★ **The Princess Bride** 1987   98 mins (cert PG)
Enchanting fairytale adventure in which abducted princess, *Robin Wright*, must be rescued by dashing hero, *Cary Elwes*.

★★★★ **The Railway Children** 1972   108 mins (cert U)
Three children adapt to new life in the country when father's imprisoned on spying charge. Little gem of a picture.

★★ **The Rescuers** 1977   75 mins (cert U)
Animated adventure from Disney studios involving the engaging exploits of trouble-shooting mice.

★★ **The Rescuers Down Under** 1990   77 mins (cert U)
More of the same. International Rescue Aid dispatches our two brave mice to save an Australian boy deep in trouble.

★★★ **Rookie of the Year** 1993   103 mins (cert PG)
A young lad's broken arm sets so that he can pitch a baseball at the speed of light. So off he goes to play with the professionals. Cute piece of whimsy from director and co-star *Daniel Stern*.

★★★ **The Sandlot Kids** 1994   101 mins (cert PG)
Sweet story about a new boy welcomed into the neighbourhood by a local gang of baseball players and the summer they spend together.

★★★★ **The Secret Garden** 1993   101 mins (cert U)
A spellbinding version of the children's story of an orphan girl sent to stay with her grieving uncle and crippled cousin. *Maggie Smith* is the haunting housekeeper.

★★★★★ **Snow White and the Seven Dwarfs** 1937   84 mins (cert U)
Disney's first – and in many ways still best-loved – full-length animated feature, not released on video until 1994. Worth the wait? Oh, sure. 57-years-old or not, Snow White stands the test of time admirably.

★★★★★ **The Thief of Baghdad** 1940   109 mins (cert U)
A magical film – the best Arabian Nights fantasy of them all. *John Justin* as the prince, *Sabu* as the thief and *Conrad Veidt* magnificent as the Vizier.

★★★ **Thumbelina** 1994   83 mins (cert U)
Not Disney, but still a very pleasing animation about a beautiful girl who's knee high to a grasshopper.

★★ **Tom and Jerry: The Movie** 1993   83 mins (cert U)
Spoilt by talking and singing. Tom and Jerry's real fans will stick to the shorts.

★★★ **War of the Buttons** 1994   94 mins (cert PG)
David Puttnam's tale of rival children's gangs in rural County Cork is pleasing and nostalgic but rather too melodramatic towards the end. (Based on French film 'La Guerre des Boutons'.)

★★★ **Watership Down** 1978   92 mins (cert U)
Animated feature adaptation of Richard Adams' bestseller. A family of rabbits face danger and death as they search for a new home. A bit violent for the very young.

★★★★ **Who Framed Roger Rabbit?** 1988   103 mins (cert PG)
Outstanding animation combined with live action marks comic caper of detective, *Bob Hoskins*, out to clear the name of the wrongly accused rabbit.

★★★ **Willow** 1988   126 mins (cert PG)
Fantasy adventure of a dwarf guarding a baby saviour with the help of *Val Kilmer* and *Joanne Whalley-Kilmer*.

★★★ **The Wind in the Willows** 1983   55 mins (cert U)
Beautiful adaptation of the great children's book. Voices are provided by *David Jason*, *Michael Hordern*, *Peter Sallis* and *Ian Carmichael*.

★★★ **The Witches** 1990   92 mins (cert PG)
At a British hotel, a small boy and his granny find themselves in the middle of a witches' convention headed by *Anjelica Huston*.

★★★★★ **The Wizard of Oz** 1939   101 mins (cert U)
Shirley Temple was initial choice for Dorothy but, mercifully, *Judy Garland* stepped into the ruby slippers for this enchanting, fantasy musical.

FOREIGN

★★★★ **A Bout de Souffle** 1959   90 mins (cert 18)
Jean-Luc Godard's stylish movie about a Parisian car thief, *Jean Paul Belmondo*, on the run with his American girlfriend, *Jean Seberg*, for killing a policeman.

★★ **L'Accompagnatrice** 1993   111 mins (cert PG)
Set in occupied France and wartime London. Singer *Elena Safonova*'s accompanist acts as go-between for her and resistance lover. Nice idea but rather flat and unconvincing.

★★★ **Agantuk** 1992   120 mins (cert U)
The last film by Indian director Satyajit Ray, about a family thrown into disarray after receiving a letter from a long lost uncle.

★★ **The Anchoress** 1993   108 mins (cert 12)
Heavy-handed 14th-century tale wherein *Natalie Morse* – who is obsessed with the Virgin Mary – is proclaimed a holy anchoress and walled up in the church. Looks pretty but lacks substance and coherence.

★★★ **The Assault** 1986   155 mins (cert PG)
Thought-provoking drama of Dutch survivor of WWII tracing events that led to the slaughter of his family. Won best foreign film Oscar.

★★★★ **Au Revoir les Enfants** 1987   107 mins (cert PG)
Classy, affecting film from Louis Malle which tells the story of a group of Jewish children at boarding school in occupied France during WWII.

★★★★ **Babette's Feast** 1987   102 mins (cert U)
Delightful adaptation of Isak Dinesen's tale of a French refugee, *Stephane Audran*, who cooks the world's greatest meal for two Danish sisters who have befriended her. A mouthwatering feast of a film.

★★★ **La Balance** 1982   102 mins (cert 18)
Violent, thrilling French crime story. Prostitute and petty criminal pressed to give evidence against crime boss. *Nathalie Baye* as the hooker.

★★★★★ **The Battleship Potemkin** 1925   86 mins (cert U)
Eisenstein's great silent movie about the crew of a Russian battleship during the mutiny at Odessa. One of the most influential films ever made.

★★★ **Belle Epoque** 1992   108 mins (cert 15)
Charming though sloppy Spanish Oscar winner about a deserter from the Civil War who finds refuge with an old painter and his four wild and beautiful daughters.

★★ **Betty Blue** 1986   121 mins (cert 18)
Visually impressive French film of mad waitress and odd-job man travelling around country. Noted for opening sex scenes. Not as good as its cult following would suggest.

★★★ **La Cage aux Folles** 1978   91 mins (cert 15)
Very funny French comedy. Two gay lovers pose as straights when the son of one of them wants to get married. (Followed by two sequels, the first of which is pretty good but forget the other one.)

★★★ **Cinema Paradiso** 1988   124 mins (cert PG)
Italian gem about young boy's love of the cinema. Steeped in charm, especially the early section with *Philippe Noiret* and young *Salvatore Cascio*. (Re-released, an hour longer, in 1993. Longer is not necessarily better.)

★★★ **Claire's Knee** 1971   106 mins (cert 12)
One of Eric Rohmer's fascinating moral tales. Engaged young man becomes obsessed with knee of girl he doesn't even like.

★★★★ **Un Coeur en Hiver** 1992   105 mins (cert 12)
Emmanuelle Béart stars in an adult, sophisticated love triangle with *Daniel Autueil* and *Andre Dussollier*. The kind of film only the French know how to make.

★★★ **Cronos** 1994   92 mins (cert 15)
Mexican variation on the vampire story involving an ancient religious icon with magic and sinister powers. Some striking images in a thoughtful tale that is less horrific than most in the genre.

★★★★ **Cyrano de Bergerac** 1990   135 mins (cert U)
Outstanding adaptation of Rostand play with *Gérard Depardieu* superb as the poet, swordsman and vicarious lover.

FOREIGN

★★★★ **Danton** 1982 136 mins (cert PG)
Gérard Depardieu is memorable in Andrzej Wajda's dramatic reconstruction of the Reign of Terror in 18th-century Paris.

★★★ **Delicatessen** 1991 97 mins (cert 15)
Shocking, funny French tale that hovers between farce and horror centred on cannibalistic inhabitants of apartment block. You don't want to make friends with the butcher.

★★★ **Diva** 1982 117 mins (cert 15)
Stylish high-tech melodrama about French music lover who is unwittingly involved with underworld after illicitly taping a diva's concert.

★★★★ **La Dolce Vita** 1960 173 mins (cert 18)
Fellini's surreal Italian drama of reporter *Marcello Mastroianni*'s adventures in decadent Roman society. Bit dated now but one of the seminal films of its time.

★★★★ **8½** 1963 138 mins (cert 15)
Portrait of a film director, *Marcello Mastroianni*, on the verge of a nervous breakdown and fantasizing about his life. Viewed by many as Fellini's masterpiece.

★★★★ **Les Enfants du Paradis** 1945 195 mins (cert PG)
Marcel Carne's marvellous theatrical extravaganza of 1840s Paris made during WWII. Poetic romance superbly conceived, superbly played.

★★★ **Fanny and Alexander** 1983 197 mins (cert 15)
Sumptuous family saga by Ingmar Bergman (his last film as a director) which deals with the fortunes of two children in turn-of-the-century Sweden. (The TV version runs for 420 minutes.)

★★★★ **Farewell, My Concubine** 1993 128 mins (cert 15)
Story of the rise and fall of two opera stars set against the background of changing China from 1920s to 1970s. A lavish costume drama well worth a look.

★★★ **La Fille de L'Air** 1993 106 mins (cert 15)
Beatrice Dalle risks family to spring her husband from jail. Based on a true story but hard to believe it's based on fact.

★★★ **Germinal** 1994   129 mins (cert 15)
Gérard Depardieu is the head of a starving family, driven by necessity to lead striking minors to rise against oppressive conditions in 19th-century France. Well-made but too fragmented adaptation of Emile Zola story.

★★★ **Golden Balls** 1994   88 mins (cert 18)
Spanish wunderkind *Bigas Luna*'s kitsch and curious tale about a stud who does everything he can to build the phallic tower of his dreams.

★★★ **High Heels** 1991   115 mins (cert 18)
Spanish director Pedro Almodovar's spicy tale of a mother and daughter's relationship helped and hindered by the death of *Victoria Abril*'s husband – her mother's one-time lover.

★★★ **Hiroshima, Mon Amour** 1960   91 mins (cert 18)
Alain Resnais' unusual, thoughtful story about love affair of French actress and Japanese architect who meet in post-war Hiroshima.

★★★ **How to Be a Woman and Not Die in the Attempt** 1993   86 mins (cert 15)
Amusing, touching Spanish film from the producers of 'Belle Epoque'. A working mother, *Carmen Maura*, finds her third husband doesn't pull his weight at home and fights back to save her self-respect.

★★ **Indochine** 1992   120 mins (cert 12)
Catherine Deneuve looks as good as ever in an epic tale set in SE Asia during the French occupation, but the story ambles nowhere in the end.

★★ **IP5** 1993   98 mins (cert 15)
Yves Montand's final performance as an elderly man searching for his lost love in the company of a graffiti artist and a Paris rapper. Bizarre and inconclusive.

★★ **Jamon Jamon** 1993   120 mins (cert 18)
Bizarre Spanish love tangle. Girl loves boy who's sleeping with her mother. Girl sleeps with boy's father. Boy's mother hires another boy to seduce girl and sleeps with him herself. All ends with brains being bashed out by legs of ham. Everyday plot really . . .

FOREIGN ■

★★★★ **Jean de Florette** 1986 122 mins (cert PG)
Beautifully shot, perfectly acted French country soap. *Gérard Depardieu* is the farmer duped by his conniving neighbour, *Yves Montand*.

★★★ **Jesus of Montreal** 1989 120 mins (cert 18)
Denis Arcaud's morality play in which actor, *Lothaire Bluteau*, portraying Jesus is mistaken for the real thing.

★★★★ **Kagemusha** 1980 181 mins (cert PG)
16th-century Japanese thief poses as dead warlord to safeguard the throne in Kurosawa's marvellous epic.

★★ **Kika** 1994 109 mins (cert 18)
Victoria Abril and *Peter Coyote* lead Pedro Almodovar's kinky tale of a makeup artist who for years has been having an affair with an American writer – and his son.

★★★ **The Legend of the Holy Drinker** 1988 120 mins (cert PG)
Affecting adaptation of Joseph Roth novella with *Rutger Hauer* as a Parisian tramp offered money by a stranger if he will give it back to a chapel when he can.

★ **Léolo** 1993 107 mins (cert 18)
Italian boy believes he was conceived by a tomato. Preferable to his family whose madness is slowly revealed in this strange drama.

★★★ **Like Water for Chocolate** 1993 114 mins (cert 15)
Intriguing feast of a movie about love, sex, food and families, starting in Mexico at the turn of the century. Quite bizarre but hypnotic.

★★★ **Man Bites Dog** 1992 96 mins (cert 18)
Hilarious, violent, pitch-black comedy about a documentary crew filming a serial killer at work. One scene is so brutal it will wipe the smile off your face, but drives the message home. Best Belgian film ever made.

★★★ **Manon des Sources** 1986 114 mins (cert PG)
Impressive sequel to 'Jean de Florette', though maybe not quite as good. *Emmanuelle Béart*, as Gérard Depardieu's daughter, seeks revenge on *Yves Montand*.

★★ **Mediterraneo** 1993   86 mins (cert 15)
During WWII eight Italian soldiers are abandoned on a Greek island. Gradually they begin to enjoy a blissful idyll. Charming but insubstantial.

★★★★ **Mephisto** 1981   144 mins (cert 15)
Klaus Maria Brandauer as the actor whose ambition leads him to sell out to the Nazis. Riveting movie which shows that Brandauer, in German, is one of the best screen actors in the world.

★★★ **Monsieur Hire** 1989   82 mins (cert 15)
Peeping Tom falls in love with beautiful neighbour involved in murder. Taut, tense adaptation of Simenon story.

★★★★ **Monsieur Hulot's Holiday** 1953   86 mins (cert U)
Jacques Tati as accident prone bachelor causing chaos at the seaside in a lovely, virtually silent, comedy.

★★★★ **My Father's Glory** 1991   105 mins (cert U)
Marcel Pagnol's utterly charming account of his childhood in southern France during the early part of century.

★★★★ **My Life as a Dog** 1985   101 mins (cert PG)
Poignant Swedish comedy about mischievous boy sent to live with aunt and uncle. Many people chose this as the best film of the 1980s.

★★★★ **The Nasty Girl** 1990   108 mins (cert 15)
Fine blend of humour and drama in young woman's attempt to uncover her hometown's guilty, Nazi past.

★★★ **Olivier, Olivier** 1992   105 mins (cert 15)
Young boy disappears in rural France only to return years later. His family welcomes him back – but is he the real Olivier? An intriguing tale.

★★★ **The Ox** 1992   92 mins (cert 12)
Based on a true story and telling of the drastic effect of the theft of a cow on a Swedish village struck by famine during 19th-century crop failure. *Max von Sydow* heads a fine cast.

★★★★ **Pandora's Box** 1929   97 mins (cert 15)
Silent German masterpiece with a legendary performance by *Louise Brooks* as the sexually provocative Lulu who ends up in the hands of Jack the Ripper.

★★★ **Pelle the Conqueror** 1988   155 mins (cert 15)
Deeply moving Swedish drama about a widower, *Max von Sydow*, and young son struggling to survive as immigrants in Denmark.

★★★ **Pixote** 1981   127 mins (cert 18)
Harrowing Brazilian exposé of plight of homeless children driven to crime, drugs and prostitution on the streets of Rio.

★★★ **Playtime** 1967   152 mins (cert U)
Monsieur Hulot finds himself in a futuristic Paris in *Jacques Tati*'s comedy delight.

★★★ **Les Quatre Cents Coups** 1959   94 mins (cert 15)
François Truffaut's innovative account of a young boy, *Jean-Pierre Léaud*, who, neglected by his parents, turns to petty crime and is sent to reform school.

★★★ **The Quince Tree Sun** 1993   139 mins (cert U)
Some may find watching grass grow more entertaining than this film about a painter painting a tree. And that's all he does. Yet it's strangely hypnotic and rather fascinating.

★★★★ **Ran** 1985   161 mins (cert 15)
Stunning Japanese version of 'King Lear' by master moviemaker Akira Kurosawa.

★★★ **Red Sorghum** 1987   92 mins (cert 15)
Evocative, moving story of a young Chinese couple in the 1920s and 1930s. Rich in detail, visually spectacular.

★★ **The Red Squirrel** 1993   65 mins (cert 15)
Convoluted Spanish story of a retired pop singer, an apparently amnesiac girl and the husband who is pursuing her. Mainly set in a campsite by a lake.

★★★★★ **La Regle du Jeu** 1939   113 mins (cert 15)
Jean Renoir's tragi-comic masterpiece about love and intrigue among houseguests at a weekend shooting party. A truly great film.

★★★ **Le Retour de Martin Guerre** 1982   123 mins (cert 15)
16th-century French tale – based on fact – of a villager, *Gérard Depardieu*, returning home a changed character. But is he really Martin Guerre? Remade as 'Sommersby'.

★★★★ **Romuald et Juliette** 1989   107 mins (cert 12)
Warm but sharp romantic comedy with lovers *Daniel Auteuil* and *Firmine Richard* crossing barriers of class and colour.

★★★ **La Ronde** 1950   110 mins (cert 18)
Max Ophul's delicious French farce in which a chain of illicit love affairs comes round full circle. Was thought dead saucy in its day.

★★★★★ **The Seven Samurai** 1954   155 mins (cert 15)
Akira Kurosawa's masterpiece from which 'The Magnificent Seven' was taken. Must be on everyone's list of the ten best.

★★★★★ **The Seventh Seal** 1957   95 mins (cert 15)
Magical, classic Swedish gem from director Ingmar Bergman. A 14th-century knight, *Max von Sydow*, plays chess with Death and gets an insight into life.

★★ **The Slingshot** 1994   102 mins (cert 12)
Swedish tale, set in the 1920s, of a young lad who, despite hostility, prejudice and tragedy, kept springing back like the catapult of the title.

★★ **Smoking/No Smoking** 1994   140/145 mins (cert PG)
Two separate films, French adaptations of Alan Ayckbourn plays, in which the same characters interpret different incidents in different ways. Quite appealing but too long and too repetitive.

★★★ **The Stolen Children** 1993   112 mins (cert 15)
Tragic but heartwarming true story about two children growing up on an immigrants' housing estate near Milan.

★★★ **The Story of Qui Ju** 1993   100 mins (cert 12)
Gong Li is splendid in this absorbing, sometimes amusing story of a Chinese village woman's stubborn fight for justice. The overview of modern China is perhaps a little too rosy but still very unusual.

★★★ **Subway** 1985   104 mins (cert 15)
Stylish French thriller by Luc Besson about a thief, *Christopher Lambert*, hiding out among the strange community living in the Paris Metro.

FOREIGN ■

★★★ **Sweet Emma, Dear Bobe** 1992   81 mins (cert 18)
Modern Hungary seen through the eyes of two young teachers struggling to make ends meet, and keep their self-respect, in Budapest.

★★★ **Tatie Danielle** 1991   112 mins (cert 15)
Delightful French comedy veers to the black as embittered widow, *Tsilla Chelton*, exorcises her anger on those around her.

★★★ **Three Colours Trilogy** 1993   88/90/89 mins (cert 15)
Krzystof Kieslowski's trilogy inspired by the colours of the French flag – White, Blue and Red – and the French watchwords: liberty, equality and fraternity. All very different, all rather elliptical but all with the power to absorb you into the characters' lives.

★★★★★ **Throne of Blood** 1957   105 mins (cert 15)
Akira Kurosawa's masterly version of 'Macbeth' in a Samurai setting. A truly great movie.

★★★ **Tie Me Up! Tie Me Down!** 1989   102 mins (cert 18)
Decidedly kinky effort from Pedro Almodovar about psychiatric patient *Antonio Banderas*' bizarre efforts to woo a porn star, *Victoria Abril*.

★★★★★ **Tokyo Story** 1953   135 mins (cert U)
Elderly Chinese couple travel from rural home to big city to see children. Greed and generation gap explored by late great director Yasujiro Ozu.

★★★ **To Live** 1994   125 mins (cert 12)
Fascinating street-level view of thirty years of modern Chinese history as witnessed by one small, sometimes tragic family. Though careful not to criticise the politics of modern China, director Zhang Yimou has been banned from making any more films for five years.

★★★ **Toto the Hero** 1991   90 mins (cert 15)
Belgian comedy/drama. Elderly Toto, believing he was given to wrong parents, seeks revenge for lost, wasted life.

★★★ **Tous les Matins du Monde** 1993   114 mins (cert 12)
Baroque 17th-century musical drama of love and betrayal starring *Gérard Depardieu* and his son *Guillaume*.

★★★ **Trop Belle Pour Toi!** 1989   91 mins (cert 18)
Gérard Depardieu in bittersweet tale of husband who chooses homely mistress over beautiful wife.

★★ **Les Visiteurs** 1994   100 mins (cert 15)
Wacky French comedy about a 12th-century knight and his servant who are mistakenly sent into the present day. Probably funny in French but not in subtitles.

★★★ **The Wedding Banquet** 1993   107 mins (cert 15)
Charming Chinese comedy/drama about a gay man's marriage of convenience to please his parents. Complications ensue when he accidentally impregnates the bride.

★★★★ **Wild Strawberries** 1957   93 mins (cert 15)
Victor Sjostrom gives wonderful performance as aged academic who relives and comes to terms with his life while travelling across Sweden in this Ingmar Bergman classic.

★★★★ **Women on the Verge of a Nervous Breakdown** 1988   89 mins (cert 15)
Glamorous, sexy Spanish farce of a pregnant soap opera star dumped by her long-term lover.

★★★★ **Yojimbo** 1961   110 mins (cert PG)
Classic samurai film with bodyguard *Toshiro Mifune* selling his services to the highest bidder. Used as model for 'A Fistful of Dollars'.

★★★ **Zéro de Conduite** 1933   47 mins (cert U)
Surrealist short film about boys' rebellion in a repressive French boarding school.

HORROR

★★★★ **An American Werewolf in London** 1981   97 mins (cert 18)
Brilliant use of soundtrack to indicate numerous changes of pace in cracking, tongue-in-cheek horror movie by John Landis.

★ **Army of Darkness: The Medieval Dead** 1993   89 mins (cert 15)
Final part of director Sam Raimi's 'Evil Dead' trilogy. Time travel caper with too little horror, too much tongue-in-cheek.

★ **Beyond Bedlam** 1994   108 mins (cert 18)
Weak attempt at a kind of British 'Silence of the Lambs'. *Elizabeth Hurley* plays the psychiatrist whose mind is invaded and haunted by psychotic *Keith Allen*. He's better than she is.

★★★ **The Birds** 1963   120 mins (cert 15)
Tippi Hedren (Melanie Griffith's mum) stars as a lonely woman attacked by killer birds in Alfred Hitchcock's shocker. Not one of Hitch's best but it could put you off feeding the dickies.

★★★ **Bram Stoker's Dracula** 1992   123 mins (cert 18)
Coppola's gothic, fairly loyal adaptation. *Gary Oldman* longs to have a nibble at the neck of *Winona Ryder*. *Anthony Hopkins* – as Van Helsing – intends to stop him. Beautiful direction, great star performances and much visual splendour.

★★★ **Cape Fear** 1961   101 mins (cert 15)
Robert Mitchum gives menacing performance as sadistic ex-con threatening the lives of lawyer, *Gregory Peck*, and his family.

★★★★ **Cape Fear** 1991   127 mins (cert 18)
Robert De Niro seeks revenge on lawyer *Nick Nolte* and family in Martin Scorsese's violent, horrifying and brilliant remake, marred by over-the-top Hollywood ending.

★★ **Carnosaur** 1993   83 mins (cert 15)
Tale of dinosaurs from schlock-horror king Roger Corman. A doctor plans to wipe out the human race in favour of prehistoric creatures.

★★★ **Carrie** 1976   97 mins (cert 18)
Lonesome, creepy child, *Sissy Spacek*, unleashes telekinetic powers against those who wronged her. Shock-horror ending is screen classic.

★ **The Crow** 1994   101 mins (cert 18)
Trashy adaptation of comic book hero who returns from the grave to wreak vengeance on his murderer. Horror and suspense are lacking as the film takes itself too seriously. Star *Brandon Lee* died when a stunt went wrong.

★★ **The Dark Half** 1993   121 mins (cert 18)
George Romero adapts a Stephen King chiller in which *Timothy Hutton* is a novelist trying to kill off his pseudonym and alter ego. But said ego refuses to die and does a bit of killing itself. *Amy Madigan* also stars.

★★ **The Devils** 1970   111 mins (cert 18)
17th-century nuns apparently possessed by the Devil in Ken Russell's once controversial, sexy shocker. Probably underrated in its time.

★★★ **Dracula** 1979   109 mins (cert 15)
Lush, romantic but rather rambling version of the old vampire story. *Frank Langella* is a sexy Dracula, *Laurence Olivier* a rather hammy Van Helsing.

★★ **The Fly** 1986   96 mins (cert 18)
Jeff Goldblum metamorphosizes into dipterous insect in David Cronenberg's snappy remake. Special effects and touches of humour make it a watchable horror.

★★★ **Halloween** 1978   91 mins (cert 18)
First – and best – of the slasher series with *Jamie Lee Curtis* as the babysitter menaced by a mysterious, homicidal lunatic. John Carpenter directed but, alas, he did not direct '2', '3' and '4', which are hardly worth bothering about.

★★ **Henry: Portrait of a Serial Killer** 1991   89 mins (cert 18)
Controversial, ultra-violent, low-budget shocker about a mass murderer. Allegedly based on real life case. Spent a long time awaiting video certification.

★★★★ **The Hitcher** 1986   97 mins (cert 18)
Rutger Hauer hauntingly good as the hitch-hiking psycho preying on the drivers who give him a lift. Some extreme violence and a lot of tension.

★★★ **The Howling** 1981   91 mins (cert 18)
Joe Dante's tongue-in-cheek story (from a John Sayles script) of California community overrun by werewolves. Led to no fewer than five sequels of which 'V: The Rebirth' and 'VI: The Freaks' are better than the rest.

★★ **Leprechaun** 1993   88 mins (cert 15)
Dan O'Grady discovers an Irish fairy but it doesn't bring much luck with it as the father and daughter take a holiday at the site of its gold.

★★★ **Mary Shelley's Frankenstein** 1994   123 mins (cert 15)
Good try, looks superb, doesn't entirely work. *Kenneth Branagh* directs and acts with panache, ably supported by a fine cast: *Robert De Niro* as the Creature, *Helena Bonham Carter* and *John Cleese* among others. Sticks faithfully to the book but is short of thrills and terror.

★★★★ **Misery** 1990   107 mins (cert 18)
Car crash leaves novelist *James Caan* imprisoned by number one fan, *Kathy Bates*, in exceptional psychological blood-curdler.

★★★ **Mother's Boys** 1994   101 mins (cert 15)
Jamie Lee Curtis, the mother from hell, returns to claim her brood after a three-year absence. *Peter Gallagher* is her long-suffering husband, *Joanne Whalley-Kilmer* his new love. Wildly silly ending rather spoils things.

★★★★ **A Nightmare on Elm Street** 1984   91 mins (cert 18)
Wes Craven's teenage nightmare terrifies thanks to the eerie effects and *Robert Englund* as the bogey man. Followed by six sequels, all progressively less good except the latest one.

★★ **Night of the Living Dead** 1990   89 mins (cert 18)
George Romero's violent, gruesome, black-and-white story of flesh-eating zombies. If you like ugly this is the film for you.

★★★ **The Omen** 1976   111 mins (cert 18)
Son of *Gregory Peck* and *Lee Remick* turns out to be the Antichrist in a gripping tale of the supernatural. The law of diminishing returns comes into play with all three sequels.

★ **Pet Sematary** 1989   102 mins (cert 18)
Family suffers all sorts of nastiness in new home behind Indian burial ground in Steven King nasty. The sequel is no better.

★★ **The Phantom of the Opera** 1989 — 91 mins (cert 18)
More on the lines of a slasher movie than an attempt to be faithful to the original novel. Well, what would you expect with Elm Street's Freddie – *Robert Englund* – involved?

★★★ **Poltergeist** 1982 — 114 mins (cert 15)
Scary goings-on when unfriendly spirits invade the home of a nice middle-class family. Nice performances, great effects. Inevitably the spirits returned, to largely similar effect, in two sequels.

★★★★ **Psycho** 1960 — 109 mins (cert 15)
Still the best of all shock-horror movies, with *Anthony Perkins* as demented Norman Bates in Hitchock classic.

★★★ **Rosemary's Baby** 1968 — 137 mins (cert 18)
Mia Farrow suffers psychological torment – and worse – when husband *John Cassavetes* becomes involved with Satanic cult in Roman Polanski's supernatural thriller.

★★★★ **The Shining** 1980 — 146 mins (cert 18)
Jack Nicholson, off-season caretaker at a hotel, goes mad in this overlong but originally underrated Stanley Kubrick chiller. Based on a Stephen King novel.

★★★★★ **The Silence of the Lambs** 1991 — 119 mins (cert 18)
A violent, shocking and outstanding film. Rookie FBI agent *Jodie Foster* hunts a serial killer with the help of incarcerated psychopath *Anthony Hopkins*. Cleaned up at the Oscars.

★★★ **Tales from the Dark Side** 1990 — 93 mins (cert 18)
Christian Slater and *Debbie Harry* contribute to four horror stories written by masters of the genre, including Conan Doyle and Stephen King.

★★ **The Unholy** 1988 — 102 mins (cert 18)
Two Roman Catholic priests have been murdered and their successor, *Ben Cross*, discovers nasty Satanic practices in his new parish. Bit daft, bit gory, but quite interesting.

★★★ **Witchboard** 1986 — 94 mins (cert 15)
A group of young friends run into trouble when they contact the spirit of a mass murderer on their ouija board.

★★★★ **Wolf** 1994   120 mins (cert 15)
Publisher *Jack Nicholson* is bitten by a wolf, loses his wife and job and turns into a werewolf. Still, as he seeks revenge, he does gain *Michelle Pfeiffer*. More a study of the animal in man than a horror movie. Brilliant support from *James Spader*.

★★★ **The Woman in Black** 1989   99 mins (cert 15)
Truly terrifying ghost story by novelist Susan Hill, cleverly adapted for the screen.

★★ **Zombies: Dawn of the Dead** 1979   126 mins (cert 18)
George Romero at it again with a lip-smacking relish of gore as the zombies look like taking over the whole of America.

MUSICALS

- ★ **Absolute Beginners** 1986 — 100 mins (cert 15)
  Stylish but unsatisfying British musical set in London in the 1950s. Box-office flop in its time. Cast includes *Patsy Kensit*, *James Fox* and *David Bowie*.

- ★★★ **All That Jazz** 1979 — 123 mins (cert 15)
  Imaginative piece starring *Roy Scheider* as choreographer Joe Gideon working himself into the grave.

- ★★★ **An American in Paris** 1951 — 113 mins (cert U)
  Pleasing setting with *Gene Kelly*, *Leslie Caron* and Gershwin tunes in great musical spectacular.

- ★★★ **Anchors Aweigh** 1945 — 139 mins (cert U)
  All-singing, all-dancing *Gene Kelly* and *Frank Sinatra* as a couple of sailors enjoying shore leave.

- ★★★ **The Band Wagon** 1953 — 112 mins (cert U)
  Lively and sophisticated backstage musical with *Fred Astaire*, *Cyd Charisse*, *Jack Buchanan* and the song 'That's Entertainment' among many others.

- ★★★ **The Barkleys of Broadway** 1949 — 109 mins (cert U)
  Final pairing of *Fred Astaire* and *Ginger Rogers*, themselves reuniting after ten years, as a showbiz couple who split up and reunite. Not their best but good, nostalgic stuff.

- ★★★ **Bird** 1988 — 154 mins (cert 15)
  Clint Eastwood's cool but affectionate look at the life of legendary jazzman Charlie Parker with *Forest Whitaker* splendid in the main role.

- ★★ **Bloodhounds of Broadway** 1989 — 93 mins (cert PG)
  Madonna and *Matt Dillon* in a loose adaptation of a Damon Runyon story. Lightweight but amusing.

- ★★ **The Blues Brothers** 1980 — 113 mins (cert 15)
  Brash John Landis comedy with *James Belushi* and *Dan Aykroyd* as musicians trying to save an orphanage. Great score. It now has a cult following but who can understand cults?

★★ **Brigadoon** 1954   108 mins (cert U)
Twee but charming musical fantasy with *Gene Kelly* as the American finding a mythical Scottish village and falling in love with *Cyd Charisse*.

★★ **The Buddy Holly Story** 1978   113 mins (cert PG)
Soundtrack's the star though *Gary Busey* is competent as the legendary but ill-fated singer.

★★★ **Cabaret** 1972   123 mins (cert 15)
Liza Minnelli stars in multiple Oscar-winning musical set in pre-war Nazi Germany. Based on Christopher Isherwood stories.

★★ **Calamity Jane** 1953   101 mins (cert U)
Doris Day as the gun totin' female who must resort to feminine wiles to win Wild Bill Hickock, *Howard Keel*, in lively Western musical.

★★★ **Carmen** 1983   102 mins (cert 15)
Life imitates art in Carlos Saura's ingenious story about a choreographer falling for leading lady as they stage Bizet's opera.

★★★ **Carousel** 1956   123 mins (cert U)
Warm and colourful version of the Rogers and Hammerstein stage hit. *Gordon MacRae* comes down from heaven for a day to help his daughter and widow *Shirley Jones*.

★★★ **A Chorus Line** 1985   111 mins (cert PG)
Richard Attenborough's underrated but often exhilarating screen version of the much-admired, long-running stage musical.

★★ **Chuck Berry: Hail! Hail! Rock and Roll** 1987   120 mins (cert PG)
Documentary about the legendary old singer. A pretty candid look at his sometimes shocking life and times.

★★★★ **The Commitments** 1991   117 mins (cert 15)
Alan Parker's funny, joyous story of a Dublin soul band, its rise and fall. A warming paean to the spirit of human optimism.

★★ **Cover Girl** 1944   107 mins (cert U)
Jolly but clichéd comedy with *Rita Hayworth* and *Gene Kelly*, partly saved by Jerome Kern and Ira Gershwin score.

★★★ **Dirty Dancing** 1987   97 mins (cert 15)
Patrick Swayze hot-hoofs his way into *Jennifer Grey*'s heart in slim but pleasing rites-of-passage musical.

★★★★ **Easter Parade** 1948   96 mins (cert U)
Lovely Irving Berlin score with *Fred Astaire*, *Judy Garland* and *Ann Miller* in showbiz setting.

★★ **Fame** 1980   133 mins (cert PG)
New York school of performing arts is the setting for Alan Parker's vibrant musical drama which spawned a successful TV spinoff.

★★★ **Fiddler on the Roof** 1971   181 mins (cert U)
Nostalgic tale of a father, *Topol*, clinging to old Jewish values and trying to marry off his daughters in changing Russia.

★★ **Flashdance** 1983   96 mins (cert 15)
Jennifer Beals dreams of making the big time as a dancer in pretty daft Adrian Lyne movie, saved by good dance sequences.

★★★★ **42nd Street** 1933   89 mins (cert U)
Warner Baxter and *Ruby Keeler* in the definitive musical about the understudy who comes back a star.

★★ **Funny Face** 1957   103 mins (cert U)
Gershwin score enhances this charming musical romance with *Fred Astaire* discovering talents of *Audrey Hepburn*.

★★ **Funny Girl** 1968   169 mins (cert U)
Touching biopic with a roller-skating *Barbra Streisand* playing Ziegfield Follies star Fanny Brice.

★★★ **Gigi** 1958   119 mins (cert PG)
'Thank heaven for little girls' – musical gem with ravishing *Leslie Caron* more interested in *Louis Jourdan* than becoming a courtesan.

★★★ **The Glenn Miller Story** 1954   116 mins (cert U)
James Stewart's warm and convincing portrayal of the famed band leader, who died mysteriously in WWII.

★★ **Grease** 1978   110 mins (cert PG)
Bland story of young love enhanced by great Bee Gees songs and enthusiastic performances from *John Travolta* and *Olivia Newton John*.

★★ **Gypsy** 1962   149 mins (cert 12)
Natalie Wood and *Rosalind Russell* star in entertaining biography of stripper Gypsy Rose Lee and her mum.

★★ **Gypsy** 1994   142 mins (cert PG)
Bette Midler plays the mother of future stripper Gypsy Rose Lee in a tuneful little film about her formative years and unconventional family life.

★★★ **A Hard Day's Night** 1964   83 mins (cert U)
The *Beatles*' first film and their best. An ingenious, black-and-white fantasy, endearingly concocted by director Richard Lester.

★★ **Hello, Dolly!** 1969   146 mins (cert U)
Gene Kelly directs *Barbra Streisand* as a meddling matchmaker in a period piece that doesn't reach expectations.

★★★★ **High Society** 1956   107 mins (cert U)
Lovely musical version of 'The Philadelphia story' with *Grace Kelly*, *Frank Sinatra*, *Bing Crosby* and Cole Porter songs – what more could you ask for?

★★★ **Holiday Inn** 1942   101 mins (cert U)
Romantic tale notable for *Bing Crosby*'s rendition of 'White Christmas'. *Fred Astaire* provides nifty footwork and Irving Berlin some great songs.

★★ **In Bed with Madonna** 1991   119 mins (cert 18)
Self-indulgent peep at musical megastar on tour. Concert footage redeems some of the overt silliness.

★★ **Jesus Christ Superstar** 1973   103 mins (cert PG)
Innovative Andrew Lloyd Webber and Tim Rice stage hit brought entertainingly to screen by Norman Jewison.

★★ **The Jolson Story** 1946   129 mins (cert U)
Al Jolson sings but *Larry Parks* acts in this biopic of the great vaudeville and Broadway singer. (The sequel – 'Jolson Sings Again' – is less good.)

★★★★ **The King and I** 1956   133 mins (cert U)
Rogers and Hammerstein charmer set in the court of Siam. Governess *Deborah Kerr* instructs royal children and falls for king, *Yul Brynner*. Packed with splendid set pieces.

★★★★ **Kiss Me Kate** 1953   111 mins (cert U)
Great Cole Porter frolic loosely based on 'The Taming of the Shrew'. *Ann Miller*, *Howard Keel* and *Ann Blyth* are all on brilliant form.

★★ **La Bamba** 1987   108 mins (cert 15)
Competent biopic about popster Ritchie Valens who made the fatal mistake of hitching a ride in Buddy Holly's plane.

★★★ **Meet Me in St Louis** 1944   113 mins (cert U)
Heartwarming *Judy Garland* vehicle based on a year in the life of a family during the St Louis World Fair, 1903.

★★★ **The Music Man** 1962   151 mins (cert U)
Rousing musical about salesman-cum-conartist, *Robert Preston*, who arrives in a small town to form a brass band.

★★★★ **My Fair Lady** 1964   175 mins (cert U)
Audrey Hepburn as the Victorian flower girl turned into a lady by professor *Rex Harrison*. Lovely score, design and costumes.

★★★ **New York, New York** 1977   137 mins (cert PG)
Saxophonist *Robert De Niro* and singer *Liza Minnelli* love and squabble through the Big Band era in Martin Scorsese's effective but over-ambitious movie.

★★★★ **Oklahoma!** 1955   145 mins (cert U)
Rogers and Hammerstein again. *Shirley Jones* is the country girl pursued by wholesome cowboy *Gordon MacRae* and evil farmhand *Rod Steiger*.

★★★★ **Oliver!** 1968   146 mins (cert U)
Lavish musical version of 'Oliver Twist'. *Mark Lester* cute as Oliver, *Ron Moody* splendid as Fagin. Great score and choreography.

★★★ **On the Town** 1949   98 mins (cert U)
Exuberant yarn about three sailors – *Gene Kelly*, *Frank Sinatra* and *Jules Munshin* – finding romance and adventure on 24-hour leave in New York.

★★★ **The Pajama Game** 1957   101 mins (cert U)
Rousing musical romance with *Doris Day* heading factory workers' demands for pay rise but falling for boss.

★★ **Pal Joey** 1957   112 mins (cert U)
Charming, libidinous heel *Frank Sinatra* uses women – *Kim Novak* and *Rita Hayworth* – in bid to build his own nightclub. Great songs, slim story.

★★ **Pink Floyd: The Wall** 1982   95 mins (cert 15)
Alan Parker's affectionate visualization of band's bestselling album. *Bob Hoskins* and *Bob Geldof* appear.

★★★ **The Pirates of Penzance** 1983   112 mins (cert U)
Colourful, lively movie of Gilbert and Sullivan's operetta. *Kevin Kline* adds sex appeal.

★★★ **Quadrophenia** 1979   120 mins (cert 18)
Mods and Rockers fight it out on Britain's beaches. *Sting* makes strong impression in acting debut.

★★★ **Round Midnight** 1986   131 mins (cert 15)
Bertrand Tavernier's loving homage to great jazz musicians, Bud Powell and Lester Young. Nice score from Herbie Hancock.

★★ **Sarafina** 1992   166 mins (cert 15)
Musical set in Soweto township where the children rose against apartheid and were massacred. *Whoopi Goldberg* as teacher. Nice songs and choreography, but would have been better shorter.

★★ **Saturday Night Fever** 1977   119 mins (cert 18)
Catchy tunes, nice dance numbers and a plot about a young Italian, *John Travolta*, who lives to dance until love shows him there is more to life.

★★★★ **Seven Brides for Seven Brothers** 1954   104 mins (cert U)
Delightful songs plus some of best choreography ever staged. *Jane Powell* as the young bride making a home for *Howard Keel* and his six brothers.

★★★★ **Show Boat** 1951   108 mins (cert U)
Splendid weepy set on the Mississippi. Heartbreak and romance for *Howard Keel*, *Kathryn Grayson* and *Ava Gardner* to the strains of Jerome Kern's beautiful score.

★★★★★ **Singin' in the Rain** 1952   102 mins (cert U)
Quite simply the best of all musicals. Great dancing by *Gene Kelly* and *Donald O'Connor*.

★★★★ **The Sound of Music** 1965 172 mins (cert U)
Sentimental saga about a convent girl, *Julie Andrews*, becoming nanny to large family in pre-war Austria. Wonderful songs.

★★★★ **South Pacific** 1958 170 mins (cert U)
Exotic Rogers and Hammerstein musical about WWII life on a Pacific island. Songs include 'Nothing Like a Dame' and 'Happy Talk'.

★★★ **A Star Is Born** 1954 169 mins (cert U)
Moving story of a rising young star, *Judy Garland*, who achieves success at the expense of the man she loves, *James Mason*. Remade, less well, with *Barbra Streisand* in 1976.

★★★ **That'll Be the Day** 1974 91 mins (cert 15)
Young lads in 1950s England use rock music to escape their humdrum lives. Stars *David Essex* and *Ringo Starr*. Dated but enjoyable.

★★★ **That's Entertainment** 1974 132 mins (cert U)
A loving eulogy to the best of MGM's musicals narrated by its stars and featuring a montage of the studio's greatest hits.

★★★ **That's Entertainment Part II** 1976 133 mins (cert U)
More of the same, only not quite so much fun. *Fred Astaire* and *Gene Kelly* link the excerpts.

★★★★ **Top Hat** 1935 100 mins (cert U)
Wonderful songs and nifty footwork lift the usual, mistaken-identity plot in *Fred Astaire* and *Ginger Rogers* romance.

★★★ **U2 – Rattle and Hum** 1988 99 mins (cert 15)
Pretty good documentary of the Irish band's 1987 tour, the concerts nicely balanced by backstage stuff about visits to Harlem and Graceland.

★★★ **West Side Story** 1961 155 mins (cert U)
'Romeo and Juliet' set to music in modern-day, gangland America. *Natalie Wood* and *Richard Beymer* are the lovers from opposing gangs.

★★★ **White Christmas** 1954 120 mins (cert U)
Army pals *Bing Crosby* and *Danny Kaye* try to boost popularity of holiday resort, aided by Irving Berlin's score.

★★★ **Woodstock** 1970   184 mins (cert U)
Seminal documentary of the famous weekend rock festival. Great footage of the *Who*, *Jimi Hendrix*, *Joe Cocker*, *Sly and the Family Stone* and others. Now rich in historical value.

★★★ **Yankee Doodle Dandee** 1942   126 mins (cert U)
James Cagney great as song-and-dance man-cum-playwright, George M Cohan, in lavish biography.

MYSTERY/THRILLER

★★ **Absence of Malice** 1981   161 mins (cert PG)
Journalist *Sally Field* is duped into writing story that discredits innocent and angry *Paul Newman*. Crisp examination of press corruption.

★★ **The Anderson Tapes** 1972   98 mins (cert PG)
Fast-moving thriller in which *Sean Connery* attempts to pull off major heist under police surveillance.

★★★ **Angel Heart** 1987   113 mins (cert 18)
Heart-stopping tension created by director Alan Parker. *Mickey Rourke* takes on *Robert De Niro* as the devil in a suspense thriller not for the faint-hearted.

★ **Another Stakeout** 1993   109 mins (cert PG)
Emilio Estevez and *Richard Dreyfuss* find themselves playing happy families with assistant DA *Rosie O'Donnell* as they seek to find a witness before the Mob gets her. Silly sequel which is short on plot, wit and inspiration – not worth waiting six years for.

★★★ **Bad Day at Black Rock** 1954   78 mins (cert PG)
Spencer Tracy encounters hostility in desert town when looking for missing Japanese farmer after WWII.

★★ **Basic Instinct** 1992   128 mins (cert 18)
Michael Douglas and *Sharon Stone* in violent, well-made but trashy anti-feminist thriller with women shown as objects of fantasy or fear. Stone's notorious flash doesn't come over so clearly (thank God) on video.

★★ **The Bedroom Window** 1987   112 mins (cert 15)
Intriguing though over-plotted thriller. Illicit lovers *Steve Guttenberg* and *Elizabeth McGovern* unwittingly involved when they witness a murder through the bedroom window.

★★ **Bellman and True** 1988   121 mins (cert 15)
Realistic suspense story of computer expert forced to aid robbery when his son is kidnapped. Fine performance by *Bernard Hill*.

- ★ **Benefit of the Doubt** 1993   92 mins (cert 18)
Donald Sutherland as a wife murderer released from jail; *Amy Irving* as the daughter whose testimony convicted him. Was he guilty or not? Twisted plot, with suggestions of incest, becomes very silly.

- ★★★ **The Big Easy** 1987   108 mins (cert 18)
Offbeat New Orleans cop *Dennis Quaid* and uptight but sexy DA *Ellen Barkin* investigate a case of police corruption. All very spicy and enjoyable.

- ★★★ **The Big Heat** 1953   90 mins (cert 15)
Fritz Lang's notable piece of film noir about a policeman, *Glenn Ford*, going undercover to get revenge on a crime ring. *Lee Marvin*, as the killer, is as sadistic as only he could be.

- ★★★★★ **The Big Sleep** 1944   99 mins (cert PG)
Howard Hawks directs *Humphrey Bogart* and *Lauren Bacall* in a convoluted investigation of sex and murder. Confusing but terrific and quite the best of all the Philip Marlowe movies.

- ★★ **Bitter Moon** 1992   139 mins (cert 18)
Roman Polanski's steamy, sexy melodrama set aboard a cruise liner. Crippled *Peter Coyote* manipulates *Emmanuelle Seigner* and *Hugh Grant*. More preposterous than erotic.

- ★★ **Black Rain** 1989   125 mins (cert 18)
Ridley Scott's violent cops and robbers thriller set in Japan is tough, long and predictable. *Michael Douglas* and *Andy Garcia* can't save it from obscurity.

- ★★ **Black Widow** 1986   103 mins (cert 15)
Debra Winger as an FBI agent on the trail of husband-killer *Theresa Russell* in Bob Rafelson's steamy thriller.

- ★★★ **Blink** 1993   100 mins (cert 18)
A blind woman, *Madeline Stowe*, partially regains her sight and witnesses a murder. Detective *Aidan Quinn* stands by her – in bed and out – as his only witness. Nicely suspenseful thriller.

- ★★★ **Blown Away** 1994   123 mins (cert 18)
Cop *Jeff Bridges* and vengeful crazy *Tommy Lee Jones* battle it out as bomb experts. Brilliant special effects – most of Boston exploding – but otherwise the film is weak.

★★★ **Blow Out** 1981   108 mins (cert 18)
Brian De Palma's sexy thriller about a sound effects man, *John Travolta*, innocently taping a murder. Good suspense, neat twists and turns.

★ **Blue Ice** 1992   105 mins (cert 15)
A really dopey thriller set in London and hardly helped by the romantic pairing of *Michael Caine* and *Sean Young*, who belong to very different generations.

★★ **Blue Velvet** 1986   120 mins (cert 18)
David Lynch's stylish, nasty story of small-town corruption and violence. *Dennis Hopper*'s psycho steals the show. Another cult movie.

★★★ **Body Heat** 1981   113 mins (cert 18)
Lawrence Kasdan's sweaty, erotic conspiracy in which *William Hurt* and *Kathleen Turner* plot to kill her husband.

★ **Body of Evidence** 1992   99 mins (cert 18)
Madonna's accused of murdering her lover through sex. Seducing her lawyer, *Willem Dafoe*, ensures she gets the best defence. Sex scenes are totally risible. Use of candle wax and crushed light bulbs makes the eyes water.

★ **Boiling Point** 1993   92 mins (cert 15)
US agent *Wesley Snipes* on trail of counterfeiters who murdered his partner. *Dennis Hopper* and *Viggo Mortenson* co-star in a flat, unimaginative thriller.

★★ **Brainscan** 1994   89 mins (cert 15)
Edward Furlong plays an interactive video game taking on the role of serial killer. Is it for real or isn't it?

★★★ **Brighton Rock** 1947   91 mins (cert PG)
Excellent version of Graham Greene's psychological thriller. *Richard Attenborough* found stardom as Pinkie.

★★★★ **Bullitt** 1968   113 mins (cert U)
Steve McQueen at his best in police drama memorable for San Francisco car chase that spawned many imitators.

★★★ **Carlito's Way** 1993   108 mins (cert 15)
Al Pacino on top form as legendary Puerto Rican crook trying to go straight in hostile New York environment in Brian De Palma's sparkling thriller.

MYSTERY/THRILLER

★★★ **The China Syndrome** 1979   122 mins (cert PG)
Accident at nuclear power station and subsequent cover up provide meaty roles for *Jane Fonda* and *Michael Douglas*.

★★★★ **Chinatown** 1974   131 mins (cert 18)
Faye Dunaway hires private eye *Jack Nicholson* to investigate skulduggery in Roman Polanski's tense, riveting mystery set in 1930s LA. A modern classic.

★★★ **Clear and Present Danger** 1994   141 mins (cert 12)
Harrison Ford as CIA operative Jack Ryan fighting the drug cartels and his own government. *Willem Dafoe* as mercenary lends a hand. Nicely made but complicated over-plotting only over-complicates.

★ **Close to Eden** 1993   110 mins (cert 15)
Melanie Griffith unbelievable as cop investigating murder among New York's reclusive Hasidic Jews. Sidney Lumet directed but it's hard to see why.

★★ **The Color of Night** 1994   123 mins (cert 18)
. . . and of *Bruce Willis*'s penis since it gets an airing in this silly, supposedly erotic thriller about shrinks and their patients. *Jane March* is the object of Willis's desire.

★★★ **Compromising Positions** 1985   98 mins (cert 15)
Housewife *Susan Sarandon* gets involved in a lively, amusing murder investigation led by detective *Raul Julia* when her dentist is killed.

★★ **Consenting Adults** 1992   100 mins (cert 15)
Kevin Kline regrets sleeping with neighbour's wife when framed for her murder. First half keeps you gripped, second half barely keeps you awake.

★★★ **The Conversation** 1974   113 mins (cert 15)
Excellent Francis Coppola story about a surveillance operator, *Gene Hackman*, becoming personally involved in a case of murder.

★★ **Criminal Justice** 1990   90 mins (cert 15)
Courtroom drama notable for *Forest Whitaker*'s performance as a black defendant accused of mugging an unsavoury young woman.

★★ **The Crush** 1993   89 mins (cert 15)
Cary Elwes finds life becomes a nightmare when 14-year-old girl develops a fatal crush on him. *Jennifer Rubin* is his long-suffering girlfriend.

★ **Crush** 1993   96 mins (cert 15)
Set in New Zealand where a car crash leaves one girl seriously injured, giving another the chance to take advantage of her absence with a reclusive novelist. Unconvincing tale of revenge.

★★ **The Darkman** 1990   91 mins (cert 15)
Violence proves no substitute for plot in feeble thriller about disfigured scientist, *Liam Neeson*, wreaking revenge.

★★★ **Dead Again** 1991   101 mins (cert 15)
Complex, intriguing plot providing dual roles for husband and wife team, *Emma Thompson* and *Kenneth Branagh*, not to mention juicy parts for *Derek Jacobi* and *Andy Garcia*.

★★★ **Dead Calm** 1989   95 mins (cert 15)
Mystery and mayhem aboard hijacked yacht with *Sam Neill* and *Nicole Kidman*. *Billy Zane* steals the show as psycho killer.

★★★ **The Deadly Affair** 1967   106 mins (cert 15)
Sidney Lumet's web of espionage starring *James Mason* as the prototype George Smiley investigating colleague's suicide. Based on John Le Carré novel.

★★ **Deadly Pursuit** 1988   110 mins (cert 15)
Killer at large in mountain expedition led by *Kirstie Alley* is pursued by detective *Sidney Poitier* and *Tom Berenger*. Known as 'Shoot to Kill' in USA.

★★★ **Deceived** 1991   108 mins (cert 15)
Goldie Hawn discovers to her peril that her late husband, *John Heard*, had a double life. Unusual thriller, nicely done.

★★★ **Defence of the Realm** 1985   96 mins (cert PG)
Government cover-up forms basis of British political conspiracy and murder story with *Gabriel Byrne* and *Denholm Elliott*.

★★ **The Desperate Hours** 1990   105 mins (cert 15)
Michael Cimino's violent but dullish remake features *Mickey Rourke* as escaped psycho holing up with hostages *Anthony Hopkins* and family.

★★ **DOA** 1988   98 mins (cert 15)
When *Dennis Quaid* discovers he's been poisoned with only 24 hours to live, he and *Meg Ryan* go after the killer. Good start, bad ending.

★★★ **Dream Lover** 1994   109 mins (cert 18)
Intriguing and erotic thriller in which architect *James Spader* is driven to distraction by his beautiful wife's mysterious past.

★★★★ **Duel** 1971   85 mins (cert PG)
Tense stuff as mild motorist *Dennis Weaver* is persecuted by berserk but anonymous truck driver. Steven Spielberg's first film reveals enviable talent for a 24-year-old.

★★ **Everybody Wins** 1990   98 mins (cert 15)
Nick Nolte and *Debra Winger* in convoluted, tiresome plot by Arthur Miller in which Nolte investigates a murky web of corruption.

★★ **Family Business** 1986   110 mins (cert 15)
Despite a cast which includes *Sean Connery*, *Dustin Hoffman* and *Matthew Broderick*, this comic thriller about a family of burglars falls flat.

★★★ **Fatal Attraction** 1987   119 mins (cert 18)
Glenn Close as obsessed, spurned mistress wreaking revenge on *Michael Douglas* and family. Gripping but overblown.

★★ **Fatal Beauty** 1987   104 mins (cert 18)
Whoopi Goldberg as Beverly Hills cop going underground to nab a cocaine ring. So-so but a failure as an attempted 'Beverly Hills Cop' seen from the distaff side.

★★ **Fatal Vision** 1984   108 mins (cert 15)
Murder/mystery based on true story of American doctor accused of murdering wife and daughters. *Karl Malden* splendid as man seeking justice.

★ **Femme Fatale** 1991   96 mins (cert 15)
Newlywed's wife mysteriously vanishes in thriller starring *Billy Zane* and *Colin Firth*. Doesn't amount to much. Billy's sister, *Liza Zane*, plays the bride.

★★★ **Final Analysis** 1991   125 mins (cert 15)
Psychiatrist *Richard Gere* gets involved with his patient *Uma Thurman*'s sister, *Kim Basinger*, but finds he's bitten off more than he can chew in a knife-edge thriller wherein no woman is quite what she seems.

★★★ **The Firm** 1993   155 mins (cert 15)
Tom Cruise as new lawyer in a firm laundering money for the Mob faces tricky quandary: to play ball with the FBI and risk losing his career or condone the corruption. *Gene Hackman*, *Holly Hunter* and *Ed Harris* co-star.

★★ **Flatliners** 1990   114 mins (cert 15)
Five medical students experiment with the after life. Despite decent cast, including *Kiefer Sutherland*, *Kevin Bacon* and *Julia Roberts*, both dark and comic moments fall flat.

★★★ **Frantic** 1988   120 mins (cert 15)
Hit-and-miss mystery by Roman Polanski in which *Harrison Ford* and *Emmanuelle Seigner* search Paris for his missing wife.

★★★ **The French Connection** 1971   104 mins (cert 18)
Narcotics cops, *Gene Hackman* and *Roy Scheider*, fighting heroin importers in NY. Good action movie with exceptional car chase.

★★★ **The French Connection II** 1975   119 mins (cert 18)
Gene Hackman reprises his role of Popeye Doyle – this time in Paris – in acceptable sequel.

★★ **Gleaming the Cube** 1989   105 mins (cert PG)
Silly murder/mystery for teenage *Christian Slater* to investigate on his skateboard. Stunts make it worth watching – just.

★★ **The Good Son** 1993   115 mins (cert 15)
In which 13-year-old multi-millionaire *Macaulay Culkin* plays the bad guy for the first time. A nice idea ineptly worked out.

★★★ **Gorky Park** 1983   102 mins (cert 15)
Intriguing spy story set in the last days of the Cold War. With *William Hurt* as the Moscow cop investigating murder.

★★ **Guilty As Sin** 1993   99 mins (cert 15)
Rebecca De Mornay as hot-shot defence lawyer hired to defend smooth wife-killer *Don Johnson* – only to find her life threatened by her terrifying client.

★★★★ **The Hand That Rocks the Cradle** 1992   110 mins (cert 15)
Rebecca De Mornay as a revengeful nanny gradually reducing *Anabella Sciorra*'s happy family life to ashes in nail-biting, sinister thriller.

★★★ **The Hard Way** 1989   111 mins (cert 15)
Movie star *Michael J Fox* attaches himself to unwelcoming hard-nosed cop *James Woods* to research a forthcoming role. Lovely performances and a lot of fun to watch.

★★ **The Hawk** 1993   86 mins (cert 15)
Helen Mirren fears her husband's the serial killer at large since her hammer is missing! She is good, the rest of the film disappoints.

★★★★ **Hidden Agenda** 1990   108 mins (cert 15)
Ken Loach's palm-sweating thriller focusing upon the British government's dirty tricks in Northern Ireland. *Brian Cox* leads an excellent cast.

★★★ **Homicide** 1991   102 mins (cert 18)
Jewish cop *Joe Mantegna* finds his loyalties are divided when he investigates sinister murder of Jewish pawn shop owner in David Mamet's grim, thoughtful thriller.

★★ **House of Cards** 1992   105 mins (cert 15)
Strange psychological drama about disturbed young girl's brush with the supernatural after her father dies. *Kathleen Turner* is the mother reluctantly accepting help from psychiatrist *Tommy Lee Jones*.

★★★ **House of Games** 1987   102 mins (cert 15)
David Mamet's ingenious tale of psychiatrist embroiled in web of mystery when she helps a conman patient. With *Lindsay Crouse* and *Joe Mantegna*.

★★ **I Love Trouble** 1994   123 mins (cert PG)
Disappointing romantic murder/mystery in which *Julia Roberts* plays a cub-reporter competing with seasoned columnist *Nick Nolte*. Neither very thrilling nor convincing as a love story.

★★ **Indecent Proposal** 1992   117 mins (cert 15)
In which billionaire *Robert Redford* offers $1 million for a night with *Demi Moore* to prove to her and hubby, *Woody Harrelson*, that money can buy anything. Hardly seems worth it. Tears before bedtime are guaranteed.

★ **The Innocent** 1994   118 mins (cert 15)
Despite *Anthony Hopkins*, *Campbell Scott* and *Isabella Rossellini*, this dated spy story promises more than it delivers.

★★★ **Internal Affairs** 1990   114 mins (cert 18)
Crooked cop *Richard Gere* is investigated by fellow officer *Andy Garcia* in tough, convincing action/drama.

★★★★ **In the Heat of the Night** 1967   109 mins (cert 15)
Bigoted southern sheriff *Rod Steiger* grudgingly accepts help of big-city black cop, *Sidney Poitier*, in murder investigation. A very superior thriller.

★★★ **The Ipcress File** 1965   109 mins (cert PG)
Michael Caine's first and best outing as Len Deighton's Cockney secret agent, Harry Palmer.

★★★ **Jacob's Ladder** 1990   113 mins (cert 18)
Psychological drama with *Tim Robbins* as a Vietnam veteran discovering source of his terrifying hallucinations. Full of interesting ideas but cops out at the end.

★★★★ **Jagged Edge** 1985   108 mins (cert 18)
Excellent, tense did-he, didn't-he suspense thriller. *Jeff Bridges* is the man accused of murdering his wife; *Glenn Close* is the lawyer defending and sleeping with him.

★★ **Jennifer 8** 1992   124 mins (cert 15)
Andy Garcia as ex-LA cop finding new job and a severed hand in new town where a killer's preying on blind women – *Uma Thurman* among them.

★★ **Johnny Handsome** 1989   94 mins (cert 15)
Unusual Walter Hill crime story in which disfigured *Mickey Rourke* gets a new face and plans revenge on *Ellen Barkin* and others who double-crossed him.

★★★ **Jumpin' Jack Flash** 1986   100 mins (cert 15)
Whoopi Goldberg as computer operator embroiled in espionage. Neat outlet for her comic flair.

★★★ **Kalifornia** 1994   110 mins (cert 18)
A couple of hitchhikers, serial killer *Brad Pitt* and bimbo girlfriend *Juliette Lewis*, turn a trip across the States into a nightmare. Violent but evocative.

★★ **Keeper of the City** 1992　　　　　　　　　　114 mins (cert 15)
Lou Gossett Jr as troubled cop hunting vigilante killer *Anthony La Paglia* in run-of-the-mill thriller.

★★★ **Key Largo** 1948　　　　　　　　　　　　　101 mins (cert PG)
Gangster *Edward G Robinson* holds *Humphrey Bogart*, *Lauren Bacall* and others captive in John Huston film noir. Wordy but nicely world-weary.

★★ **Kill Me Again** 1989　　　　　　　　　　　　96 mins (cert 18)
Violent but stylish thriller with *Val Kilmer* as a Reno private eye and *Joanne Whalley-Kilmer* (his wife) as a steamy femme fatale. A much better than average mystery tale.

★★ **A Kiss Before Dying** 1991　　　　　　　　　92 mins (cert 18)
Psychopath *Matt Dillon* uses wife, *Sean Young*, to achieve greedy ambitions. Poor remake of goodish 1956 movie.

★★★★ **Klute** 1971　　　　　　　　　　　　　　140 mins (cert 18)
Everyone's dream hooker *Jane Fonda* is menaced by a psychopath. *Donald Sutherland* as the helpful cop in a tense, first-rate thriller.

★★ **The Lady in White** 1989　　　　　　　　　103 mins (cert 15)
Eerie and enjoyable thriller in which *Lukas Haas* (the kid from 'Witness') is threatened by a strangler when his friends lock him in school as a Halloween prank.

★★★★ **The Last Seduction** 1994　　　　　　　　98 mins (cert 18)
Thrilling mystery with some great lines. *Linda Fiorentino* is oustanding as the feisty, sassy, double-crossing villainess who always gets her man – and more. *Bill Pullman* and *Peter Berg* support.

★★★ **The Late Show** 1977　　　　　　　　　　　93 mins (cert 15)
Excellent, witty, well-plotted murder/mystery. *Art Carnie* as the aged private eye, *Lily Tomlin* his infuriating client.

★★★★ **Laura** 1944　　　　　　　　　　　　　　85 mins (cert U)
Marvellous romantic thriller. *Gene Tierney* as the supposed murder victim with whose picture detective *Dana Andrews* falls in love.

★ **The Lawnmower Man** 1992　　　　　　　　　105 mins (cert 15)
Virtual reality makes household machines run amok in this silly, ineffectual thriller. A good idea sadly wasted – as is *Pierce Brosnan*.

★★★ **Legal Eagles** 1986   116 mins (cert PG)
Not bad mystery teams DA *Robert Redford* with lawyer *Debra Winger* and her flaky client *Darryl Hannah* on a murder trail.

★★ **The Little Drummer Girl** 1984   130 mins (cert 15)
Pretty wooden adaptation of John Le Carré's spy novel. *Diane Keaton* miscast as American girl caught up in espionage.

★★★ **Lost Horizon** 1937   132 mins (cert U)
Air-crash survivor *Ronald Colman* discovers strange Tibetan land of love, peace and longevity in this haunting Frank Capra drama.

★★ **Love at Large** 1990   97 mins (cert 15)
Thin comic thriller. PI *Tom Berenger*, hired by mysterious *Anne Archer*, discovers that he's being shadowed by another PI, *Elizabeth Perkins*.

★★ **Mad Dog and Glory** 1993   96 mins (cert 18)
In which meek and mild police photographer *Robert De Niro* is given *Uma Thurman* by mean mafioso *Bill Murray*, who then reneges on the deal. Disappointing considering cast. Comedy never funny, violence too heavy handed.

★★★ **Malice** 1993   111 mins (cert 18)
Alec Baldwin, *Nicole Kidman* and *Bill Pullman* in well-plotted suspense thriller set in a New England college town, where a brilliant surgeon, a college dean and his beautiful wife are drawn into a web of intrigue and deception.

★★★★ **The Maltese Falcon** 1941   80 mins (cert U)
Classic, evergreen film noir/mystery from John Huston. Great performances by *Humphrey Bogart* – as Sam Spade – *Sidney Greenstreet*, *Peter Lorre* and *Mary Astor*.

★★★ **Manhattan Murder Mystery** 1994   105 mins (cert 12)
Woody Allen and *Diane Keaton* think their next door neighbour's a killer and try to prove it, 'Rear Window' style. Co-starring *Anjelica Huston* and *Alan Alda*.

★★★ **Marathon Man** 1976   126 mins (cert 18)
Absorbing thriller in which graduate student *Dustin Hoffman* is unwittingly embroiled in the hunt for a Nazi war criminal, *Laurence Olivier*.

★ **Miami Blues** 1990   97 mins (cert 18)
Psycho criminal *Alec Baldwin* and naive prostitute *Jennifer Jason Leigh* are doggedly pursued by victimised cop, *Fred Ward*. Performances better than plot.

★★★★ **Missing** 1982   122 mins (cert 15)
Excellent political thriller about a father, *Jack Lemmon*, trying to uncover mystery surrounding his son's disappearance in Chile.

★★★★ **Mona Lisa** 1986   104 mins (cert 18)
London underworld provides the backdrop for romantic thriller with *Bob Hoskins*, *Cathy Tyson* and *Michael Caine*.

★★ **The Morning After** 1986   103 mins (cert 15)
Disappointing considering Sidney Lumet directs. *Jane Fonda* wakes up next to a mysterious dead man. *Jeff Bridges* helps solve the problem.

★★ **Mortal Thoughts** 1991   102 mins (cert 15)
Demi Moore and *Glenn Headley* attempt to cover up the murder of Headley's brutish husband, *Bruce Willis*. Stylish, well-plotted but uninvolving.

★★★ **Murder on the Orient Express** 1974   131 mins (cert PG)
Albert Finney as Hercule Poirot solving murder aboard train. Superb supporting cast all do their bit.

★★ **Narrow Margin** 1990   97 mins (cert 15)
Fairly tense thriller with DA *Gene Hackman* trying to protect murder witness *Anne Archer* on a perilous train trip through the Rockies.

★★★ **Needful Things** 1994   120 mins (cert 15)
A mysterious man opens a local shop full of nick-nacks and all hell breaks loose in the community. A devilish performance from *Max von Sydow* with a nice touch of humour.

★★ **Night and the City** 1992   98 mins (cert 15)
Unattractive characters and dark settings do little to enhance the appeal of a sleazy lawyer, *Robert De Niro*, moving into the world of boxing promotion and trouble with his girlfriend's money. *Jessica Lange* and Bob too classy for this.

★★★★ **Night of the Hunter** 1955   98 mins (cert PG)
Robert Mitchum as psychotic preacher on the prowl. Suspenseful examination of good and evil. Only film Charles Laughton directed.

★★★ **A Night to Remember** 1943   91 mins (cert PG)
Mystery writer and wife, *Brian Aherne* and *Loretta Young*, investigate murder in a lively comedy/thriller.

★★ **No Mercy** 1986   108 mins (cert 18)
Richard Gere, a policeman bent on revenge, distracted by pouting *Kim Basinger* in a violent thriller with a New Orleans setting.

★★★ **Notorious** 1946   101 mins (cert U)
Romantic Hitchcock thriller set in Rio and involving *Cary Grant*, *Ingrid Bergman* and Nazi plots.

★★★ **No Way Out** 1987   114 mins (cert 15)
Sex, suspense, murder and cover-up within US Government. *Kevin Costner*, *Gene Hackman* and *Sean Young* in ménage-à-trois.

★★ **Out for Justice** 1991   91 mins (cert 18)
Steven Seagal (still walking like there's something up his bottom) as a formulaic cop fighting Brooklyn baddy and old school friend. Slick, fast-paced and action-packed though totally mindless.

★★ **Pacific Heights** 1990   102 mins (cert 15)
Psychological battle begins as smooth lodger *Michael Keaton* persecutes his landlords, *Melanie Griffith* and *Matthew Modine*.

★★★ **The Parallax View** 1974   102 mins (cert 15)
Warren Beatty stars in this intriguing conspiracy theory tale, apparently inspired by John F Kennedy's assassination.

★ **Paris Trout** 1992   100 mins (cert 18)
Bigoted *Dennis Hopper* goes on a shooting spree when a black customer refuses to pay for a second-hand car. *Barbara Hershey* is Hopper's abused wife.

★★ **The Pelican Brief** 1994   135 mins (cert 12)
Disappointing version of John Grisham thriller. Weak performance from *Julia Roberts* as law student uncovering dirty dealings that go right to the top of government. *Denzel Washington* is much better as the journalist who helps her.

★★★★ **Play Misty for Me** 1971   102 mins (cert 18)
Spurned lover *Jessica Walker* obsessively seeks revenge on DJ *Clint Eastwood*. This is 'Fatal Attraction' but earlier and better.

★★ **The Presidio** 1988   98 mins (cert 15)
Formula thriller with soldier, *Sean Connery*, and local cop, *Mark Harmon*, clashing during army base murder investigation.

★★★ **Presumed Innocent** 1990   126 mins (cert 15)
Gripping did-he, didn't-he story about an attorney, *Harrison Ford*, as the suspect when his girlfriend is murdered.

★★ **Prime Suspect** 1982   100 mins (cert PG)
Adequate, made-for-TV movie in which an innocent member of the public is persecuted after young girl's murder.

★★★ **Prizzi's Honour** 1985   129 mins (cert 15)
Blackly comic Mafia movie in which rival hit-persons, *Jack Nicholson* and *Kathleen Turner*, fall in love.

★★★ **The Public Enemy** 1931   83 mins (cert 15)
Splendid early gangster movie – the one in which *James Cagney* shoves a grapefruit into *Mae Clark*'s face.

★★ **The Public Eye** 1992   99 mins (cert 15)
Joe Pesci as 1940s photographer embroiled in Mafia murders and trying to save threatened nightclub owner, *Barbara Hershey*. Should have been better.

★★★ **Q & A** 1990   132 mins (cert 18)
Intelligent investigation of deep-rooted corruption within NY police force. *Nick Nolte* the bent copper; *Timothy Hutton* the crusading DA.

★ **Raising Cain** 1992   92 mins (cert 15)
Psychological thriller with *John Lithgow* as a father with split personalities who kidnaps children to experiment on them. Uneasy balance of comedy and violence.

★★ **The Real McCoy** 1993   104 mins (cert 12)
Kim Basinger as cat burglar forced into doing one last job by evil *Terence Stamp*. *Val Kilmer* is her hapless partner, we the hapless audience.

★★★ **Rear Window** 1954   112 mins (cert PG)
Hitchcock at his most stylish. Incapacitated *James Stewart* witnesses murder across the street. *Grace Kelly* helps him investigate.

★★★★ **Rebecca** 1940   130 mins (cert PG)
Daphne Du Maurier's romantic saga of young bride haunted by memory of husband's first wife. Directed by Hitchcock with *Joan Fontaine* and *Laurence Olivier*.

★★ **Red Rock West** 1993   98 mins (cert 15)
Nicolas Cage and *Dennis Hopper* lead excellent cast in story of a drifter looking for work in a small town and being mistaken for a hired killer.

★ **Ricochet** 1992   110 mins (cert 18)
Predictable story about a psychopath hunting the man who imprisoned him. *Denzel Washington* and *John Lithgow* star.

★★ **Rising Sun** 1993   129 mins (cert 18)
Call-girl's murder in LA HQ of Japanese conglomerate leads to investigation by Japanophile *Sean Connery* and cop *Wesley Snipes*. Good, over-involved thriller which was accused of Japan-bashing.

★ **The Rookie** 1990   115 mins (cert 18)
Clint Eastwood as a veteran cop, *Charlie Sheen* his apprentice partner in a feeble thriller.

★★ **Ruby** 1992   110 mins (cert 15)
Danny Aiello stars as Jack Ruby in British director John Mackenzie's docudrama about the man who shot Lee Harvey Oswald.

★★ **The Russia House** 1990   123 mins (cert 15)
Sean Connery as London publisher embroiled in wordy, post-Cold War Anglo-Russian espionage. *Michelle Pfeiffer* is the Moscow love interest.

★★★ **Scarface** 1983   170 mins (cert 18)
Lengthy, violent remake of the old Howard Hawkes' gangster movie, with *Al Pacino* in the Paul Muni role.

★★★★ **Sea of Love** 1989   113 mins (cert 18)
Scintillating, sexy thriller with *Al Pacino* investigating a series of murders and falling for chief suspect, *Ellen Barkin*.

★★★★ **Serpico** 1973   130 mins (cert 18)
Al Pacino as an honest cop fighting alone against corruption in the NYPD in Sidney Lumet's gritty, disturbing adaptation of a true story.

★★★ **Shallow Grave** 1995   93 mins (cert 18)
Highly impressive debut thriller by Danny Boyle. *Kerry Fox* and flatmates dispose of crooked lodger *Keith Allen*'s body and his money when he overdoses. But they reckon without the police and Allen's murderous accomplices.

★★ **Shattered** 1991   106 mins (cert 15)
Tom Berenger suffers from amnesia after a car crash. The plot thickens when he hires detective *Bob Hoskins* to find out what happened. *Greta Scacchi*, *Corbin Bernsen* and *Joanne Whalley-Kilmer* also involved.

★★ **Single White Female** 1992   108 mins (cert 18)
Palm-sweating thriller of a woman's obsession with her flatmate, spoilt by a daft ending. *Jennifer Jason Leigh* is obsessed; *Bridget Fonda* is terrorised.

★★ **Sleeping With the Enemy** 1991   100 mins (cert 15)
Murderous husband *Patrick Bergin* hunting runaway wife *Julia Roberts* in a dreary tale. Can't see why he should want to catch her.

★★ **Sliver** 1993   115 mins (cert 18)
Thin murder mystery. *Sharon Stone* pursued by *William Baldwin* and *Tom Berenger*, one of whom is a Peeping Tom. Steamy and sexy but hugely unerotic.

★ **Society** 1989   99 mins (cert 18)
Teenage mystery, merely worth mentioning for shocking special effects – everything else is bland and dull.

★★★★ **Someone to Watch Over Me** 1987   106 mins (cert 15)
Sensational blend of romance and suspense as married cop *Tom Berenger* falls in love with the witness he's protecting, *Mimi Rogers*.

★★★ **Spellbound** 1945   111 mins (cert PG)
Hitchcock's romantic thriller wherein psychoanalyst *Ingrid Bergman* falls in love with her boss, *Gregory Peck*, while helping him prove he's not a murderer.

★★★ **Stakeout** 1987   117 mins (cert 12)
Witty thriller in which policeman *Richard Dreyfuss* falls for *Madeleine Stowe*, the woman he's meant to be watching. *Emilio Estevez* is his disapproving partner.

★★ **Stepfather** 1987   86 mins (cert 18)
Chilling performance from *Terry O'Quinn* as a man who marries widows with children in search of the perfect family, only to erupt into murderous rages when they disappoint. Followed by two inferior sequels.

★★★★ **The Sting** 1973   129 mins (cert 15)
Paul Newman and *Robert Redford* plan elaborate ruse to con crooked businessman *Robert Shaw*. Great fun but you'll need your wits about you to keep up with the plot.

★★★ **Storyville** 1992   110 mins (cert 15)
Passion, sex and political skulduggery as lawyer turned politician, *James Spader*, lands in deep trouble.

★★★ **Strangers on a Train** 1951   101 mins (cert PG)
Snappy Hitchcock direction. *Robert Walker* proposes that he and *Farley Granger* should exchange murders in order to avoid suspicion.

★★★★ **Suspect** 1987   121 mins (cert 15)
Intriguing suspense thriller about lawyer, *Cher*, defending deaf mute, *Liam Neeson*, on a murder charge with the illegal help of juror, *Dennis Quaid*.

★★ **Target** 1985   118 mins (cert 15)
Average spy thriller with *Gene Hackman* and son, *Matt Dillon*, frantically searching Paris for missing wife/mother – *Gayle Hunnicutt*.

★★ **Teen Agent** 1991   89 mins (cert PG)
Schoolboy *Richard Grieco* is mistaken for a CIA agent while on a school trip to Paris. No brain-stretcher but OK for the kids.

★★★ **10 Rillington Place** 1970   111 mins (cert 15)
Solid account of the John Christie/Timothy Evans murder case in 1940s. *Richard Attenborough*, *Judy Geeson* and *John Hurt* give their all.

★★★★★ **The 39 Steps** 1935   81 mins (cert U)
Cracking tale of murder, espionage and romance. Hitchcock directs, *Robert Donat* and *Madeleine Carroll* star. A classic not to be confused with the able, but uninspired Robert Powell version.

★★★★ **The Thomas Crown Affair** 1968   102 mins (cert PG)
Sharp, sexy thriller featuring *Steve McQueen* as a gentleman bank robber, *Faye Dunaway* as the insurance investigator out to catch him and a great Oscar-winning song – 'Windmills of Your Mind'.

★★ **Thunderheart** 1992   114 mins (cert 15)
A half-Sioux FBI man, *Val Kilmer*, is sent to a Navajo settlement where murder and mystery abound. No big surprise at the end, though.

★★★ **Tiger Bay** 1959   105 mins (cert 15)
A lonely girl, *Hayley Mills*, is abducted by a murderer on the run. Sensitive story, nicely performed. Hayley's daddy, *John Mills*, also stars.

★★★★ **To Catch a Thief** 1955   97 mins (cert U)
Fun and suspense from Hitchcock. Retired cat-burglar *Cary Grant*, suspected of robberies on the Riviera, tracks down the real culprit. *Grace Kelly* is the wealthy love interest.

★★★ **The Trouble with Harry** 1955   99 mins (cert PG)
This offbeat Hitchcock comedy/thriller about the problem of disposing of a corpse stars *John Forsyth* before his hair turned prematurely blue in 'Dynasty'.

★★★ **Turner and Hooch** 1989   99 mins (cert PG)
Entertaining comedy/thriller concerning fastidious cop *Tom Hanks* and his slobbering dog.

★ **Twin Peaks: Fire Walk with Me** 1992   134 mins (cert 18)
Prequel to David Lynch's cult TV series recounting the events leading to Laura Palmer's murder. Should have been much better than it is.

★★ **The Two Jakes** 1990   137 mins (cert 15)
Disappointing sequel to 'Chinatown'. *Jack Nicholson* stars and directs but still can't make the thriller thrill.

★ **Undercover Blues** 1994   90 mins (cert 12)
Happily married spies *Dennis Quaid* and *Kathleen Turner*, plus baby, embroiled in fatuous espionage caper.

★★ **Unlawful Entry** 1992   111 mins (cert 18)
Kurt Russell and *Madeleine Stowe* terrorised by psycho policeman, *Ray Liotta*. Good idea, feebly handled.

★★★★ **The Vanishing** 1988   106 mins (cert 15)
George Sluizer's riveting chiller about a young Dutchman's search for his girlfriend after her kidnap in France. Mystery, tension and a truly shocking ending.

★★ **The Vanishing** 1993   110 mins (cert 15)
Same story as above, same director too. But now it's set in America with *Kiefer Sutherland* as the bereaved boyfriend, *Jeff Bridges* the weird kidnapper. Hollywood takes over, tension and suspense vanish.

★★ **Vertigo** 1958   127 mins (cert PG)
Flawed but enjoyable Hitchcock mystery with *James Stewart* as ex-cop hired to keep an eye on friend's wife, *Kim Novak*.

★★ **VI Warshawski** 1991   89 mins (cert 15)
Kathleen Turner does her best as a wise-cracking private eye but the film falls flat, thanks to a limp script.

★★ **When Sleeping Dogs Lie** 1994   88 mins (cert 15)
Middling thriller in which a writer, *Dylan McDermott*, is persuaded by his agent, *Sharon Stone*, to write a novel about a violent serial killer. *Tom Sizemore* is the mysterious guy who arrives offering help.

★★ **White Nights** 1985   135 mins (cert PG)
Thriller starring *Gregory Hines* and Russian ballet star, *Mikhail Baryshnikov*, planning to defect from USSR to America.

★★★ **White Sands** 1992   101 mins (cert 15)
Pacy thriller with *Willem Dafoe* as a deputy sheriff involved with murder, money and mysterious *Mary Elizabeth Mastrantonio*.

★★★ **The Wicker Man** 1973   86 mins (cert 15)
Palm-sweating tale of Scottish policeman, *Edward Woodward*, investigating the disappearance of a child on an eerie island.

MYSTERY/THRILLER

★★ **Without a Clue** 1988   107 mins (cert PG)
Sherlock Holmes send-up. Holmes, *Michael Caine*, is really a drunken actor fronting for true genius Doctor Watson, *Ben Kingsley*.

★★★★ **Witness** 1985   112 mins (cert 15)
Magnetic combination of action, romance, suspense and thrills. Cop *Harrison Ford* uncovers high level corruption while hiding out with murder witness in the Amish community.

★★★ **Witness for the Prosecution** 1957   113 mins (cert U)
Agatha Christie plot expertly adapted by Billy Wilder. Good performances by *Charles Laughton*, *Marlene Dietrich* and *Tyrone Power*.

★★ **Year of the Dragon** 1985   125 mins (cert 18)
Michael Cimino's violent, untidy tale of drug warfare in New York's Chinatown. *Mickey Rourke* is the investigating cop.

★ **The Young Americans** 1993   104 mins (cert 15)
Harvey Keitel as New York cop in London to expose drug racket. Recruits the help of local lad, *Craig Kelly*, who's reluctant to grass. Bleak but some interesting shots of London.

★ **Young Soul Rebels** 1991   100 mins (cert 18)
Black British drama/murder story about two DJs – one straight, the other gay – at a funky pirate radio station. Set in 1970s.

SCI-FI/FANTASY

★★ The Abyss 1989 — 140 mins (cert 12)
'Alien' underwater but to poor effect. A group of oil rig workers trying to rescue sunken nuclear sub. But something else lurks in the murky depths – not suspense, that's for sure.

★★ The Abyss: Special Edition 1992 — 171 mins (cert 12)
The director, James Cameron, saw fit to add 31 minutes to an already overlong film. Main additions are to the special effects which are technically brilliant.

★★★★ Alien 1979 — 117 mins (cert 18)
Terrifying galaxy adventure of epic proportions aboard a plagued spaceship. *Sigourney Weaver*, *Tom Skerritt* and *John Hurt* are excellent. Fine special effects.

★★★ Aliens 1986 — 137 mins (cert 18)
Not quite up to the original. More violence than plot but still exciting stuff.

★★ Alien 3 1992 — 110 mins (cert 18)
Law of diminishing returns comes in when Ripley, *Sigourney Weaver*, is forced to confront alien again on a penal reform planet run by *Brian Glover*, ministered to by doctor *Charles Dance*.

★★ Alien Nation 1988 — 86 mins (cert 18)
Aliens have landed and settled in LA. *James Caan* is a police officer investigating murder with *Mandy Patinkin* as his alien partner.

★★★★ Back to the Future 1985 — 116 mins (cert PG)
Michael J Fox is sent to the past to ensure his future in a terrific movie. First and best of the series. *Christopher Lloyd* is fine as the mad inventor of the De Lorean-based time machine.

★★ Back to the Future Part II 1989 — 107 mins (cert PG)
Too fast, too complex, too harsh sequel has *Fox* and *Lloyd* zipping back and forth through time like yo-yos.

★★★ Back to the Future Part III 1990 — 118 mins (cert PG)
On form again, *Fox* and *Lloyd* are zapped back to the Wild West where the Doc finds romance with *Mary Steenbergen*. Better than 'II', not as good as 'I' and a nice point to end the series.

★★ **Barbarella** 1968   98 mins (cert 18)
Pre-feminist *Jane Fonda* explodes onto the screen as a sexy adventuress leched over by inhabitants of strange 41st-century planet. Very sexy for its time, less so now.

★★★ **Batman** 1989   126 mins (cert 12)
Michael Keaton's moody hero is overshadowed by *Jack Nicholson*'s hammy Joker. Nicholson and dark, impressive gothic sets dominate the film.

★★★ **Batman Returns** 1992   127 mins (cert 12)
Michael Keaton still low-key as he fights such adversaries as the Penguin *Danny DeVito*, Catwoman *Michelle Pfeiffer* and evil entrepreneur *Christopher Walken*. Catwoman rules, OK?

★ **Batteries Not Included** 1987   106 mins (cert PG)
Aliens help poverty-stricken oldies battle to keep their home in thin extra-terrestrial comedy.

★★★ **Blade Runner** 1982   118 mins (cert 15)
Impressive, futuristic thriller in which a cop, *Harrison Ford*, tracks down escaped robots, *Rutger Hauer*, *Sean Young* and *Darryl Hannah*. But wait and see . . .

★★★★ **Blade Runner: The Director's Cut** 1992   116 mins (cert 15)
Shorter and much better than the version originally released, now that Ridley Scott has tightened things up and got rid of that unnecessary, intrusive voice-over narration.

★★ **Body Snatchers** 1993   83 mins (cert 15)
Abel Ferrara's remake of the classic 1956 B-pic, 'Invasion of the Bodysnatchers'. Now set on an army base in the USA but it no longer seems to have much point.

★★ **Brazil** 1985   142 mins (cert 15)
Terry Gilliam's futuristic social satire with *Robert De Niro*, *Jonathan Pryce* and *Bob Hoskins* achieved cult status in America. Brilliant – but only in parts.

★★★★ **Close Encounters of the Third Kind** 1977   135 mins (cert PG)
Fantastic, thought-provoking Steven Spielberg sci-fi about non-threatening aliens landing in America. Great special effects.

★★★ **The Dark Star** 1974   84 mins (cert PG)
John Carpenter's very inventive film about a group of slobs cruising space and blowing up obsolete planets. This was Carpenter's first feature.

★★ **Dark Universe** 1993   87 mins (cert 15)
Emilio Estevez stars in a melodrama about an alien-infected spaceship that can't reach earth. A billionaire decides to launch his own rescuing space shuttle. Okay but nothing special.

★★ **Dune** 1984   131 mins (cert 15)
David Lynch's attempt to bring Frank Herbert's fantasy of a futuristic galactic empire to the screen was reckoned a failure in its time but it's still a bold attempt.

★★★★ **The Empire Strikes Back** 1980   124 mins (cert U)
Great action-packed sequel to 'Star Wars', reuniting cast and crew with added special effects.

★★★★★ **ET The Extra Terrestrial** 1982   115 mins (cert U)
The greatest fantasy movie ever about a little boy and his friendship with a stranded alien. Spielberg's direction plus story and acting are quite superb. Second only to 'Jurassic Park' in box-office takings.

★★★ **Fantastic Voyage** 1966   100 mins (cert U)
Shrunken *Raquel Welch* is injected into ailing doctor's bloodstream to save his life. Preposterous but quite thrilling sci-fi adventure.

★★ **Fire in the Sky** 1992   107 mins (cert 15)
Allegedly true story of a lumberjack who is abducted by aliens. *D B Sweeney* and *James Garner* lend scant credibility to a drama otherwise impossible to believe.

★★ **Flash Gordon** 1980   115 mins (cert PG)
Comic strip hero brought to life by *Sam J Jones* in lavish sci-fi adventure. Good designs, score and supporting cast.

★★★★ **Forbidden Planet** 1956   98 mins (cert U)
Classic sci-fi version of 'The Tempest' with *Leslie Nielsen* as the commander of a spaceship arriving at a remote, almost deserted, planet.

★★★★ **Ghostbusters** 1984   107 mins (cert PG)
Who you gonna call if plagued by ghosts? *Dan Aykroyd, Harold Ramis* and the wonderful *Bill Murray*. Rib-tickling comedy with scary special effects.

★★★ **Ghostbusters II** 1989   108 mins (cert PG)
Old gang return with fewer laughs, more violence as they battle a New Year's Eve explosion of spirits.

★★★ **Highlander** 1986   116 mins (cert 15)
Action/adventure pairing of immortal 16th-century *Sean Connery* and modern day pupil *Christopher Lambert*. Enjoyable fantasy hokum.

★ **Highlander II – The Quickening** 1990   100 mins (cert 12)
Confused sequel quite unworthy of *Christopher Lambert* and *Virginia Madsen*. One can only wonder what huge amounts of money prompted *Sean Connery* to star again.

★★★ **Iceman** 1984   99 mins (cert 15)
Prehistoric man is alive and well and living in Antarctica where he's discovered by *Timothy Hutton*. Quite intriguing piece of sci-fi.

★★★ **Innerspace** 1987   120 mins (cert PG)
Astronaut *Dennis Quaid* is miniaturized and accidentally injected into body of hypochondriac *Martin Short*. Fast and funny. Quaid and wife *Meg Ryan* fell in love on the set of this film. Ahhh.

★★★★ **Invasion of the Bodysnatchers** 1956   80 mins (cert PG)
Don Siegel's highly effective sci-fi story of unfriendly aliens taking over bodies of town's inhabitants. Seen at the time as a grim warning against Communist infiltration.

★★★ **Invasion of the Bodysnatchers** 1978   115 mins (cert 15)
Philip Kaufman's update of the original tale, now set in San Francisco and starring *Donald Sutherland*. Still very effective but loses something in the absence of the old Red scare.

★★ **Mindwarp** 1993   96 mins (cert 18)
Post-apocalyptic science fantasy – toxic zones, mutant cannibals, religious nutters and a rebellious girl, *Marta Alicia*. *Bruce Campbell* stars.

★★ **Paperhouse** 1988   94 mins (cert 15)
Engaging psychological study of pre-pubescent who enters imaginary world of her own drawings.

★★★ **The Philadelphia Experiment** 1984   101 mins (cert PG)
Engaging science fiction adventure in which two US sailors, *Michael Pare* and *Bobby Di Cicco*, slip through a time warp and are transported from WWII to modern times.

★★★★ **Return of the Jedi** 1983   133 mins (cert PG)
Final part of 'Star Wars' trilogy, with Luke Skywalker and co up against giant Deathstar. Special effects great as ever.

★★ **Return of the Swamp Thing** 1989   88 mins (cert 12)
Vegetable superhero rescues distressed damsel, *Heather Locklear*, from evil *Louis Jourdan*. Cheap and rather cheerful.

★★ **Rollerball** 1975   129 mins (cert 15)
James Caan as the star of an ultra-violent sport in a futuristic society where all other violence is banned.

★★ **The Running Man** 1987   103 mins (cert 18)
Imaginative, futuristic thriller in which a TV quiz show is a matter of survival. *Arnold Schwarzenegger* is the contestant battling for life.

★★ **The Shadow** 1994   107 mins (cert 12)
Alec Baldwin is the comic strip character who seems to be Batman's poor relation. It looks good but somehow it doesn't quite work.

★★★ **Short Circuit** 1986   98 mins (cert PG)
A cutesy robot comes to life to the surprise of its creator, *Steve Guttenberg*. Acceptable sci-fi comedy.

★★ **Short Circuit 2** 1988   106 mins (cert PG)
Agreeable sequel, this time with the robot hitting the streets of New York for some 'urban input'.

★★★ **Starman** 1984   115 mins (cert PG)
Jeff Bridges is the appealing alien, *Karen Allen* the widow who helps him elude the police and the army to get him back to his own planet.

SCI-FI/FANTASY ■

★★ **Star Trek: The Motion Picture** 1979   132 mins (cert U)
Disappointing film version of the marvellous TV series. The Starship Enterprise crew battle to save earth from threatening force field. 'Star Trek II', 'III' and 'V' not up to much either. But . . .

★★★ **Star Trek IV: The Voyage Home** 1986   119 mins (cert PG)
. . . is much more fun and contains a strong ecological message as the Enterprise lands on 20th-century Earth to save the whale. And . . .

★★★★ **Star Trek VI: The Undiscovered Country** 1991   110 mins (cert PG)
. . . is better still, though in this, supposedly the last episode, the crew are now so old that what they really need is an intergalactic zimmerframe. Still, this is the most enjoyable adventure of Kirk and company.

★★★★ **Star Wars** 1977   121 mins (cert U)
Marvellous sci-fi adventure. *Mark Hamill*, *Harrison Ford*, *Carrie Fisher*, *Alec Guinness* and robots, R2D2 and C-3PO, in hugely imaginative space-age Western.

★★ **Stay Tuned** 1992   89 mins (cert PG)
Couch potatoes *John Ritter* and *Pam Dawber* must survive 24 hours appearing on Hellvision if they're to be returned home alive. Some good spoofs and numerous throw-away lines.

★★★ **Superman** 1978   142 mins (cert PG)
Much as you'd expect. *Christopher Reeve* as Superman, *Margot Kidder* as Lois Lane. *Gene Hackman* makes a very good comic villain. Enjoyable, unsophisticated fun.

★★★ **Superman II** 1980   127 mins (cert PG)
Richard Lester takes over the direction from Richard Donner and adds more visual flair to this tale in which Superman loses his powers and falls in love with Lois Lane.

★★ **Superman III** 1983   125 mins (cert PG)
Getting a bit silly now. The new villain is *Robert Vaughn*, the new lady is *Annette O'Toole* and *Richard Pryor* is woefully wasted.

★ **Superman IV: The Quest for Peace** 1987   89 mins (cert PG)
Forget it. *Christopher Reeve* co-wrote this earnest story about Superman tackling the nuclear menace. Most of the fun has gone, despite the return of *Gene Hackman*.

★★★★ **The Terminator** 1984   108 mins (cert 18)
Arnold Schwarzenegger as a Terminator/android sent back from the future to kill the boy who will grow up to save mankind from the rule of machines. Very fast, very violent, very stylish.

★★★★ **Terminator 2** 1991   136 mins (cert 15)
Arnie's back – this time as a goody protecting his former intended victim from an even more evil Cyborg. Story takes back seat to special effects even better than in the original.

★★★ **They Live** 1988   94 mins (cert 18)
John Carpenter sci-fi chiller about aliens taking over Earth – and only *Roddy Piper* and his friends can see them.

★★★ **Timescape** 1991   90 mins (cert 15)
Small-town America is visited by a group from the future. To avert doom, widower *Jeff Daniels* has to interfere with the fabric of time itself.

★★★ **Total Recall** 1990   109 mins (cert 18)
Arnold Schwarzenegger provides the brawn, special effects the brain, in violent futuristic thriller in which technology can inject memories into minds.

★★ **The Toxic Avenger** 1985   76 mins (cert 18)
Soufflé-light spoof on comic strip heroes. A wimpy janitor falls into a tub of nuclear waste and emerges both toxic and crusading.

★★ **The Toxic Avenger Part II** 1989   95 mins (cert 18)
Same sort of thing – only this time Toxic is up against an evil Japanese conglomerate.

★ **The Toxic Avenger Part III** 1989   89 mins (cert 18)
And more or less the same again but too slapdash, too hurriedly made.

★★★★★ **2001: A Space Odyssey** 1968   160 mins (cert U)
Stanley Kubrick's ground-breaking account of a space journey, jeopardized when the computer takes control. Best seen in the cinema, though.

★★★ **2010: The Year We Make Contact** 1984   112 mins (cert PG)
Good sequel, this time directed by Peter Hyams, with a multi-national group of astronauts trying to discover what happened to the space mission of '2001'.

★★★ **Universal Soldier** 1991 103 mins (cert 18)
Dolph Lundgren the baddie, *Jean-Claude Van Damme* the good guy, battle it out as state-of-the-art soldiers in surprisingly good futuristic thriller. Similar to 'The Terminator' in look and action.

★★ **The War of the Worlds** 1953 85 mins (cert PG)
Martians invade Earth. *Gene Barry* and *Les Tremayne* star in commendable version of H G Wells story. Oscar-winning special effects.

★★★ **Westworld** 1973 89 mins (cert PG)
Ambitious thriller set in a future where a Disneyland for adults is staffed by robots, one of which looks just like *Yul Brynner*.

★★ **When Worlds Collide** 1951 82 mins (cert U)
Corny, end-of-the-world fable, distinguished by Oscar-winning special effects.

★★★ **Zardoz** 1974 105 mins (cert 15)
Sean Connery and *Charlotte Rampling* in futuristic tale of civilisation in a state of post-cataclysm. The visuals are better than the plot.

WESTERNS

★★ The Alamo 1960 — 154 mins (cert PG)
John Wayne's long, earnest version of America's Dunkirk-like defeat in the old West. Also stars *Richard Widmark* and *Laurence Harvey*.

★★★ Bad Girls 1993 — 100 mins (cert 15)
Bunch of female outlaws – *Andie MacDowell*, *Madeleine Stowe*, *Mary Louise Parker* and *Drew Barrymore* – go after the crook who's stolen their money. Sassy women with different goals. Intriguing, if a little clichéd.

★★★★ The Big Country 1958 — 165 mins (cert PG)
Pleasing direction by William Wyler of a sweeping, overlong Western. Seafaring man *Gregory Peck* comes ashore to be shown country ways (and dirty tricks) by the likes of *Jean Simmons*, *Charlton Heston* and *Burl Ives*.

★★★★★ Butch Cassidy and the Sundance Kid 1969 — 110 mins (cert PG)
Unbeatable romantic, funny, action/Western. Inspired pairing of *Paul Newman* and *Robert Redford* as lawless buddies.

★★★ Cat Ballou 1965 — 96 mins (cert PG)
Highly engaging spoof Western. *Jane Fonda* as school teacher turned outlaw; *Lee Marvin* a glorious drunken gunfighter.

★★ Cheyenne Autumn 1964 — 170 mins (cert U)
John Ford's last, oddly pessimistic account of Cheyenne tribe's journey back to original settlement. *Richard Widmark* heads excellent cast.

★★ The Cowboys 1972 — 128 mins (cert PG)
John Wayne forced to take group of young boys on cattle drive – and thereby help them grow up – in slow, earnest story.

★★★★ Dances with Wolves 1990 — 179 mins (cert 12)
Oscar-winning directorial debut by star *Kevin Costner* in post-Civil War epic. Near-4hr version also available and equally worth seeing.

★★★ Duel in the Sun 1946 — 125 mins (cert PG)
King Vidor Western with *Gregory Peck* and *Joseph Cotten* fighting over half-breed, *Jennifer Jones*. Sometimes known as 'Lust in the Dust'.

★★★★ **A Fistful of Dollars** 1964   100 mins (cert 15)
'Man with no name' *Clint Eastwood* blows into Mexican border town torn apart by feud. First of Sergio Leone's spaghetti Westerns. Film that made Eastwood a star.

★★★ **For a Few Dollars More** 1965   130 mins (cert 15)
Bounty hunters, *Lee Van Cleef* and the laconic *Clint Eastwood*, in violent sequel to 'A Fistful of Dollars'. Plenty of shootouts.

★★ **Fort Apache** 1948   128 mins (cert U)
Unusual John Ford Western – an action/drama revolving around conflict between martinet cavalry officer, *Henry Fonda*, and pragmatic subordinate, *John Wayne*.

★★★★ **The Good, the Bad and the Ugly** 1967   180 mins (cert 18)
Clint Eastwood, 'The Good' of the title, *Lee Van Cleef* 'The Bad' and *Eli Wallach* 'The Ugly' in top-rate spaghetti Western.

★★★★ **High Noon** 1952   85 mins (cert U)
Classic adventure with *Gary Cooper*, the sheriff, single-handedly facing the vengeful bad guys on Main Street. Unmissable stuff.

★★★ **High Plains Drifter** 1973   105 mins (cert 18)
Mystical Western with *Clint Eastwood* as an avenging angel cleaning up a corrupt town.

★★★ **How the West Was Won** 1962   165 mins (cert PG)
Spectacular saga covering three generations. Narrated by *Spencer Tracy* and starring hordes of the great screen cowboys – *Wayne, Peck, Stewart, Fonda, Widmark*, etc.

★★★ **Jesse James** 1939   103 mins (cert U)
Colourful, romanticized version of life of the notorious outlaw. *Tyrone Power* as Jesse, *Henry Fonda* as brother Frank.

★★ **The Left-Handed Gun** 1958   102 mins (cert PG)
First method Western. Psychological study of exploits of Billy the Kid, nicely played by *Paul Newman*.

★★★★ **Little Big Man** 1970   150 mins (cert 15)
Epic, imaginative saga focusing upon the reminiscences of a 120-year-old half-breed, *Dustin Hoffman*, who – among other things – survived the battle of Little Big Horn.

★★★★★ **The Magnificent Seven** 1960   138 mins (cert PG)
Smashing adaptation of Kurosawa's 'The Seven Samurai'. Hired guns protect Mexican village from gang of bandits. Stars *Yul Brynner*, *Steve McQueen*, *Charles Bronson*, et al. Excellent.

★★ **Major Dundee** 1965   134 mins (cert 18)
Sam Peckinpah directed this disturbing, uneven drama about Confederate pioneers sent to quell the Apaches. Much messed about by Columbia. *Charlton Heston* and *Richard Harris* star.

★★★ **A Man Called Horse** 1970   114 mins (cert 15)
Gory but gripping study of Sioux culture. Captured *Richard Harris* undergoes torture to prove manhood.

★★★★ **The Man from Laramie** 1955   104 mins (cert U)
Absorbing *James Stewart* Western sees him out for revenge when his brother is murdered.

★★★ **Maverick** 1994   127 mins (cert PG)
Mel Gibson, *Jodie Foster* and *James Garner* are delightful in jokey Western about gamblers and conmen, inspired by the old TV series. Fun, fast and furious.

★★★★ **Once Upon a Time in the West** 1968   165 mins (cert 15)
Sergio Leone's testament to the Wild West, with *Henry Fonda* cast (unusually) as cold-blooded killer.

★★★ **One-Eyed Jacks** 1961   141 mins (cert 15)
Outlaw *Marlon Brando* seeks revenge on double-crossing partner *Karl Malden*. Moody atmosphere; good direction by Brando.

★★ **The Outlaw** 1943   126 mins (cert U)
Once notoriously sexy, now tame Western. *Jane Russell* almost falling out of her bra (specially made for her) during a tumble in the hay with Billy the Kid.

★★★★ **The Outlaw Josey Wales** 1976   135 mins (cert 18)
Great Western from *Clint Eastwood* as a family man turned vigilante when wife and kids are murdered by union soldiers.

★★ **Paint Your Wagon** 1969   166 mins (cert PG)
Nice looking musical Western. *Lee Marvin* and *Clint Eastwood* buy the same wife – *Jean Seberg* – at auction.

★★ **Pale Rider** 1985   115 mins (cert 15)
Enigmatic, slightly pretentious Western. *Clint Eastwood* as a mysterious stranger helping miners in their struggle against a large corporation.

★★ **Posse** 1993   109 mins (cert 15)
An earnest black Western, not uninteresting but slow and heavy on the clichés. *Mario Van Peebles* and friends chased across the West by mad colonel *Billy Zane*.

★★★★ **Red River** 1948   133 mins (cert U)
Epic movie by Howard Hawkes. A cattle drive sparks conflict between leader, *John Wayne*, and rebel, *Montgomery Clift*.

★★★ **Rio Bravo** 1959   141 mins (cert PG)
Enjoyable Howard Hawkes Western in which an ill-assorted quartet of lawmen, hired guns and drunks – led by *John Wayne* – fight off the bad guys.

★★★ **Rio Grande** 1950   105 mins (cert U)
Last of John Ford's splendid cavalry trilogy. *John Wayne* licks new cavalry recruits – one of them his son – into shape in post-Civil War era.

★★★★★ **The Searchers** 1956   119 mins (cert U)
The finest of all Westerns. Racist *John Wayne* seeks his niece *Natalie Wood*, kidnapped by marauding Indians, in order to kill her. *Jeffrey Hunter* wants to save her.

★★★★★ **Shane** 1953   118 mins (cert U)
One of the classic Westerns. *Alan Ladd*'s arrival disturbs the lives of the homesteaders he's come to protect. *Jack Palance* is marvellous as the chief heavy.

★★★★ **She Wore a Yellow Ribbon** 1949   103 mins (cert U)
Lavish, satisfying homage from the master, John Ford. Stars *John Wayne* as the cavalry officer reluctant to retire while the Apaches are on the war-path.

★★★ **The Shootist** 1976   99 mins (cert PG)
Touching performance by *John Wayne* as a dying gunfighter looking for a place to lay his holster. *James Stewart* and *Lauren Bacall* also feature. Deeply nostalgic.

★★★ **Silverado** 1985   133 mins (cert PG)
Not at all a bad Western with *Kevin Kline*, *Kevin Costner* and *John Cleese* heading a cast that sometimes looks uncomfortable in the old West.

★★★★★ **Stagecoach** 1939   99 mins (cert U)
The first great Western from John Ford with *John Wayne* as the Ringo Kid and *Claire Trevor* the tart-with-a-heart, aboard a stagecoach threatened by Red Indians.

★★★★ **Support Your Local Sheriff** 1969   93 mins (cert PG)
Charming parody pits reluctant sheriff *James Garner* against a lawless mining town, as he drifts through on his way to Australia.

★★★ **They Died With Their Boots On** 1941   140 mins (cert U)
Hollywood's lavish, whitewashed version of the Little Big Horn battle with *Errol Flynn* as Colonel Custer, *Olivia de Havilland* his worried wife.

★★★ **Tombstone** 1993   101 mins (cert 15)
The other Wyatt Earp film and not bad either. Faithful account of before, during and after the OK Corral shoot-out.

★★★ **True Grit** 1969   128 mins (cert U)
John Wayne's only Oscar-winning performance as a crusty old marshal helping a young girl, *Kim Darby*, get revenge for her father's death.

★★★★★ **Unforgiven** 1992   131 mins (cert 15)
Clint Eastwood's marvellous, revisionist Western with superb performances from Eastwood, *Morgan Freeman* and *Gene Hackman*. Terrific atmosphere.

★★★★★ **The Wild Bunch** 1969   144 mins (cert 18)
Violent, riveting Sam Peckinpah Western set in 1914, when the few remaining outlaws find the rules have changed.

★★★★ **Winchester '73** 1950   92 mins (cert U)
Fine, intelligent example of the Western genre. *James Stewart* tracks his stolen gun across the prairies.

★★★★ **Wyatt Earp** 1994   190 mins (cert 12)
Lawrence Kasdan's epic tale of the legendary lawman, *Kevin Costner*, and his brothers. Film-stealing performance from *Dennis Quaid* as Doc Holliday, a part for which he lost 44 lbs in weight.

★★★ **Young Guns** 1988   107 mins (cert 18)
Brat Pack Western explores the romantic myth surrounding Billy the Kid. *Keifer Sutherland*, *Charlie Sheen* and *Emilio Estevez* – as Billy – are the young outlaws.

★★ **Young Guns II** 1990   104 mins (cert 12)
Pretty fair sequel to the above. *Christian Slater* joins cast; *Charlie Sheen* leaves it. Rest of team remain the same.

INDEX

A Bout de Souffle 116
Above the Rim 58
Above Us the Waves 1
Absence of Malice 139
Absolute Beginners 131
The Abyss 159
The Abyss: Special Edition 159
Accident 58
Accidental Hero 58
Accidental Tourist 58
L'Accompagnatrice 116
The Accused 58
Ace Ventura: Pet Detective 24
Adam's Rib 24
The Addams Family 105
Addams Family Values 105
Adventures in Babysitting 24
The Adventures of Baron Munchausen 24
The Adventures of Huckleberry Finn 105
The Adventures of Priscilla, Queen of the Desert 24
The Adventures of Robin Hood 1
The African Queen 1
After Darkness 58
After Hours 24
Agantuk 16
The Age of Innocence 58
Agnes of God 58
Air America 1
Airheads 24
Airplane! 24
Airplane II: The Sequel 24
The Air Up There 105
Aladdin 105
The Alamo 167
Alice 25
Alice Doesn't Live Here Any More 58
Alien 159
Aliens 159
Alien 3 159
Alien Nation 159
Alive 1
All About Eve 59
All of Me 25
All Quiet on the Western Front 1
All That Jazz 131
All the President's Men 59
All This and Heaven Too 59
Always 59

Amadeus 59
American Graffiti 25
American Heart 59
An American in Paris 131
An American Tail 105
An American Tail II: Fievel Goes West 105
An American Werewolf in London 126
The Anchoress 116
Anchors Aweigh 131
The Anderson Tapes 139
And Now for Something Completely Different 25
And the Band Played On 59
Angel Heart 139
Angie 59
Anna Karenina 59
Annie Hall 25
Another Country 59
Another 48 Hours 1
Another Stakeout 139
The Apartment 25
Apocalypse Now 1
Arachnophobia 105
The Aristocats 105
Army of Darkness: The Medieval Dead 126
Arsenic and Old Lace 25
Arthur 25
Arthur II: On the Rocks 25
The Assassin 1
Assassin of the Tsar 60
The Assault 116
Atlantic City 60
Attack of the 50 Foot Woman 2
Aunt Julia and the Scriptwriter 60
Au Revoir les Enfants 116
Awakenings 60

Babette's Feast 116
Baby Boom 25
Baby It's You 26
The Baby of Macon 60
Baby's Day Out 106
Baby: Secret of the Lost Legend 106
Backbeat 60
Backdraft 2
Back in the USSR 2
Back to the Future 159
Back to the Future Part II 159
Back to the Future Part III 159
The Bad and the Beautiful 60
Bad Behaviour 26
Bad Day at Black Rock 139

Bad Girls 167
Badlands 60
Bad Lieutenant 60
La Balance 116
The Ballad of Little Jo 61
Bambi 106
Bananas 26
The Band Wagon 131
Barbarella 160
Barefoot in the Park 26
The Barkleys of Broadway 131
Barry Lyndon 61
Barton Fink 26
Basic Instinct 139
Batman 160
Batman Returns 160
Batteries Not Included 160
The Battleship Ptomekin 117
Beaches 61
The Bear 106
Beauty and the Beast 106
Bedknobs and Broomsticks 106
The Bedroom Window 139
Beethoven 106
Beethoven's 2nd 106
Beetlejuice 26
Belle Epoque 117
Bellman and True 139
The Belly of an Architect 61
Benefit of the Doubt 140
Ben Hur 2
Benny and Joon 61
The Best Years of Our Lives 61
Betsy's Wedding 26
Betty Blue 117
Beverly Hills Cop 2
Beverly Hills Cop 2 2
Beverly Hills Cop 3 2
Beyond Bedlam 126
Big 106
The Big Blue 61
The Big Chill 61
The Big Country 167
The Big Easy 140
The Big Heat 140
The Big Picture 26
The Big Sleep 140
Bill and Ted's Bogus Journey 107
Bill and Ted's Excellent Adventure 107
Billy Bathgate 61
Billy Liar 62
Biloxi Blues 26
Bird 131
Bird on a Wire 27
The Birds 126

173

Birdy 62
Bitter Moon 140
Black Narcissus 62
Black Rain 140
Black Widow 140
Blade Runner 160
Blade Runner: The Director's Cut 160
Blank Cheque 107
Blazing Saddles 27
Blink 107
Bloodhounds of Broadway 131
Blown Away 140
Blow Out 141
Blue Ice 141
The Blues Brothers 131
Blue Velvet 141
Bob Roberts 27
Bodies Rest and Motion 62
The Bodyguard 62
Body Heat 141
Body of Evidence 141
Body Snatchers 160
Boiling Point 141
Boomerang 27
Born on the Fourth of July 62
The Bounty 2
Boxing Helena 62
Boyz N the Hood 62
Brainscan 141
Bram Stoker's Dracula 126
Brazil 160
Breakfast at Tiffany's 62
The Breakfast Club 63
Brideshead Revisited 63
The Bridge on the River Kwai 2
A Bridge Too Far 3
Brief Encounter 63
Brigadoon 132
Bright Lights, Big City 63
Brighton Rock 141
Bringing Up Baby 27
Broadcast News 27
Broadway Danny Rose 27
A Bronx Tale 63
The Browning Version 63
The Buddy Holly Story 132
Buffy the Vampire Slayer 107
Bugsy 63
Bull Durham 63
Bullitt 141
Bus Stop 63
Buster 63
Butch Cassidy and the Sundance Kid 167
The Butcher's Wife 64

Cabaret 132
Cadillac Man 27
La Cage aux Folles 117
The Caine Mutiny 64
Cal 64
Calamity Jane 132
California Man 27
California Suite 27
The Candidate 64
Cape Fear (1961) 126
Cape Fear (1991) 126
Captain America 107
Captain Blood 3
Carlito's Way 141
Carmen 132
Carnosaur 126
Carousel 132
Carrie 126
Carry On Columbus 28
Carry On Up the Khyber 28
Carve Her Name with Pride 64
Casablanca 64
Cat Ballou 167
Catch 22 64
Cat on a Hot Tin Roof (1958) 64
Cat on a Hot Tin Roof (1976) 64
The Cement Garden 64
The Cemetery Club 65
Champions 107
Chaplin 65
Chariots of Fire 65
The Chase 28
Chasers 28
Cheyenne Autumn 167
Children of a Lesser God 65
The China Syndrome 142
Chinatown 142
A Chorus Line 132
A Chorus of Disapproval 28
A Christmas Carol 107
Christopher Columbus: The Discovery 3
Chuck Berry: Hail! Hail! Rock and Roll 132
Cinema Paradiso 117
Citizen Kane 65
City Lights 28
City of Joy 65
City Slickers 28
City Slickers II: The Legend of Curly's Gold 28
Claire's Knee 117
Clear and Present Danger 142
The Client 65
Cliffhanger 3

Clockwise 28
Close Encounters of the Third Kind 160
Close My Eyes 65
Close to Eden 142
Cocktail 65
Cocoon 107
Cocoon: The Return 107
Un Coeur en Hiver 117
The Colditz Story 3
The Color of Money 65
The Color of Night 142
The Color Purple 66
Colors 66
Comfort and Joy 29
The Commitments 132
Company Business 29
The Company of Wolves 66
Compromising Positions 142
The Concierge 29
Consenting Adults 142
The Conversation 142
The Cook, the Thief, His Wife and Her Lover 66
Cool Hand Luke 66
Cool Runnings 29
Cool World 107
Cop and a Half 108
Corrina, Corrina 66
The Cotton Club 66
Cousins 66
Cover Girl 132
The Cowboys 167
Crazy People 29
Crimes and Misdemeanours 29
Criminal Justice 142
Crocodile Dundee 108
Crocodile Dundee II 108
Cronos 117
Crossing Delancey 29
The Crow 127
The Cruel Sea 3
The Crush 143
Crush 143
Cry Freedom 66
The Crying Game 66
A Cry in the Dark 67
Curly Sue 108
Cyrano de Bergerac 117

Dad 67
The Dam Busters 3
Dances with Wolves 167
Dance with a Stranger 67
Dangerous Game 67
Dangerous Liaisons 67
A Dangerous Woman 67
Danton 118
The Dark Crystal 108

The Dark Half 127
The Darkman 143
The Dark Star 161
Dark Universe 161
Darling 67
Daughters of the Dust 67
Dave 29
David Copperfield 108
A Day at the Races 29
The Day of the Jackal 67
Days of Heaven 68
Days of Thunder 3
Dazed and Confused 68
D-Day the Sixth of June 3
The Dead 68
Dead Again 143
Dead Calm 143
Deadly Advice 30
The Deadly Affair 143
Deadly Pursuit 143
Dead Men Don't Wear Plaid 30
Dead Poets Society 68
The Dead Pool 3
Death Becomes Her 30
Death in Venice 68
Deceived 143
The Deer Hunter 68
Defence of the Realm 143
Delicatessen 118
Demolition Man 4
Dennis 108
The Desert Fox 4
The Desert Rats 4
The Desperate Hours 143
Desperately Seeking Susan 30
The Devils 127
Diamonds Are Forever 4
Dick Tracy 108
Die Hard 4
Die Hard 2 4
Diner 68
Dirty Dancing 133
The Dirty Dozen 4
Dirty Harry 4
Dirty Rotten Scoundrels 30
Distant Voices, Still Lives 68
The Distinguished Gentleman 30
Diva 118
DOA 144
The Doctor 68
Doctor Zhivago 68
Dog Day Afternoon 69
La Dolce Vita 118
The Doors 69
Do the Right Thing 69
Double Impact 4
Down and Out in Beverly Hills 30

Dracula 127
Dragnet 30
Dragon: The Bruce Lee Story 5
Dream Lover 144
The Dream Team 30
The Dresser 69
Driving Miss Daisy 69
Dr No 5
Dr Strangelove 30
A Dry White Season 69
Duel 144
Duel in the Sun 167
Dumbo 108
Dune 161

The Eagle Has Landed 5
Earth Girls Are Easy 31
Easter Parade 133
East of Eden 69
Easy Rider 69
Educating Rita 69
Edward Scissorhands 108
8½ 118
18 Again! 31
Eight Men Out 69
Eight Seconds 70
81 Charing Cross Road 70
El Cid 5
The Electric Horseman 70
Elenya 70
The Elephant Man 70
The Emerald Forest 70
Empire of the Sun 70
The Empire Strikes Back 161
Enchanted April 70
The End of the Golden Weather 70
An Enemy of the People 70
Les Enfants du Paradis 118
The Enforcer 5
An Englishman Abroad 71
The Entertainer 71
Equinox 71
Erik the Viking 31
Escape from Alcatraz 5
Escape from Sobibor 5
ET The Extra Terrestrial 161
Everybody Wins 144
Every Which Way But Loose 31
Excalibur 5
The Exterminator 5

The Fabulous Baker Boys 71
The Falcon and the Snowman 71
Fallen Angels 71
The Fallen Idol 71
Falling Down 71

Fame 133
Family Business 144
Fanny and Alexander 118
Fantasia 108
Fantastic Voyage 161
Far and Away 71
Farewell, My Concubine 118
Far From the Madding Crowd 72
Fatal Attraction 144
Fatal Beauty 144
Fatal Instinct 31
Fatal Vision 144
Father of the Bride 31
The Favour 31
Fearless 72
Fear of a Black Hat 31
Femme Fatale 144
Ferngully: The Last Rain Forest 109
A Few Good Men 72
Fiddler on the Roof 133
The Field 72
Field of Dreams 109
La Fille de L'Air 119
Filofax 31
Final Analysis 145
Firefox 5
Fire in the Sky 161
The Firm 145
The First of the Few 6
A Fish Called Wanda 31
The Fisher King 72
A Fistful of Dollars 168
Flashdance 133
Flash Gordon 161
Flatliners 145
Flesh and Bone 72
The Flintstones 109
The Fly 127
The Fool 72
For a Few Dollars More 168
Forbidden Planet 161
Forever Young 72
For Queen and Country 72
Forrest Gump 32
Fort Apache 168
The Fortune Cookie 32
48 Hours 6
42nd Street 133
For Your Eyes Only 6
1492: The Conquest of Paradise 73
Four Weddings and a Funeral 32
Frances 73
Frankie and Johnny 73
Frantic 145

Free Willy 109
The French Connection 145
The French Connection II 145
The French Lieutenant's Woman 73
The Freshman 32
Fried Green Tomatoes at the Whistle Stop Cafe 73
From Here to Eternity 6
From Russia With Love 6
The Front 73
Frozen Assets 32
The Fugitive 6
Full Metal Jacket 6
Funny Face 133
Funny Girl 133
FX: Murder by Illusion 6
FX 2: The Deadly Art of Illusion 6

Gallipoli 7
Gandhi 73
The General 32
Germinal 119
Geronimo 7
The Getaway 7
Getting Even with Dad 109
Gettysburg 7
Ghengis Cohn 32
Ghost 32
Ghostbusters 162
Ghostbusters II 162
Giant 73
Gigi 133
Gleaming the Cube 145
Glengarry Glen Ross 74
The Glenn Miller Story 133
Gloria 74
Glory 7
The Godfather 7
The Godfather Part II 7
The Godfather Part III 7
The Gods Must Be Crazy 32
Golden Balls 119
The Golden Voyage of Sinbad 109
Goldfinger 7
The Gold Rush 33
Gone With the Wind 74
Goodbye Mr Chips 74
Goodfellas 8
Good Morning Vietnam 33
The Good Son 145
The Good, the Bad and the Ugly 168
Gorillas in the Mist 74
Gorky Park 145
The Graduate 74
Grand Canyon 74

Grand Hotel 74
The Grapes of Wrath 74
Grease 133
Great Balls of Fire! 74
The Great Escape 8
Great Expectations 109
The Great Mouse Detective 109
Greedy 33
Green Card 33
Gregory's Girl 33
Gremlins 109
Gremlins 2: The New Batch 109
Greystoke: The Legend of Tarzan 8
The Grifters 75
Groundhog Day 33
Grumpy Old Men 33
Guess Who's Coming to Dinner 33
Guilty As Sin 145
Guilty by Suspicion 75
Gunga Din 8
The Guns of Navarone 8
Gypsy (1962) 134
Gypsy (1994) 134

Hairspray 33
Halloween 127
Hamlet (1948) 75
Hamlet (1991) 75
A Handful of Dust 75
The Handmaid's Tale 75
The Hand That Rocks the Cradle 146
Hangin' with the Homeboys 75
Hannah and Her Sisters 34
A Hard Day's Night 134
Hard Target 8
The Hard Way 146
Harvey 34
Havana 75
The Hawk 146
Hear My Song 34
The Heartbreak Kid 34
Heartbreak Ridge 8
Heartburn 75
Heart Condition 34
Heat and Dust 75
Heathers 75
Heaven and Earth 76
Hello, Dolly! 134
Henry and June 76
Henry: Portrait of a Serial Killer 127
Henry V (1944) 76
Henry V (1989) 76
Hidden Agenda 146
High Anxiety 34

High Heels 119
High Hopes 34
Highlander 162
Highlander II – The Quickening 162
High Noon 168
High Plains Drifter 168
High Sierra 8
High Society 134
Hiroshima, Mon Amour 119
The Hitcher 127
Hocus Pocus 110
Hoffa 76
Holiday Inn 134
Home Alone 110
Home Alone 2: Lost in New York 110
A Home of Our Own 76
Homer and Eddie 76
Homeward Bound: The Incredible Journey 110
Homicide 146
Honey, I Blew Up the Kid 110
Honey, I Shrunk the Kids 110
Honeymoon in Vegas 34
Hook 110
Hope and Glory 34
Hostile Hostages 35
Hot Shots 35
Hot Shots Part Deux 35
House of Cards 146
House of Games 146
House of the Spirits 76
Housesitter 35
Howards End 76
The Howling 128
How the West Was Won 168
How to Be a Woman and Not Die in the Attempt 119
How to Get Ahead in Advertising 35
The Hudsucker Proxy 35
The Hunchback of Notre Dame 77
The Hunt for Red October 8
Husbands and Wives 35
The Hustler 77

Ice Cold in Alex 9
Iceman 162
If . . . 77
I Love Trouble 146
I Love You to Death 35
I'm Alright Jack 35
I'm Gonna Git You, Sucka 36
The Importance of Being Ernest 36

In Bed with Madonna 134
Indecent Proposal 146
Indiana Jones and the Last
  Crusade 9
Indiana Jones and the
  Temple of Doom 9
Indian Runner 77
Indiscreet 36
Indochine 119
Inherit the Wind 77
The Inner Circle 77
Innerspace 162
The Innocent 147
Innocent Blood 36
An Innocent Man 9
Innocent Moves 77
The Inn of the Sixth
  Happiness 77
Internal Affairs 147
Intersection 77
In the Heat of the Night 147
In the Line of Fire 9
In the Name of the Father 77
Into the West 9
Invasion of the Bodysnatchers
  (1956) 162
Invasion of the Bodysnatchers
  (1978) 162
In Which We Serve 9
The Ipcress File 147
IP5 119
Ironweed 78
The Italian Job 9
It Could Happen to You 36
It Happened One Night 36
It's a Wonderful Life 110
I Was Monty's Double 9

Jacknife 78
Jack the Bear 78
Jacob's Ladder 147
Jagged Edge 147
Jamon Jamon 119
Jane Eyre 78
Jason and the Argonauts
  111
Jaws 9
Jaws 2 10
Jean de Florette 120
Jennifer 8 147
The Jerk 36
Jesse James 168
Jesus Christ Superstar 134
Jesus of Montreal 120
The Jewel of the Nile 10
JFK 78
Joe Versus the Volcano 36
Johnny Handsome 147
Johnny Suede 78
The Jolson Story 134
Josh and SAM 78

The Joy Luck Club 78
Juice 78
Julia 79
Julius Caesar 79
Jumpin' Jack Flash 147
The Jungle Book 111
Jungle Fever 79
Jurassic Park 111
Just Like a Woman 36
Just One of the Girls 36

Kagemusha 120
Kalifornia 147
The Karate Kid 10
Keeper of the City 148
Key Largo 148
Kickboxer 10
Kika 120
The Killing Fields 79
Killing Zoe 79
Kill Me Again 148
Kindergarten Cop 10
Kind Hearts and Coronets
  37
The King and I 134
King Kong 10
King of New York 10
King of the Hill 79
King Ralph 37
A Kiss Before Dying 148
Kiss Me Kate 135
Kiss of the Spider Woman
  79
Klute 148
K9 10
Kramer vs Kramer 79
The Krays 10
Kuffs 11

La Bamba 135
Labyrinth 111
Lady and the Tramp 111
Ladybird, Ladybird 79
The Lady in White 148
The Ladykillers 37
Lake Consequence 79
Last Action Hero 11
The Last Boy Scout 11
The Last Days of Chez Nous
  80
The Last Detail 80
The Last Emperor 80
Last Exit to Brooklyn 80
The Last of the Mohicans 11
LA Story 37
The Last Picture Show 80
The Last Seduction 148
Last Tango in Paris 80
The Last Temptation of
  Christ 80
The Late Show 148

Laura 148
The Lavender Hill Mob 37
The Lawnmower Man 148
Lawrence of Arabia 11
A League of Their Own 37
Leap of Faith 37
The Left-Handed Gun 168
Legal Eagles 149
The Legend of the Holy
  Drinker 120
Lenny 80
Lenny: Live and Unleashed
  37
Léolo 120
Leon the Pig Farmer 37
Leprechaun 128
Lethal Weapon 11
Lethal Weapon 2 11
Lethal Weapon 3 11
Let Him Have It 80
Letter to Brezhnev 38
A Letter to Three Wives 80
Licence to Kill 11
Life Is Sweet 38
Lightning Jack 38
Light Sleeper 81
Like Father Like Son 38
Like Water for Chocolate 120
The Lion in Winter 81
Little Big Man 168
Little Buddha 38
Little Caesar 12
Little Dorrit 81
The Little Drummer Girl
  149
Little Man Tate 81
The Little Mermaid 111
The Little Princess 111
The Little Shop of Horrors
  38
Little Women 81
Live and Let Die 12
Local Hero 111
Lolita 81
The Loneliness of the Long
  Distance Runner 81
The Lonely Passion of Judith
  Hearne 81
The Long and the Short and
  the Tall 12
The Long Day Closes 82
The Longest Day 12
The Long Good Friday 12
Longtime Companion 82
Look Back in Anger 82
Look Who's Talking 38
Look Who's Talking Too 38
Look Who's Talking Now 38
The Lord of the Flies 82
Lorenzo's Oil 82
Lost Horizon 149

Lost in Yonkers 38
Love and Death 39
Love and Human Remains 39
Love at First Bite 39
Love at Large 149
Love Field 82
The Lover 82
Love Story 82
Love Streams 82
Lucas 83

Mac 83
Macbeth 83
Madame Sousatzka 83
Mad Dog and Glory 149
Made in America 39
Madhouse 39
Mad Max 12
Mad Max 2: The Road Warrior 12
Mad Max 3: Beyond Thunderdome 12
The Magic Box 83
The Magnificent Seven 169
Magnum Force 12
Major Dundee 169
Major League 39
Major League II 39
Malcolm X 83
Malice 149
The Maltese Falcon 149
The Mambo Kings 83
Man Bites Dog 120
A Man Called Horse 169
A Man for all Seasons 83
The Man from Laramie 169
Manhattan 39
Manhattan Murder Mystery 149
The Man in the Moon 83
The Man in the White Suit 39
Manon des Sources 120
Man Trouble 40
The Man Without a Face 84
The Man with Two Brains 40
Map of the Human Heart 84
Marathon Man 149
Married to the Mob 12
Mary Poppins 111
Mary Shelley's Frankenstein 128
M*A*S*H 84
Mask 84
The Mask 40
Matewan 84
Matinee 40
Maverick 169
M Butterfly 84

Mean Streets 13
Medicine Man 84
Mediterraneo 121
Meeting Venus 84
Meet Me in St Louis 135
Memoirs of an Invisible Man 40
Memphis 84
Memphis Belle 13
Men Don't Leave 84
Mephisto 121
Mermaids 40
Metropolitan 40
Miami Blues 150
Micki + Maude 40
A Midnight Clear 85
Midnight Express 85
Midnight Run 40
Midnight Sting 41
A Midsummer Night's Sex Comedy 41
Mighty Ducks II 112
Millers Crossing 85
Mindwarp 162
Miracle on 34th Street (1947) 112
Miracle on 34th Street (1994) 112
Misery 128
The Misfits 85
Miss Firecracker 85
Missing 150
The Mission 85
Mississippi Burning 85
Mississippi Masala 85
Mo' Better Blues 85
The Moderns 85
The Molly Maguires 86
Mommie Dearest 86
Mo' Money 86
Mona Lisa 150
Monkey Trouble 41
Monsieur Hire 121
Monsieur Hulot's Holiday 121
A Month in the Country 86
Monty Python and the Holy Grail 41
Monty Python's Life of Brian 41
Monty Python's The Meaning of Life 41
Moonraker 13
Moonstruck 112
The Morning After 150
Mortal Thoughts 150
Mother's Boys 128
Mountains of the Moon 86
Mr Baseball 41
Mr Deeds Goes to Town 41
Mr Jones 86

Mr Nanny 112
Mr Saturday Night 41
Mrs Doubtfire 42
Mrs Miniver 86
Mr Smith Goes to Washington 86
Mr Wonderful 42
Much Ado About Nothing 42
The Muppet Christmas Carol 112
Murder by Death 42
Murder on the Orient Express 150
The Music Box 86
The Music Man 135
Mutiny on the Bounty (1935) 13
Mutiny on the Bounty (1962) 13
My Beautiful Launderette 87
My Blue Heaven 42
My Cousin Vinny 42
My Fair Lady 135
My Father's Glory 121
My Father the Hero 42
My Favourite Year 42
My Girl 112
My Girl 2 112
My Left Foot 87
My Life as a Dog 121
My Own Private Idaho 87
My Stepmother Is an Alien 42
The Mystery of Edwin Drood 87
Mystic Pizza 87

Naked 43
The Naked Gun 43
The Naked Gun 2½ 43
The Naked Gun 33⅓ 43
Naked in New York 43
Naked Lunch 87
The Name of the Rose 13
Narrow Margin 150
Nashville 43
The Nasty Girl 121
The National Health 43
National Lampoon's Animal House 43
National Lampoon's Christmas Vacation 43
National Lampoon's European Vacation 44
National Lampoon's Loaded Weapon 44
National Lampoon's Vacation 44
The Natural 87
Navy Seals 13

Needful Things 150
Network 87
The Neverending Story 112
The Neverending Story 2 113
The Neverending Story 3 113
Never Say Never Again 13
New Jack City 13
New York, New York 135
New York Stories 87
Next of Kin 13
Nicholas and Alexandra 88
Nico: Above the Law 14
Night and the City 150
A Night at the Opera 44
The Nightmare Before Christmas 113
A Nightmare on Elm Street 128
Night of the Hunter 151
Night of the Living Dead 128
Night on Earth 88
A Night to Remember 151
9½ Weeks 88
9 to 5 44
Ninotchka 44
No Escape 14
No Highway 88
No Mercy 151
Norma Rae 88
North 113
North by Northwest 14
Northwest Frontier 14
No Surrender 88
Notorious 151
Not Without My Daughter 88
No Way Out 151
Nowhere to Run 14
Now, Voyager 88
Nuns on the Run 44
The Nun's Story 88
Nuts in May 44

Octopussy 14
The Odd Couple 44
An Officer and a Gentleman 88
Of Mice and Men 89
Oklahoma! 135
Old Gringo 89
Oliver! 135
Oliver Twist 89
Olivier, Olivier 121
The Omen 128
Once Around 89
Once Upon a Forest 113

Once Upon a Time in the West 169
On Christmas Eve 113
On Deadly Ground 14
One-Eyed Jacks 169
One Flew Over the Cuckoo's Nest 89
On Golden Pond 89
Only Angels Have Wings 89
On the Town 135
On the Waterfront 89
Ordinary People 89
Orlando 90
Oscar 44
Other People's Money 45
An Outcast of the Islands 90
Out for Justice 151
The Outlaw 169
The Outlaw Josey Wales 169
Out of Africa 90
Outrageous Fortune 45
Overboard 45
The Ox 121

Pacific Heights 151
The Package 14
Painted Heart 90
Paint Your Wagon 169
The Pajama Game 135
Pale Rider 170
Pal Joey 135
Pandora's Box 121
The Paper 90
Paperhouse 163
Paradise 90
The Parallax View 151
Parenthood 45
Paris, Texas 90
Paris Trout 151
A Passage to India 90
Passenger 57 14
Passion Fish 90
Passport to Pimlico 45
Patriot Games 15
Peggy Sue Got Married 45
The Pelican Brief 151
Pelle the Conqueror 122
A Perfect World 15
Peter Pan 113
Peter's Friends 45
Pet Sematary 128
The Phantom of the Opera 129
Philadelphia 91
The Philadelphia Experiment 163
The Philadelphia Story 45
The Piano 91
Picnic at Hanging Rock 91
Pink Floyd: The Wall 136

The Pink Panther 45
The Pink Panther Strikes Again 45
Pinocchio 113
The Pirates of Penzance 136
Pixote 122
Places in the Heart 91
Planes, Trains and Automobiles 46
Platoon 15
The Playboys 91
The Player 46
Play It Again, Sam 46
Play Misty for Me 152
Playtime 122
Plaza Suite 46
Point Break 15
Police Academy 46
Poltergeist 129
The Pope Must Die 46
The Pope of Greenwich Village 46
The Poseidon Adventure 15
Posse 170
Postcards from the Edge 91
The Power of One 91
Predator 15
Predator 2 15
The Presidio 152
Presumed Innocent 152
Pretty Woman 46
Prick Up Your Ears 91
Pride and Prejudice 91
The Prime of Miss Jean Brodie 46
Prime Suspect 152
The Prince of Tides 91
The Princess and the Goblin 113
The Princess Bride 114
A Private Function 46
The Private Life of Sherlock Holmes 47
Private's Progress 47
Prizzi's Honour 152
Proof 92
Prospero's Books 92
Psycho 129
The Public Enemy 152
The Public Eye 152
Pumping Iron 92
Pump Up the Volume 47
Punchline 47
The Purple Rose of Cairo 47

Q & A 152
Quadrophenia 136
Les Quatre Cents Coups 122
Queen Christina 92
Quick Change 47

The Quiet Man 92
Quigley Down Under 15
The Quince Tree Sun 122

The Rachel Papers 92
Radio Days 47
A Rage in Harlem 15
Raging Bull 92
Raiders of the Lost Ark 15
The Railway Children 114
Raining Stones 47
Rain Man 92
Raising Arizona 47
Raising Cain 152
Rambling Rose 92
Ran 122
Rapid Fire 16
Reach for the Sky 16
Reality Bites 92
The Real McCoy 152
Rear Window 153
Rebecca 153
Rebel Without a Cause 93
The Red Badge of Courage 16
Red Heat 16
Red River 170
Red Rock West 153
Reds 93
The Red Shoes 93
Red Sorghum 122
The Red Squirrel 122
Regarding Henry 93
La Regle du Jeu 122
The Remains of the Day 93
Renaissance Man 47
Repo Man 48
The Rescuers 114
The Rescuers Down Under 114
Le Retour de Martin Guerre 122
Return of the Jedi 163
Return of the Swamp Thing 163
Revenge 16
Reversal of Fortune 93
Richard III 93
Rich in Love 93
Ricochet 153
The Right Stuff 16
Rio Bravo 170
Rio Grande 170
Rising Sun 153
Risky Business 48
The River 93
A River Runs Through It 94
The River Wild 16
Road House 16
The Roaring Twenties 16

Robin and Marian 94
Robin Hood 17
Robin Hood: Men in Tights 48
Robin Hood: Prince of Thieves 17
Robocop 17
Robocop 2 17
Robocop 3 17
The Rocketeer 17
The Rocking Horse Winner 94
Rocky 17
Rocky 2 17
Rocky 3 17
Rocky 4 17
Rocky 5 18
The Rocky Horror Picture Show 48
Roger & Me 94
Rollerball 163
Romancing the Stone 18
Roman Holiday 94
Romeo Is Bleeding 18
Romero 94
Romper Stomper 18
Romuald et Juliette 123
La Ronde 123
The Rookie 153
Rookie of the Year 114
Room Service 48
A Room With a View 94
Rosalie Goes Shopping 94
Rosemary's Baby 129
Rosencrantz and Guildenstern Are Dead 48
Round Midnight 136
Roxanne 48
Ruby 153
Rumble Fish 18
The Running Man 163
Running on Empty 94
Rush 94
The Russia House 153
Ruthless People 48
Ryan's Daughter 95

Sabrina Fair 48
The Saint of Fort Washington 95
Salaam Bombay! 95
Salvador 95
Same Time Next Year 95
The Sandlot Kids 114
Sarafina 136
Saturday Night and Sunday Morning 95
Saturday Night Fever 136
Scandal 95
Scarface 153
Scenes from a Mall 48

Scent of a Woman 95
Schindler's List 95
Scrooged 49
The Sea Hawk 18
Sea of Love 153
The Searchers 170
Second Best 96
The Secret Garden 114
Secret Honor 96
The Secret Life of Walter Mitty 49
The Secret of My Success 96
See No Evil, Hear No Evil 49
Serial Mom 49
Serpico 154
Seven Brides for Seven Brothers 136
The Seven Samurai 123
The Seventh Seal 123
The Seven Year Itch 49
sex, lies and videotape 96
The Shadow 163
Shadowlands 96
A Shadow of Doubt 96
Shadows and Fog 49
Shag 49
Shallow Grave 154
Shane 170
Shanghai Surprise 18
Shattered 154
Shawshank Redemption 96
The Sheltering Sky 96
She's Gotta Have It 49
She's Having a Baby 49
She Wore a Yellow Ribbon 170
The Shining 129
Shining Through 18
Shirley Valentine 96
The Shooting Party 97
The Shootist 170
Shopping 97
Short Circuit 163
Short Circuit 2 163
Short Cuts 97
Shout 97
Show Boat 136
Sibling Rivalry 50
Silas Marner 97
The Silence of the Lambs 129
Silkwood 97
Silverado 171
Singin' in the Rain 136
Singles 97
Single White Female 154
Sirens 97
Sister Act 50
Sister Act 2: Back in the Habit 50

The Six Wives of Henry VIII 97
Sleeper 50
Sleeping With the Enemy 154
Sleepless in Seattle 50
Sleep with Me 98
The Slingshot 123
Sliver 154
Smoking/No Smoking 123
The Snapper 50
Sneakers 18
Sniper 18
Snow White and the Seven Dwarfs 114
Soapdish 50
Society 154
Soft Top, Hard Shoulder 50
So I Married an Axe Murderer 50
Some Like It Hot 50
Someone to Watch Over Me 154
Sommersby 98
Son of the Pink Panther 51
Sophie's Choice 98
The Sound Barrier 19
The Sound of Music 137
South Central 19
Southern Comfort 19
South Pacific 137
Spartacus 19
The Specialist 19
Speed 19
Spellbound 154
Splash 51
Splitting Heirs 51
Spymaker: The Secret Life of Ian Fleming 19
The Spy Who Loved Me 19
Stagecoach 171
Staggered 51
Stakeout 155
Stalag 17 19
Stand and Deliver 98
Stand By Me 98
Stanley and Iris 98
A Star Is Born 137
Starman 163
Star Trek: The Motion Picture 164
Star Trek IV: The Voyage Home 164
Star Trek VI: The Undiscovered Country 164
Star Wars 164
Stay Tuned 164
Steel Magnolias 98
Stella 98
St Elmo's Fire 98

Stepfather 155
Stepping Out 99
The Sting 155
The Stolen Children 123
Stop! or My Mom Will Shoot 51
The Story of Qui Ju 123
Storyville 155
Straight Out of Brooklyn 99
Straight Talk 51
Strangers on a Train 155
Strapless 99
A Streetcar Named Desire 99
Streets of Fire 20
Strictly Ballroom 51
Striking Distance 20
Suburban Commando 51
Subway 123
Sunset Boulevard 99
Superman 164
Superman II 164
Superman III 164
Superman IV: The Quest for Peace 164
Super Mario Brothers 20
Support Your Local Sheriff 171
Suspect 155
Sweet Emma, Dear Bobe 124
Swing Kids 99
Switch 52
Switching Channels 52

The Taking of Pelham 123 20
A Tale of Two Cities 20
Tales from the Dark Side 129
The Talk of the Town 52
Talk Radio 99
The Tall Guy 52
The Taming of the Shrew 52
Tango 52
Tango and Cash 20
Target 155
Tatie Danielle 124
Taxi Driver 99
Teenage Mutant Ninja Turtles 20
Teenage Mutant Ninja Turtles II 20
Teenage Mutant Ninja Turtles III 20
Teen Agent 155
The Ten Commandments 20
Tender Mercies 99
10 Rillington Place 155
The Terminator 165

Terminator 2 165
Terms of Endearment 100
Texasville 100
That'll Be the Day 137
That's Entertainment 137
That's Entertainment Part II 137
Thelma and Louise 21
These Foolish Things 100
They Died With Their Boots On 171
They Live 165
They Shoot Horses, Don't They? 100
The Thief of Baghdad 114
Things Change 52
The Third Man 100
The 39 Steps 156
This Boy's Life 100
This Is My Life 52
This Is Spinal Tap 52
The Thomas Crown Affair 156
Three Colours Trilogy 124
Three Men and a Baby 52
Three Men and a Little Lady 53
The Three Musketeers (1973) 21
The Three Musketeers (1993) 21
Three Ninja Kids 21
Three of Hearts 53
Threesome 53
Throne of Blood 124
Throw Momma from the Train 53
Thumbelina 114
Thunderball 21
Thunderheart 156
Tie Me Up! Tie Me Down! 124
Tiger Bay 156
The Time Bandits 53
Timescape 165
Tin Men 53
The Titfield Thunderbolt 53
To Be or Not To Be (1942) 53
To Be or Not To Be (1983) 53
To Catch a Thief 156
To Die For 53
To Have and Have Not 21
To Kill a Mockingbird 100
Tokyo Story 124
To Live 124
Tom and Jerry: The Movie 115
Tom & Viv 100

181

Tombstone 171
Tom Jones 54
Too Hot to Handle 54
Tootsie 54
Top Gun 21
Top Hat 137
Top Secret! 54
Tora! Tora! Tora! 21
Torch Song Trilogy 101
To Sir With Love 101
Total Recall 165
Toto the Hero 124
Tous les Matins du Monde 124
The Towering Inferno 21
A Town Like Alice 22
The Toxic Avenger 166
The Toxic Avenger Part II 165
The Toxic Avenger Part III 165
Toys 54
Toy Soldiers 22
Trading Places 54
The Treasure of the Sierra Madre 101
Trespass 22
The Trial 101
Trop Belle Pour Toi! 125
The Trouble with Harry 156
True Grit 171
True Identity 54
True Lies 22
True Romance 22
Truly, Madly, Deeply 101
Turner and Hooch 156
Twelve Angry Men 101
Twelve O'Clock High 22
Twin Peaks: Fire Walk with Me 156
Twins 54
The Two Jakes 156
2001: A Space Odyssey 165
2010: The Year We Make Contact 165

The Ugly American 101
The Unbearable Lightness of Being 101
Uncle Buck 54
Undercover Blues 157
Under Fire 101
Under Siege 22
Unforgiven 171
The Unholy 129
Universal Soldier 166
Unlawful Entry 157
Untamed Heart 101
The Untouchables 22
Used People 54
U2 – Rattle and Hum 137

Valmont 102
Vampire's Kiss 55
The Vanishing (1988) 157
The Vanishing (1993) 157
The Verdict 102
Vertigo 157
Vice Versa 55
A View to a Kill 23
Vincent and Theo 102
Les Visiteurs 125
Vital Signs 102
Viva Zapata! 23
V I Warshawski 157

Wall Street 102
War and Peace 23
War Games 55
War of the Buttons 115
The War of the Roses 55
The War of the Worlds 166
The Waterdance 102
Watership Down 115
Wayne's World 55
Wayne's World 2 55
The Wedding Banquet 125
Welcome Home, Roxy Carmichael 55
West Side Story 137
Westworld 166
What About Bob? 55
Whatever Happened to Baby Jane? 55
What's Eating Gilbert Grape? 102
What's Love Got To Do With It? 102
What's Up Doc? 55
When a Man Loves a Woman 102
When Harry Met Sally 56
When Sleeping Dogs Lie 157
When Worlds Collide 166
Where Angels Fear to Tread 103
Whisky Galore 56
White Christmas 137
White Hunter, Black Heart 103
White Men Can't Jump 56
White Mischief 103
White Nights 103
White Palace 103
White Sands 157
Who Framed Roger Rabbit? 115
Who's Afraid of Virginia Woolf? 103

Whose Life Is It Anyway? 103
The Wicker Man 157
Widow's Peak 56
Wild at Heart 103
The Wild Bunch 171
The Wild One 23
Wild Strawberries 125
Wild West 56
Willow 115
Wilt 56
Winchester '73 171
The Wind in the Willows 115
Wings of the Apache 23
The Winslow Boy 103
Wish You Were Here 56
Witchboard 129
The Witches 115
The Witches of Eastwick 56
With Honors 103
Withnail & I 56
Without a Clue 158
Witness 158
Witness for the Prosecution 158
The Wizard of Oz 115
Wolf 130
The Woman in Black 130
Women on the Verge of a Nervous Breakdown 125
The Wooden Horse 23
Woodstock 138
Working Girl 56
A World Apart 103
Wrestling Ernest Hemingway 104
Wuthering Heights 104
Wyatt Earp 71

Yankee Doodle Dandee 138
Yanks 104
The Year of Living Dangerously 104
Year of the Dragon 158
Yojimbo 125
The Young Americans 158
Young Frankenstein 57
Young Guns 172
Young Guns II 172
The Young Lions 23
Young Soul Rebels 158
You Only Live Twice 23

Zardoz 166
Zelig 57
Zéro de Conduite 125
Zombies: Dawn of the Dead 130
Zulu 23
Zulu Dawn 23